THE FIELD ARMIES OF THE EAST ROMAN EMPIRE, 361–630

This book presents a new history of the leadership, organization, and disposition of the field armies of the east Roman empire between Julian (361–363) and Herakleios (610–641). To date, scholars studying this topic have privileged a poorly understood document, the *Notitia dignitatum*, and imposed it on the entire period from 395 to 630. This study, by contrast, gathers all of the available narrative, legal, papyrological, and epigraphic evidence to demonstrate empirically that the *Notitia* system emerged only in the 440s and that it was already mutating by the late fifth century before being fundamentally reformed during Justinian's wars of reconquest. This realization calls for a new, revised history of the eastern armies. Every facet of military policy must be reassessed, often with broad implications for the period. The volume provides a new military narrative for the period 361–630 and appendices revising the prosopography of high-ranking generals and arguing for a later *Notitia*.

ANTHONY KALDELLIS is Professor of Classics at the University of Chicago. He has written on many aspects of Byzantine history, literature, and culture, including the reception of the classical tradition, identities (*Romanland*, 2019), monuments (*The Christian Parthenon*, Cambridge University Press, 2009), and politics (*The Byzantine Republic*, 2015). He has completed a new history of Byzantium (*The New Roman Empire*, forthcoming) and is the host of the popular podcast *Byzantium & Friends*.

MARION KRUSE is an Associate Professor of Classics at the University of Cincinnati. His research focuses on Roman and Byzantine history and historiography, and he has published on topics ranging from Prokopios' *Wars of Justinian* to the prosopography of the eleventh century. His first book, *The Politics of Roman Memory* (2019), examines the role of memory in eastern Roman responses to the fall of the western empire, especially in the *Novels* of Justinian.

THE FIELD ARMIES OF THE EAST ROMAN EMPIRE, 361–630

ANTHONY KALDELLIS

University of Chicago

MARION KRUSE

University of Cincinnati

Shaftesbury Road, Cambridge CB2 8EA, United Kingdom

One Liberty Plaza, 20th Floor, New York, NY 10006, USA

477 Williamstown Road, Port Melbourne, VIC 3207, Australia

314–321, 3rd Floor, Plot 3, Splendor Forum, Jasola District Centre, New Delhi – 110025, India

103 Penang Road, #05–06/07, Visioncrest Commercial, Singapore 238467

Cambridge University Press is part of Cambridge University Press & Assessment, a department of the University of Cambridge.

We share the University's mission to contribute to society through the pursuit of education, learning and research at the highest international levels of excellence.

www.cambridge.org
Information on this title: www.cambridge.org/9781009296939

DOI: 10.1017/9781009296892

First published 2023
First paperback edition 2024

A catalogue record for this publication is available from the British Library

Library of Congress Cataloging-in-Publication data
NAMES: Kaldellis, Anthony, author. | Kruse, Marion (Marion Woodrow), author.
TITLE: The field armies of the East Roman Empire, 361–630 / Anthony Kaldellis, University of Chicago, Marion Kruse, University of Cincinnati.
DESCRIPTION: Cambridge, United Kingdom ; New York : Cambridge University Press, 2023. | Includes bibliographical references and index.
IDENTIFIERS: LCCN 2022058754 | ISBN 9781009296946 (hardback) | ISBN 9781009296939 (paperback) | ISBN 9781009296892 (ebook)
SUBJECTS: LCSH: Rome – Army. | Rome – History, Military – 30 B.C.-476 A.D. | Byzantine Empire – History – To 527. | Byzantine Empire – History, Military.
CLASSIFICATION: LCC U35 .K35 2023 | DDC 355.00937–dc23/eng/20221223
LC record available at https://lccn.loc.gov/2022058754

ISBN   978-1-009-29694-6   Hardback
ISBN   978-1-009-29693-9   Paperback

Contents

Preface

This book offers a new reconstruction of the institutional history of the field armies of the east Roman empire in late antiquity. It differs significantly from the reconstruction found in almost all scholarship. Traditionally, historians have relied on a relatively static model for the organization of the field armies, based on the system found in the *Notitia dignitatum*. This is a list in Latin of the main offices and military commands of the late Roman state, divided between eastern and western commands. The eastern section in the *Notitia* is generally dated to the 390s and provides the institutional framework within which historians have reconstructed late Roman military history down to the early seventh century. Our reconstruction, by contrast, argues that the late Roman command system was in a process of continual evolution, always adapting to a changing strategic and political environment. The *Notitia* captures only a snapshot of one particular moment in that history, a couple of decades at most, starting in the 440s. Military units continued to be redeployed after that, and their overall organization was significantly reformed, not just tinkered with, by Justinian. By the second half of the sixth century, the organization of the Roman military began to degrade at an alarming rate, so that the army that faced the Persians and Arabs in the early seventh century bore little relationship, even on an institutional level, to what we see in the *Notitia*.

The armies and military history of the later Roman empire have received extensive attention from historians. This is largely because they lie at the heart of the narrative of "The Fall of the Roman Empire," an event to which many modern societies ascribe great importance. The explanation for the Fall is a Holy Grail sought after by legions of historians. Yet, whatever broader causes are identified as operating in the background of events, historians must at some point grapple with how they shaped what the Roman armies did, or failed to do, in dealing with the foreign armies who broke the empire apart and conquered its territories, namely the Vandals, Goths, Huns, and Franks in the fifth-century west and the Huns, Avars, Slavs, Persians, and Arabs in the seventh-century east.

We know about the late Roman armies from many narrative sources as well as from laws, papyri, and inscriptions. An especially important source is the *Notitia dignitatum*, an administrative blueprint that lists all the units that served under the generals of the Roman high command. Countless books and articles have been published on every conceivable aspect of the late Roman military. Narrative histories of the empire in this period, between the fourth and seventh centuries, are published every year, and these, in turn, rely on the conclusions of a huge mass of technical studies about the size and organization of the late Roman army. Yet it is the argument of this book that this body of scholarship rests on a fundamental misreading of the evidence, especially a misuse of the *Notitia*. Once this error is identified and corrected, the armies and military history of the eastern empire take on a significantly different appearance. Moreover, a cascade of other corrections follows, for example regarding military planning, strategy, diplomacy, the state economy, and the like, though our focus here will be on correcting the original error from which all the rest proceed.

The specific problem at the heart of our discussion may not at first appear to be that large, but once we grasp its implications for any particular subperiod between the fourth and seventh centuries, we realize that its military history has to be rewritten. What, then, is the problem?

The late Roman army consisted of two kinds of units. On the one hand, there were the mobile field armies that contained better-paid, more experienced soldiers commanded by the top brass, and, on the other hand, there were the frontier units (usually called *limitanei*). The latter were the first line of defense and patrolled the border under the command of local *duces* (*dux* in the singular). This book will focus on the former type of force, namely the field armies that fought most of the wars, civil and foreign, and whose actions form the core of the military narrative provided by our sources. In the eastern empire, a formalized system of five field armies appeared at some point: one for Illyricum, one for Thrace, two "praesental" armies stationed in the provinces around the capital (Constantinople), and one for the east (Oriens). These armies were led by generals called *magistri militum* (abbreviated here as MM), and the exact title of each of these generals was inflected by the name of his regional command, so, for example, the general for Oriens was called *magister militum per Orientem*. We abbreviate their titles as MMI, MMT, MMP I and II, and MMO.[1]

---

[1] *magister militum per Illyricum*; *magister militum per Thracias*; *magister militum praesentalis*; *magister militum per Orientem*.

We know about these armies primarily through narrative sources, though those sources tend to refer to their generals, who were important men in the political life of the empire, more often than to the armies themselves. This is why the prosopography of the generals has been so crucial for reconstructing the history of the field armies: Scholars assume that commands (usually named in the titles that the generals bore) imply the existence of the armies that they commanded. Our second major source is the *Notitia*. The titles given to military generals in the narrative sources often match or resemble their titles in the *Notitia* closely enough that we can be reasonably confident that they are referring (independently) to the same reality. Moreover, specific units that are attested in the *Notitia* are also mentioned in papyri and inscriptions, thereby establishing a presumption in favor of the reliability of the document's contents.[2]

The *Notitia* is also a crucial source for the estimates that scholars have made for the size of the field armies. Although the document itself does not give unit sizes, by collecting scattered pieces of evidence and making informed estimates, experts have concluded that each of these five field armies had a paper (notional) strength of between 17,000 and 24,000 men.[3] As it happens, our narrative sources occasionally give us plausible figures for the size of these armies on the march and these figures match the totals at which experts have (mostly independently) arrived, thereby confirming the soundness of the methodology. (At other times, the sources give wildly inflated figures, which we discard.) As we have not found all references to these high but plausible figures collected in one place, we group them in a note here.[4] Those reported figures are usually somewhat lower than the notional ones, but that is because units were not always kept up to strength and a general did not always take his entire force on campaign, even when it was fully up to strength. Soldiers could be left

---

[2] See, for example, Kaiser, "Egyptian Units."

[3] For example, Jones, *Later Roman Empire*, 680–683; Treadgold, *Byzantium and Its Army*, 44–49; Lee, *War in Late Antiquity*, 74–78.

[4] We have, then, a plan for 12,000 led by the MMT, a praesental army of 26,000, and "another army" likely of the same size as the praesental army (i.e., the second praesental army) in Thrace in 478 (Malchos, *History* fr. 18.2); 15,000 led by the MMI in 499 (Marcellinus Comes, *Chronicle* s.a. 499.1); 40,000 led by the two MMPs and 13,000 led by the MMO in 503 (pseudo-Joshua the Stylite, *Chronicle* 54); 20,000 under the MMO in 531 (Prokopios, *Wars* 1.18.5); 15,000 led by the MMI in 548 (Prokopios, *Wars* 7.29.3); 18,000 in Italy under Narses in the 550s (Agathias, *Histories* 2.4.10; this Italian command was, of course, not part of the *Notitia* structure, but the figure indicates the size a field army could still attain at that time); and 20,000 led by the MMO and 20,000 led by the MMA, the general of the Armenian army created by Justinian in 591 (Theophylaktos, *History* 5.9.4; *Chronicle to 1234* 7–8, tr. Palmer, pp. 116–117; cf. also pseudo-Sebeos, *History* 11 [77]).

behind for logistical, strategic, and fiscal reasons and also because of disease.

We take no issue with this reconstruction, which we summarize because it is part of the necessary background. Problems arise, however, when we ask when, how, and why this system came into being and when, how, and why it unraveled. In other words, we specifically take issue with the early and later part of the story (i.e., AD 361–450 and 506–630, respectively) and less so with the middle part. The astute reader of Note 4 will notice, for example, that these field armies are attested at full strength only after the 440s and rarely after the reign of Justinian. This uneven distribution points toward our thesis that the *Notitia* system came into being later in the fifth century than previously supposed and gradually changed into something different in the later sixth century. Let us take each of these periods in turn and state what this book argues.

According to a nearly universal consensus in the scholarship – one to which we have found no significant dissent – the *Notitia* reflects the command structure of the two halves of the empire in the year 395, give or take a few years. That was also the year when the emperor Theodosius I died after arranging for the division of the Roman empire, leaving his son Arcadius as emperor in the east (based in Constantinople) and his other son Honorius as emperor in the west (based in Rome and Ravenna). This historical development is reflected in the structure of the *Notitia*, which is divided into eastern and western sections, each of which has its own complete list of offices and command structures. While we do not know who drafted this document, why, or for whom, the eastern part is supposed to reflect the original moment (ca. 395) more or less faithfully, whereas the western part was supposedly revised in some respects down to ca. 425. Moreover, this document is understood to be a largely reliable blueprint of the Roman administration at that moment when the two empires set out on their divergent political, military, and historical trajectories. As a result, the military history of the eastern empire in the years and centuries after 395 – indeed, all aspects of its state apparatus and behavior – have been written by historians in such a way as to fit the framework provided by the *Notitia*. That is, historians have assumed that the *Notitia* accurately describes the reality hidden behind the occasional imprecision of our sources and they have used the document to correct, interpret, or fill in the gaps in our sources.

However, when taken on their own terms and not read through the filter of the *Notitia*, neither the military history nor the command structure of the eastern empire in the years between 395 and the 440s corresponds to the norms laid out in the *Notitia*. That is, there is no evidence in *any of our sources* apart from the *Notitia* itself that the *Notitia* system was put into place before the end of the reign of Theodosius II. Thus, historians have to go out of their way to square the circle and force the two to match or else to explain why the structures laid out in the *Notitia* had not yet been implemented. To give an extreme example, historians have had to postulate that an entire Roman province (Macedonia Salutaris), which is unattested by any source other than the *Notitia*, popped up briefly in the later fourth century, disappeared again (to avoid the fact that it certainly did not exist in 412), and then reappeared later in the fifth century with a slightly different name. All this is done to preserve the early dating of the eastern *Notitia*. And this is only one example among many such distortions that have been perpetrated in order to maintain the early dating.

Closer to our point of focus is the following problem. In the standard reference book for this period, the *Prosopography of the Later Roman Empire* (or *PLRE*), the titles of military officials have been changed from what the sources actually call them to what they would have been called were the *Notitia* system in effect, thus distorting the actual nature of the high command to reflect the *Notitia*. In fact, as we show, the pre-*Notitia* system lasted far longer than anyone has suspected, in some respects down to the 440s in fact. (The same distortion appears in the standard German prosopography of the late Roman generals, found in the *Real-Enkyklopädie*.) Thus, through the anachronistic rubrics that it uses for many offices, the *PLRE*, monumental and indispensable though it is, perpetrates the sin of circular logic: officials mentioned in the sources must hold the offices named in the *Notitia*; and, conversely, because officials are assigned to the posts that are named in the *Notitia*, the document must have an early date. The result is a systemic distortion in our field's most authoritative prosopographic reference work.

This book is, to our knowledge, the first attempt in a century to avoid the circular logic of the *Notitia*. Given the uncertainties of the document's date, empirical methodology dictates that we treat the *Notitia* and the other sources (especially the narrative sources and the laws) as separate and try to ascertain when they first overlap. Following this method, we argue that the eastern command system reflected in the *Notitia* came into effect in the 440s, after an unusually long period of peace and relative demilitarization in the early fifth century, and that it was implemented largely in response to the threat posed by Attila and the Huns. This realization has required us to do two things: first, to enter into the highly technical domain of *Notitia* studies to show that nothing prevents us from dating the eastern portion of the document to the 440s, and that the external evidence compels us to date it that late (indeed, in making this case we realized that arguments for an early date have been reverse-engineered in order to support the early date); and, second, to reconstruct anew the command structure and military history of the eastern empire without imposing the *Notitia* framework onto all of its phases.

As a result, both ended up looking quite different from the standard picture that we are accustomed to seeing in modern textbooks. We therefore argue in favor of a "long fourth century" when it comes to military matters, one that lasted until the 440s. It was marked by ad hoc and not "named" regional commands, as well as fewer and smaller armies. The *Notitia* system of five field armies and their named commands was introduced in the 440s, after a gradual military buildup.

At the other end of our period, we find that the *Notitia* system did not last very long, as the Roman command system was in a continual process of evolution. We believe that by the 490s it was already evolving into something different. But this development too is hidden in the modern scholarship, which assumes that the *Notitia* structure remained in place throughout the sixth century and even into the seventh, albeit expanded by the creation of three new field armies by Justinian, specifically for Armenia (in 528), North Africa (after its reconquest in 534), and Italy (after its final conquest in 552). Therefore, what we find in book after book are maps and lists according to which the eastern empire had *eight* field armies in 565 for a combined total of ca. 150,000 men under arms (not including the *limitanei*, who become increasingly hard to track in the evidence).[5] Happily, this estimate exactly matches the claim made by the historian Agathias, writing in Constantinople around 580, that toward the end of his reign Justinian had 150,000 soldiers, in contrast to previous emperors who had 645,000.[6] Agathias does not say whether the figure of 150,000 includes both the field armies and the *limitanei*, or only the former. Nor does he reveal who the previous emperors were who had so many more soldiers or where he got his figures. His testimony has, however, anchored the belief that Justinian had eight field armies within the realm of mathematical plausibility.

The present book argues that Justinian created his new field armies largely by cannibalizing the two praesental forces, which, we demonstrate, never appear in the empire's military history as integral armies after 506. This resolves

---

[5] For such maps and lists in English publications that are accessible, but written by experts, see Treadgold, *Byzantium and Its Army*, 62; Haldon, *Warfare*, 72–73, 100; Decker, *Byzantine Art of War*, 17.

[6] Agathias, *Histories* 5.13.7–8.

one of the fundamental tensions in modern accounts between the eastern empire's ostensible disposition of armies (on the one hand) and the fact that the praesental armies – two of them at 20,000 men apiece, in theory – never appeared when the capital itself was threatened, whether by the rebel Vitalianus in the mid-510s, the Huns in 559, or the Avars in the late sixth and early seventh centuries. We can, in fact, trace in the sources the gradual dismemberment of the praesental forces and their distribution to the east (Armenia) and west (Italy). Thus, by repurposing central armies to the new, expanded periphery, Justinian's wars of conquest and annexation left the Balkans more exposed to attack when the Avars, opponents more formidable than any in the region during Justinian's reign, arrived. We also trace the factors that led to a gradual diminution in the size of the east Roman field armies, until Herakleios, in his war against the Persian empire in the early seventh century, was fighting with the functional equivalent of only two field armies.

Thus, the "classical" phase of the mobile army system, as reflected in the *Notitia*, barely lasted for fifty years and not, as our field has been claiming, for more than two centuries. Many head-scratching puzzles and discrepancies in this phase of Roman military history vanish when we realize that we have made an error in the dating of one document, to which we have given far more historical weight and normative status than it deserves. A host of errors flowed outward from that original one, but fortunately they can be cleared up.

A Note on the Structure of the Book

The core of the book consists of a new history of the eastern field armies and their commanders, which explains how and when the overall structures of command changed. The argument, however, requires some technical discussions, including (a) a discussion of the dating of the eastern *Notitia* (Appendix 4); (b) countering the pervasive but incorrect assumption that *magistri militum* at the court in Constantinople must be fit into one of the "named" regional positions (MMI, MMT, MMP I and II, or MMO) and the equally incorrect assumption that the existence of those generals implies the existence of their respective field armies (Appendix 2); (c) providing a new prosopography of the generals of the later fourth century to show that the *Notitia* does not reflect the military realities of the reign of Theodosius I and therefore could not have been implemented or even planned by him (Appendices 1–2); and (d) providing a prosopography of the MMPs, arguing that far fewer generals are known to have held this office than is assumed by the editors of the *PLRE* and none of them before the 440s (Appendix 3).

The bibliography on the late Roman army, the military history of the later empire, and the *Notitia dignitatum* is vast. In our citations, we restrict ourselves to the absolute minimum that is necessary to make our case. As we are rebuilding the history of the eastern field armies from the ground up, our focus will remain on the citation and analysis of the relevant sources as well as the critical evaluation of those works of scholarship that erected the modern house of cards.

Note on Terminology and Spelling

Throughout the period we cover, Roman field armies were supplemented by soldiers drawn from barbarian (i.e., non-Roman) populations both inside and outside of the empire, such as Isaurians and Goths. These soldiers are not our focus as they were generally enrolled into units distinct from the field armies. It is often important to distinguish these barbarian units from Roman forces but doing so is complicated by the fact that they entered Roman service under a variety of arrangements and that some of these, such as the system of *foederati*, were in flux during precisely this period. We have therefore borrowed the term "auxiliary" from the early empire as a general term to describe non-Roman forces aligned with, but not integrated into, the Roman armies.

Our preference for the spelling of the names of east Romans would be to transliterate them from the Greek (e.g., Prokopios) and not to use the Latin versions (Procopius), and we do this for authors of this period who wrote in Greek. But, as this is a study of military history, a domain in which even the eastern empire maintained Latinate traditions until the sixth century, we spell the names of state and military officials in Latin form until the end of the reign of Justinian (AD 565), by which time almost all state operations were conducted in Greek, so from that point on we use the Greek spellings (e.g., Herakleios). For place-names, we transliterate from the local language – Latin in the west, Greek in the east – save when this would cause undue confusion (e.g., Constantinople, not Konstantinoupolis).

Acknowledgments

We are grateful to Brian Swain, Alexander Sarantis, and the anonymous referees of Cambridge University Press for their useful suggestions, for information and references that bolstered our argument, and for objections that led us to rethink and reformulate certain aspects of it. Our thanks also go out to Michael Sharp of Cambridge University Press, whose professionalism and judgment are pillars of the practice of rigorous peer review in our field. His service as *magister doctorum* is much appreciated and not taken for granted.

Marion Kruse is grateful to Erica Andrist for the summer that she sacrificed so this book could be written.

Abbreviations

ACO   *Acta Conciliorum Oecumenicorum,* ed. E. Schwartz, 3 vols. in ser. 1 (Berlin 1913–1937).

CIG   *Corpus inscriptionum graecarum,* 4 vols. (Berlin 1828–1877).

CIL   *Corpus inscriptionum latinarum,* 17 vols. (Berlin 1893–1986).

CJ   *Codex Iustinianus (Justinianic Code)*

CTh   *Codex Theodosianus (Theodosian Code)*

MAMA 1 *Monumenta Asiae Minoris Antiqua,* v. 1: W. M. Calder, *Eastern Phrygia* (Manchester 1928).

MAMA 3 *Monumenta Asiae Minoris Antiqua,* v. 3: J. Keil and A. Wilhelm, *Denkmäler aus dem rauhen Kilikien* (Manchester 1931).

MM   *magister militum* ("master of soldiers")

MMA *magister militum per Armeniam*

MMI   *magister militum per Illyricum*

MMO *magister militum per Orientem*

MMP *magister militum praesentalis*

MMT *magister militum per Thracias*

MVM *magister utriusque militiae* ("master of both infantry and cavalry forces")

ND Occ. *Notitia dignitatum: Occidens*

ND Or. *Notitia dignitatum: Oriens*

PG   J.-P. Migne, ed., *Patrologia Graeca,* 161 vols. (Paris 1857–1866).

PL   J.-P. Migne, ed., *Patrologia Latina,* 217 vols. (Paris 1841–1855).

PLRE I A. H. M. Jones, J. R. Martindale, and J. Morris, *The Prosopography of the Later Roman Empire, Volume I: A.D. 260–395* (Cambridge 1971).

PLRE II   J. R. Martindale, *The Prosopography of the Later Roman Empire, Volume II: A.D. 395–527* (Cambridge 1980).

PLRE III   J. R. Martindale, *The Prosopography of the Later Roman Empire, Volume III: A.D. 527–641* (Cambridge 1992).

P. Oxy.   *The Oxyrhynchus Papyri*, ed. B. P. Grenfell et al., 85 vols. (London 1898–2008).

TIB   *Tabula imperii byzantini*, 18 vols. (some still in preparation) (Vienna 1976–present).

Maps

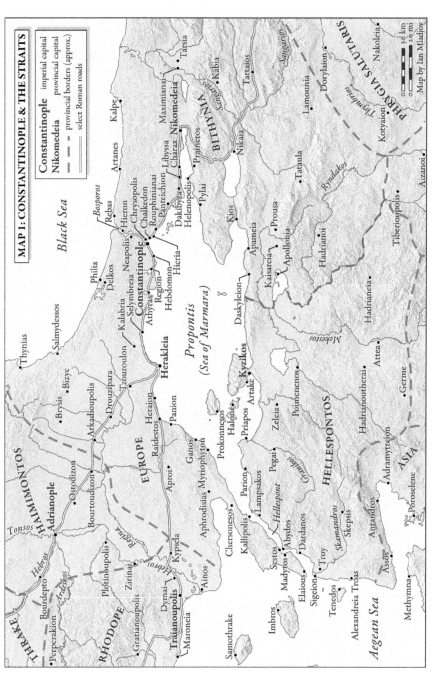

1 Constantinople and the straits

MAP 1: CONSTANTINOPLE & THE STRAITS

Constantinople imperial capital
Nikomedeia provincial capital
- - - - provincial borders (approx.)
———— select Roman roads

Map by Ian Mladjov

THRAKE
HAIMIMONTOS
Adrianople
Tonsos
Hebros
Bourdepto
Perperakion
Ardeskos
Plotinoupolis
Gratianoupolis
Zirinai
Dymai
Traianoupolis
Hebros
Kypsela
Ainos
Regina
Maroneia
Aphrodisias
Myriophyton
RHODOPE
Samothrake
Imbros
Chersonesos
Kallipolis
Parion
Lampsakos
Madytos
Sestos
Abydos
Dardanos
Elaious
Sigeion
Troy
Skamandros
Skepsis
Alexandreia Troas
Antandros
Assos
Tenedos
Methymna
Aegean Sea

Ostodizon
Bourtoudizon
Arkadioupolis
Brysis
Bizye
Drouzipara
Tzouroulon
Kalabria
Salmydessos
Thynias
EUROPE
Herakleia
Heraion
Raidestos
Panion
Aproi
Ganos
Prokonnesos
Halone
Priapos
Pegai
Poimenenos
Granikos
Zeleia
Artake
Kyzikos
HELLESPONTOS
Hadrianoutherai
Attea
Germe
Hadrianeia
ASIA
Poroselene
Adramytteion

Black Sea
Bosporos
Rebas
Hieron
Chrysopolis
Chalkedon
Rouphinianai
Panteichion
Dakibyza
Helenopolis
Philia
Delkos
Neapolis
Selymbreia
Constantinople
Athyras
Region
Hebdomon
Hieria
Propontis
(Sea of Marmara)
Daskyleion
Nekestos

Artanes
Kalpe
Tarsia
Maximianai
Charax **Nikomedeia**
Libyssa
Praenetos
Pylai
BITHYNIA
Kios
Nikaia
Apameia
Kaisareia
Prousa
Apollonia
Hadrianoi
Rhyndakos
Tiberioupolis
Sangarios
Kabia
Tattaios
Tataula
Lamounia
Dorylaion
Nakoleia
Kotyaion
Tymphrios
PHRYGIA SALUTARIS
Aizanoi

30 km
20 mi

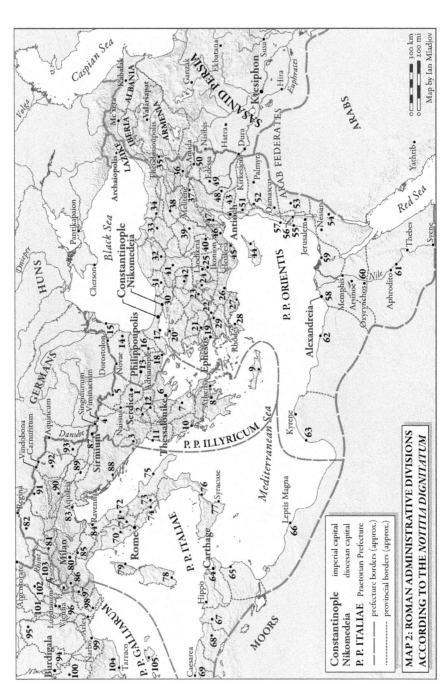

2 Roman administrative divisions according to the *Notitia dignitatum*

MAP 2: ROMAN ADMINISTRATIVE DIVISIONS
ACCORDING TO THE *NOTITIA DIGNITATUM*

Constantinople   imperial capital
Nikomedeia   diocesan capital
P. P. ITALIAE   Praetorian Prefecture
———   prefecture borders (approx.)
------   provincial borders (approx.)

Map by Ian Mladjov

KEY TO MAP 2, ROMAN ADMINISTRATIVE DIVISIONS ACCORDING TO THE *NOTITIA DIGNITATUM*

PRAETORIAN PREFECTURE OF ILLYRICUM

DIOCESE OF DACIA
1 Dacia Mediterranea (Serdica)
2 Dardania (Scupi)
3 Praevalitana (Doclea)
4 Moesia I (Viminacium)
5 Dacia Ripensis (Ratiaria)

DIOCESE OF MACEDONIA
6 Macedonia I (Thessalonike)
7 Thessalia (Larissa)
8 Achaia (Corinth)
9 Creta (Gortyna)
10 Epirus Vetus (Nikopolis)
11 Epirus Nova (Dyrrachion)
12 Macedonia II Salutaris (Stobi)

PRAETORIAN PREFECTURE OF ORIENS

DIOCESE OF THRACIAE
13 Thracia (Philippoupolis)
14 Moesia II (Markianoupolis)
15 Scythia Minor (Tomis)
16 Haemimontus (Adrianople)
17 Europa (Herakleia)
18 Rhodope (Traianoupolis)

DIOCESE OF ASIANA
19 Asia (Ephesos)
20 Hellespontus (Kyzikos)
21 Lydia (Sardeis)
22 Phrygia Pacatiana (Laodikeia)
23 Phrygia Salutaris (Synnada)
24 Pisidia (Antiocheia)
25 Lycaonia (Ikonion)
26 Pamphylia (Perge)
27 Lycia (Myra)
28 Insulae (Rhodes)
29 Caria (Aphrodisias)

DIOCESE OF PONTICA
30 Bithynia (Nikomedeia)
31 Honorias (Klaudioupolis)
32 Paphlagonia (Gangra)
33 Helenopontus (Amaseia)
34 Pontus Polemoniacus (Neokaisareia)
35 Armenia Interior (Theodosioupolis)
36 Sophene et Gentes (Arsamosata)
37 Armenia II (Melitene)
38 Armenia I (Sebasteia)
39 Cappadocia I (Kaisareia)
40 Cappadocia II (Tyana)
41 Galatia I (Ankyra)
42 Galatia II Salutaris (Pessinous)

DIOCESE OF ORIENS
43 Syria I (Antioch)
44 Cyprus (Konstanteia)
45 Isauria (Seleukeia)
46 Cilicia I (Tarsos)
47 Cilicia II (Anazarbos)
48 Euphratensis (Hierapolis)
49 Osrhoene (Edessa)
50 Mesopotamia (Amida)
51 Syria II Salutaris (Apameia)
52 Phoenice Libanensis (Emesa)
53 Arabia (Bostra)
54 Palaestina III Salutaris (Petra)
55 Palaestina I (Kaisareia)
56 Palaestina II (Skythopolis)
57 Phoenice (Tyre)

DIOCESE OF AEGYPTUS
58 Aegyptus (Alexandria)
59 Augustamnica (Pelousion)
60 Arcadia (Oxyrynchos)
61 Thebais (Ptolemais)
62 Libya Inferior (Paraitonion)
63 Libya Superior (Berenike)

PRAETORIAN PREFECTURE OF ITALIA

DIOCESE OF AFRICA
64 Africa Zeugitana (Carthage)
65 Byzacena (Hadrumetum)
66 Tripolitania (Leptis Magna)
67 Numidia (Constantina)
68 Mauretania Sitifensis (Sitifis)
69 Mauretania Caesariensis (Caesarea)

DIOCESE OF ITALIA
70 Tuscia et Umbria (Volsinii)
71 Valeria (Reate)
72 Picenum Suburbicarium (Asculum)
73 Samnium (Beneventum)
74 Campania (Capua)
75 Apulia et Calabria (Barium)
76 Lucania et Brutti (Rhegium)
77 Sicilia (Syracuse)
78 Sardinia (Carales)
79 Corsica (Aleria)
80 Liguria (Milan)
81 Raetia I (Curia)
82 Raetia II (Augusta Vindelicum)
83 Venetia et Histria (Aquileia)
84 Flaminia et Picenum (Ravenna)
85 Aemilia (Placentia)
86 Alpes Cottiae (Segusio)

DIOCESE OF ILLYRICUM (PANNONIAE)
87 Pannonia II (Sirmium)
88 Dalmatia (Salonae)
89 Savia (Siscia)
90 Noricum Mediterraneum (Virunum)
91 Noricum Ripense (Ovilava)
92 Pannonia I (Savaria)
93 Valeria Ripensis (Sopianae)

PRAETORIAN PREFECTURE OF GALLIAE

DIOCESE OF SEPTEM PROVINCIAE*
94 Aquitania II (Burdigala)
95 Aquitania I (Biturigum)
96 Viennensis (Vienna)
97 Alpes Maritimae (Ebrodunum)
98 Narbonensis II (Aquae Sextiae)
99 Narbonensis I (Narbo)
100 Novempopulana (Elusa)

DIOCESE OF GALLIAE*
101 Lugdunensis I (Lugdunum)
102 Maxima Sequanorum (Vesontio)
103 Alpes Graiae et Poeninae (Darantasia)

DIOCESE OF HISPANIAE
104 Tarraconensis (Tarraco)
105 Balearica (Palma)

* Treated jointly in the Notitia Dignitatum.

Compiled by Ian Mladjov

CHAPTER I

The High Command from Julian to Theodosius I (361–395)

The traditional narrative of the late east Roman military recognizes two major phases. In the first phase, the emperor Diocletian (284–305) codified and expanded military innovations that had evolved during the series of military and political crises that afflicted the empire during the third century. The result was a new overall structure for the Roman military. In particular, Diocletian is credited with initiating the division of the Roman army into two broad groups: mobile field armies (the *comitatus*, whose soldiers were the *comitatenses*) and frontier soldiers (*limitanei*).[1] The *limitanei* were intended to suppress small-scale raiding and generally defend and patrol the borders of the empire, while the mobile field armies represented the main battle forces of the empire and accompanied each emperor during his travels along the frontier as he took on major invaders and domestic usurpers.[2]

The second phase, still according to the standard narrative, begins with the battle of Adrianople in 378, when the field armies of the eastern empire were crushed by the Goths. After the battle, Theodosius I (379–395) assumed the throne in the east and, allegedly, undertook a massive reorganization of the east Roman military, a snapshot of which is preserved in the *Notitia dignitatum*, a list of offices, provinces, and military units broadly agreed to date to the end of his reign or the beginning of that of his son Arcadius (395–408). The *Notitia* system reflects a division of the *comitatus* into five regional armies: Illyricum, Thrace, Oriens, and two praesentals (i.e., "armies in the presence of the emperor") that were likely stationed around Constantinople, in eastern Thrace and Bithynia.[3] This system is

---

[1] Initially, the *limitanei* units were called *ripenses*. The former term appeared slightly later but is more widely used in scholarship: Lee, *War in Late Antiquity*, 11; *ripensis* appears in 325: *CTh* 7.20.4; *limitaneus* appears in 363: *CTh* 12.1.56.

[2] Distinctions between the two types of units were not at first firm: Brennan, "Zosimos II.34.1."

[3] The seminal account of this process is Hoffmann, *Das spätrömische Bewegungsheer*, chaps. 9–10, on which see Appendix 4.

believed to have continued to operate in the east until the reign of Herakleios (610–641) when the Avar and Slavic conquest of the Balkans and the Islamic conquest of Egypt, Palestine, and Syria forced the east Romans to radically reimagine their military system.

The reign of the emperor Theodosius I therefore plays an epochal role in the history of the east Roman military. However, this reconstruction is built on shaky ground. To begin with, our best guide to the Roman military of the fourth century, the history of Ammianus Marcellinus, a retired officer with a keen interest in military affairs, ends in 378 with the battle of Adrianople. Our sources for the reign of Theodosius itself are far less interested in, and detailed about, military affairs. We rely, for instance, on court panegyrics to reconstruct basic information about that emperor's major Gothic war of 379–382.[4] Militarily, therefore, the last quarter of the fourth century is an obscure period.

Traditionally, scholars have looked to the *Notitia dignitatum* to illuminate the changes taking place in this period and fill in the gaps, in particular between Theodosius' Gothic settlement of 382 and his departure for the west in 394 to suppress the usurper Eugenius. Scholars who argue for an early date for the *Notitia* and the military system it describes assign responsibility for the major relevant reforms to Theodosius I. This assignment is not driven by the testimony of the sources, whether explicit or inferred from changing patterns in appointments, but is instead the result of self-imposed necessity. The *Notitia* clearly does not reflect the military system operating in Ammianus' narrative, which ends in 378, while the *Notitia* is dated by most scholars to 395 or shortly thereafter. Thus, scholars assign the reforms to Theodosius I. This assignment is enabled by our poor sources for the Theodosian army, which allows the *Notitia* to fill in the gaps left by our otherwise meager evidence. Moreover, historians link this alleged reform to a polemical passage in Zosimos, where they see a reference to the establishment of the *Notitia* system. However, a careful evaluation of the sources, one that does not assume an early date for the *Notitia*, reveals that there is no evidence to suggest that anything like the *Notitia* system was in place by 395, either in the offices of the Roman high command or in the organization and deployment of the armies.

This book argues that there is no indication that the system described by the eastern *Notitia* came into effect before the 440s and, moreover, that

---

[4] Our chief narrative sources are Zosimos' *New History* and the *Ecclesiastical Histories* of Sozomenos and Sokrates. These are supplemented by the fragments of the historian Eunapios, the panegyrics of Themistios, and the laws of Theodosius I preserved in the *Theodosian Code*, which was compiled under his grandson, Theodosius II, in 438. For the reign in general, see Leppin, *Theodosius der Grosse*.

there is much positive evidence that it did come into effect in that later decade. This requires that the document be redated accordingly.[5] In turn, deprived of the evidence of the *Notitia*, the traditional understanding of the Theodosian military reforms becomes immediately untenable. In fact, pulling the *Notitia* out of the equation has profound consequences that extend back well before the reign of Theodosius itself because scholars have imposed aspects of the *Notitia* system even onto the army of Valens (364–378). However, the contemporary sources for all these reigns – straight through to the 440s – show that the *Notitia* structure was not in effect. This chapter will, for the first time, present this evidence without trying to force it teleologically into the mold of the *Notitia*.

As mentioned, the armies of the fourth-century Roman empire were divided into mobile field armies and *limitanei*. The field armies were led by the emperor or by top-tier generals, whose titles were *magistri peditum* ("masters of the infantry"), *magistri equitum* ("masters of the cavalry"), or the generic *magistri militum* ("masters of the soldiers," which is first attested in 349 and abbreviated here as MM).[6] The field armies were not tied to (or named after) specific regions but operated on an ad hoc basis wherever there was need to repel an invader or suppress a usurper. They might be stationed for long periods in regular trouble spots, but they also expected to be moved around a lot, anywhere from Britain to Syria. Like their armies, the field army generals were less often posted on a permanent basis to specific regions than dispatched to deal with specific crises. They too were transferred across the empire during their careers.[7] To be sure, some regions, such as Illyricum and Thrace, were frequent trouble spots during this period, so the field armies were often operating there, but there is no evidence that specific commands or armies were formally or regularly designated for them, such as we find in the *Notitia* and in the command system that was in effect after the 440s.

It is conventional in the scholarship to refer to the armies that accompanied the emperor as "praesental" or *in praesenti* (i.e., "in the emperor's presence"). The term is unobjectionable if used in a descriptive, nontechnical sense.[8] The Latin participle *praesens* means "to be present," or "here and now," as did the Latin adverb *praesto*. Thus, Constantine in 326

---

[5] For the date of the *ND Or.*, see Appendix 4 and Chapter 2.

[6] See *CTh* 8.7.3 (of 349). The appearance of the later fourth-century title of *magister utriusque militum* ("master of both branches of soldiers") is discussed later in this chapter.

[7] See, for instance, the career of Ursicinus, who served as a *magister* in the east, Gaul, and in the emperor's presence: *PLRE* I, 985–986 (Ursicinus 2).

[8] For example, Elton, *Warfare in Roman Europe*, 208 and in many other places in the book.

referred to his elite soldiers as "always present" with him (*praesto sunt semper*).[9] In 398, Arcadius issued a law in Constantinople restricting the side-jobs that soldiers could undertake "who are present (*praesentes*) in our divine following (*obsequium*) … when our court (*comitatus*) is present (*praesens*) in this City."[10] This use of the participle was not technical, as shown by the fact that the emperor uses it both for the soldiers (present at the court) and himself (present in the City). Likewise, Ammianus could refer to the praetorian prefects attached to the emperor's court as *praesens*.[11] This remains a descriptive usage and he never uses the term *praesentalis*.[12] Before the 440s, the term *praesentalis* does not appear in these officers' titles, for example, when those titles are attested in the laws.[13] However, the term suddenly appears in that way in the 440s as part of a military reorganization in the east, as we will show in Chapter 2.

Until the reign of Constantius II (337–361), the offices of *magister equitum* and *magister peditum* were separate and singular, that is there was never more than one *magister equitum* and one *magister peditum* for each emperor, though Constantius' cousin Julian appears to have had only *magistri equitum* during his time as Caesar in Gaul in the 350s (and only one at a time).[14] Moreover, despite their titles, which distinguish between infantry and cavalry commands, it does not appear that, by the reign of Constantius II at the latest, the *magistri* commanded only cavalry or infantry units, at least not when detached from the emperor's presence.[15] It is not clear if this was also the case under Constantine I.

The structure of the high command began to shift again during the reign of Julian (361–363). During his march eastward to confront Constantius II

---

[9] *CTh* 3.26.1.   [10] *CJ* 12.35.13.

[11] Ammianus Marcellinus, *Res gestae* 14.1.10 (Thalassius) and 23.5.6 (Sallustius).

[12] Although the term *praesentalis* appears in the chapter description of Ammianus Marcellinus, *Res gestae* 20.2, neither the chapter divisions nor these headings are original: Kelly, "Adrien de Valois."

[13] *Pace* Jones, *Later Roman Empire*, 124, 340, 342, 373, 609; and Southern and Dixon, *Late Roman Army*, 19: the generals "added the words *in praesenti* or *praesentalis* to their titles to indicate that they served directly under the Emperor" (also 58). On the same page (19), they say that "in the west, the *magister peditum praesentalis* held the title Patricius from 416 onwards," citing *CTh* 15.14.14. The law is addressed to the *patricius* and MM Constantius, to whom Southern and Dixon give the title *magister peditum praesentalis*, which is not present in the law and unattested for that Constantius (= *PLRE* II, 322–323). For the top general in the west holding the court rank of patrician, see Jones, *Later Roman Empire*, 176, 343–344, 241, 243–244.

[14] Jones, *Later Roman Empire*, 124–126. We follow here the reconstruction of offices of the *PLRE* I, 1113–1114, which is based on the firm evidence of Ammianus. The singularity of the offices is implied by Ammianus, who explicitly frames new *magistri* as successors, for example, Ammianus, *Res gestae* 15.5.21, 16.2.8, 18.2.7, 18.5.5, 20.9.5.

[15] See, for example, the *magister equitum* Arbetio's campaign against the Alamanni in 355: Ammianus, *Res gestae* 15.4.

in 361, Julian appointed two *magistri equitum*, Nevitta and Iovinus.[16] As no *magistri peditum* are attested under Julian, it appears that the total number of *magistri* continued to be two.[17] Let us focus, then, on Nevitta and Iovinus. After the death of Constantius in November 361, Nevitta remained at Julian's side through to the Persian campaign of 363, while Iovinus was given a sequence of two regional commands, first in Illyricum and then in Gaul, whose nomenclature (at least as conveyed in Ammianus' literary narrative) anticipates, but is not identical to, that of the regional field armies found later in the *Notitia*. Specifically, Ammianus calls Iovinus *magister equitum per Illyricum* and then *magister armorum per Gallias*.[18] Ammianus does not explicitly say why Julian needed a more-or-less designated commander for those regions, but their strategic sensitivity for the emperor is apparent. Illyricum was the crucial node between the western and eastern empires, where the civil war between Julian and Constantius II had largely played out. Julian had massively overextended his forces in Illyricum, partly under Iovinus himself, in order to surprise his cousin. As soon as the war was over, Julian needed to lock that region down. As for Gaul, Julian, who intended to stay in the east without a western co-emperor or Caesar, needed a reliable general there. Unfortunately, we have no indication as to the size and nature of the forces that Iovinus commanded in those two posts.

Despite the relative continuity and stability of these offices, their precise nomenclature was in flux during the second half of the fourth century. In Ammianus, who often employs an informal military argot in place of technical titles, we find several generals with the title *magister armorum*, which is unattested in official sources such as the *Theodosian Code* but demonstrably equivalent, in Ammianus' usage, to *magister equitum*.[19]

---

[16] Nevitta: Ammianus, *Res gestae* 21.8.1 and 3; Iovinus: ibid. 21.12.2.

[17] Zosimos lists an additional three officers who managed the retreat of Julian's Persian expedition and are thought to be *magistri* by modern scholars: Victor (στρατηγός τοῦ πεζοῦ, which is taken to be *magister peditum*) and Hormisdas and Arinthaeus (στρατηγός τῆς ἵππου, which is taken to be *magistri equitum*): Zosimos, *New History* 3.13.3. However, Zosimos is either mistaken or, more likely, is using the term στρατηγός loosely. Ammianus, who was an eyewitness and participant in these events, never gives these three commanders the title of *magister*. Moreover, Ammianus' description does not suggest that they held top-level commands. Hormisdas and Arinthaeus were jointly in command of cavalry forces, suggesting that they did not each hold the top post, while Victor is given equal billing with Dagalaifus and Secundinus (the *dux* of Osdruena). Later in the campaign, Ammianus calls Victor a *comes* and *dux*, which does not suggest a *magister* command: Ammianus, *Res gestae* 24.4.13, 24.4.31, 24.6.4, and 24.6.13. The *PLRE* interprets *dux* as a generic term for commander and makes Victor a *comes rei militaris*: *PLRE* I, 957–959 (Victor 4).

[18] Ammianus, *Res gestae* 22.3.1 and 26.5.2, respectively.

[19] Equivalent: Ammianus, *Res gestae* 21.8.1 and 3. See also our discussion of Traianus on pp. 106–109. The term is also used by Cassiodorus in the sixth century when referring to high-ranking

During the same period, official sources begin to mention individual generals with the compound title *magister equitum et peditum* ("master of the cavalry and infantry"). Silvanus, for example, is addressed in nearly contemporary laws of about 350 as both *magister equitum et peditum* and *magister militum*, and he appears by implication in Ammianus to have been *magister armorum*, as that was the title given by the historian to his "successor" Ursicinus.[20] These titles seem to have been used interchangeably. Iovinus is likewise called *magister armorum* in Ammianus, but addressed by two laws of 365 as *magister equitum* and *magister equitum et peditum*, and again in 367 as *magister equitum*.[21] It is noteworthy that in all of these cases, the new and enhanced titles are given only to generals whose base title was *magister equitum* and never to those whose base title was *magister peditum*.[22] It therefore seems likely that the new compound title, *magister equitum et peditum* (or, colloquially, *magister armorum*), was introduced in the mid-fourth century and was equivalent in rank to *magister equitum*. Still, as we will see, both *magistri equitum* and *magistri peditum* continue to be attested separately into the late fourth and early fifth century.

Although the *magistri* sat atop the military hierarchy of the later fourth century, there was, just below them, a corps of senior officers known by the title *comites rei militaris* or "counts of military affairs."[23] Although their responsibilities could vary widely, many of these men were senior military commanders whose remit placed them just below the *magistri*.[24] For example, Sebastianus and the future usurper Procopius were both *comites* when they were given charge of an army of 30,000 men during Julian's Persian expedition in 363.[25] *Comites* also occupied regional commands

---

commanders in the fourth century: Cassiodorus, *Tripartite Ecclesiastical History* 6.1.24 (translating Sokrates, *Ecclesiastical History* 3.1.32) and 10.24.2 (translating Sozomenos, *Ecclesiastical History* 8.25).

[20] *Magister equitum et peditum*: *CTh* 7.1.2; *magister militum*: *CTh* 8.7.3; *magister armorum*: Ammianus, *Res gestae* 15.5.21, 24, and 36.

[21] *Magister armorum*: Ammianus, *Res gestae* 26.5.2; 365: *CTh* 7.1.7 and 8.1.10; 367: *CTh* 7.1.9–10. The manuscripts for *CTh* 7.1.7 and 8.1.10 read *Iovio* and there was a Iovius who served as *quaestor* under Julian, however we follow the *PLRE* in amending these references to Iovinus: *PLRE* I, 462–463 (Iovinus 6) and I, 464 (Iovius 2).

[22] Ursicinus would later become *magister peditum* under Constantius II, but this was a demotion brought about by his enemies at court, and Ammianus, his partisan, continues to refer to him by the presumably higher rank of *magister armorum*: Ammianus, *Res gestae* 31.13.18.

[23] The first attested *comes rei militaris* is likely Gratianus, the father of the emperors Valentinian (364–375) and Valens (364–378), though Ammianus reports his office as *comes praefuit rei castrensi per Africam*: Ammianus, *Res gestae* 30.7.3.

[24] For the range of their responsibilities, see Jones, *Later Roman Empire*, 125 n. 26.

[25] Sebastianus: Ammianus, *Res gestae* 23.3.5; Procopius: ibid. 26.6.2.

along the frontier, a role that anticipated the MMs who oversaw regional field armies in the *Notitia*, and this was sometimes reflected in their titles (or, at least, Ammianus' descriptions of their responsibilities).[26] The *comites rei militaris* introduced flexibility into a military system dominated by the two *magistri*, and allowed emperors to place multiple independent armies in the field simultaneously, when necessary.

The picture so far presented accords generally with the scholarly consensus. Our reconstruction begins to diverge, however, in the aftermath of Julian's Persian expedition of 363. Our sources report that Julian invaded Persia with an army of roughly 65,000 soldiers, a number that is credible, though just barely, for the mobile forces at the empire's disposal. This was quite possibly the largest army ever fielded by the late Roman state.[27] Despite this massive army, the expedition ended in disaster with the death of Julian in battle and a hasty peace arranged by his short-lived successor Jovian (363–364). After Jovian's death, the army chose Valentinian as emperor (364–375) and he subsequently elevated his brother Valens (364–378). The brothers then divided the empire and the army. Unknown to them, they were laying the foundations for the distinct military establishments that would develop in significantly different directions in the eastern and western halves of the empire over the coming century:

> Iovinus, who had already been promoted to *magister armorum per Gallias* by Julian, went to Valentinian, whose decisions in these matters were final, as did Dagalaifus, whom Jovian had made a *rector militiae*. As for the east, Victor, who had also been promoted by the decision of the aforementioned emperor [i.e., Jovian],[28] was appointed to follow Valens, and Arinthaeus went with him. For Lupicinus was guarding the eastern districts having already been promoted to *magister equitum* in the same way by Jovian.[29]

Ammianus is here somewhat imprecise about the offices of the high command. Iovinus is called *magister armorum*, that is a *magister equitum et*

---

[26] *Comes per Thraciam/Thracias*: Ammianus, *Res gestae* 21.12.22 and 26.7.5; *comes* in charge of the army in Illyricum: ibid. 26.5.2; Prosper, a *comes*, *pro magistro equitum . . . militem regens* in Gaul: ibid. 24.11.5 (*comes*) and 15.13.3 (*pro magistro equitum*).

[27] Zosimos, *New History* 3.13; for estimates of the size of Julian's army, see Paschoud, *Zosime*, vol. 2, pt. 1, 110–111.

[28] Proximity points to "the aforementioned emperor" being Jovian, according with Ammianus' description of the Persian expedition, which should be preferred over that of Zosimos: see note 17. *Pace* den Boeft et al., *Philological and Historical Commentary . . . XXVI, ad* 5.2.

[29] Ammianus, *Res gestae* 26.5.2: *Et Valentiniano quidem, cuius arbitrio res gerebatur, Iovinus evenit dudum promotus a Iuliano per Gallias magister armorum, et Dagalaifus, quem militiae rectorem provexerat Iovianus: in orientem vero secuturus Valentem ordinatus est Victor, ipse quoque iudicio principis ante dicti provectus, cui iunctus est Arintheus. Lupicinus enim pridem a Ioviano pari modo promotus magister equitum partes tuebatur eoas.*

peditum, but Dagalaifus' office is more obscure. He is called a *rector militiae* ("overseer of the soldiery"), which is not an official title, but it does parallel the title that Ammianus gives him earlier in the same book, *rector equestris militiae* ("overseer of the cavalry soldiery"), which is apparently synonymous with *magister equitum.*[30] Thus, there appear to have been two *magistri equitum* or *magistri equitum et peditum* under the emperor Jovian (363–364), just as there had been during Julian's revolt, though it is possible, given Ammianus' imprecision with titles, that Dagalaifus was, in fact, a *magister peditum.*[31] Both of these men went west with Valentinian as his two *magistri.* But Jovian had apparently introduced an innovation: in addition to those two generals, he had appointed Lupicinius as *magister equitum* with a command that Ammianus marks out as exceptional, for he was specifically responsible for the "districts of Oriens" (*partes Eoae*). The historian here uses a transliteration of ἑῷα, the Greek term for *Oriens,* making Lupicinus a forerunner of the *magister militum per Orientem,* which, as we will see, was the first of the regional field army commands listed by the *Notitia* to be implemented in the eastern empire (though this happened a generation after Lupicinus' command).

The ranks of Victor and Arinthaeus are not explicitly mentioned in the passage quoted above, but for the year 366/7 we receive explicit confirmation from Ammianus that Victor was *magister equitum* and Arinthaeus *magister peditum.*[32] It is thus likely that both men held these offices beginning in 364, when we have a law addressing Victor as *magister militum.*[33] Thus Valens, like his brother, also had two top-level *magistri* with him, but he also inherited Lupicinus' third command "in the east."

The high command of the brother emperors in 364 anticipates the lines along which the Roman military would evolve in the coming century. Each of the two emperors continued to be served by two *magistri* – Iovinus and Dagalaifus in the west, Victor and Arinthaeus in the east. At the same time, the central command was beginning to be supplemented by regional *magistri,* with Iovinus posted to Illyricum and Gaul under Julian, and Lupicinus posted to Oriens under Jovian and Valens. We should not, of course, understand Ammianus' geographic descriptions as accurate reflections of official titles or strictly delineated areas of responsibility. That is,

---

[30] *Rector equestris militiae*: Ammianus, *Res gestae* 26.4.1; *magister equitum*: ibid. 26.1.6. Ammianus uses the term *rector* for a range of offices: see also Appendix 1 on the offices of Traianus and Profuturus.

[31] This is the reconstruction of the *PLRE,* but Dagalaifus' office is not explicitly attested after 364: *PLRE* I, 239 (Dagalaifus 2). He is called only *magister militum* in the one law addressed to him, which dates to 366: *CTh* 7.20.9.

[32] Ammianus, *Res gestae* 27.5.1, 27.5.4.   [33] *CTh* 7.4.12.

we cannot reconstruct the precise remit of Lupicinus' command or the extent to which Iovinus' command was geographically delimited (if it was at all). But Ammianus' testimony does offer us insight into the perceptions of this system held by an informed and interested contemporary observer, and it is clear that he understood certain magisterial commands to be linked, at least de facto, to specific regions.

Victor continued in his position as *magister equitum* until at least 378, but the final secure attestation of Arinthaeus is during his consulship in 372, when papyri show that he was still *magister peditum*.[34] Lupicinus, meanwhile, is last attested in office during the revolt of Procopius in 365–366 and was certainly replaced by 371, when one Iulius is explicitly attested as *magister equitum et peditum* by a firmly dated inscription in the east (Palestine).[35] Iulius continued to serve until the battle of Adrianople in 378 and beyond, assuming that he is to be identified with the Iulius whom Ammianus, in another nontechnical descriptor, calls *magister militiae trans Taurum* ("master of the soldiery beyond the Taurus"). In the aftermath of the battle, Iulius coordinated the ambush and slaughter of many Goths serving in Roman armies throughout *Oriens* (*orientales provinciae*).[36] Iulius was thus the successor to Lupicinus' ad hoc eastern command. This, then, was the shape of Valens' high command when the Goths arrived on the Danube in 376: the highest-ranking general was the *magister equitum* Victor, a long-serving veteran who had occupied the post for at least twelve years; the post of *magister peditum* appears to have been left vacant following the death of the equally experienced Arinthaeus; and the eastern frontier, though under Valens' direct supervision in 376, retained a distinct military apparatus under Iulius, a regional *magister equitum et peditum*.

In 376, a group of Goths, under pressure in their homeland from the recently arrived Huns, famously approached the Roman *limitanei* on the Danube and petitioned to cross into Roman territory. These Goths sought lands and safety in the empire in return for providing military service to the emperor, a trade that Germanic tribes had been making with Rome for centuries. The emperor Valens, preoccupied with a war against Persia and

---

[34] Μαγίστρος τῆς πεδικῆς δυνάμεως: see the papyri cited at *PLRE* I, 103. He had been deployed to Armenia the previous year: Ammianus, *Res gestae* 27.12.13. For his death, see Appendix 1.

[35] Lupicinus: Ammianus, *Res gestae* 26.8.4 and 26.9.1; Iulius: *CIL* 3: 88. Iulius was in Palestine overseeing a construction project by the *Equites VIIII Dalmatae*, a unit that is later found under the command of the MMP I in the *Notitia*: *ND Or.* 5.37.

[36] *Magister militiae trans Taurum*: Ammianus, *Res gestae* 31.16.8; for the slaughter, see also Zosimos, *New History* 4.26; Zuckerman, "Cappadocian Fathers," 480–486.

an uprising in Isauria,[37] granted them entry, whereupon mismanagement and exploitation by imperial officials drove the Goths to armed resistance. More Goths crossed the destabilized Danube defenses, and disaffected members of Roman society (such as slaves) made common cause with the invaders. The result was widespread destruction in Thrace.

By 377, Valens had sent his *magister equitum* Victor to sue for peace with Persia in order to lead his forces west and deal with the Gothic threat.[38] In the meantime, Valens sent on ahead two commanders, Profuturus and Traianus, and he wrote to the emperor of the west, his nephew Gratian (367–383), asking for reinforcements.[39] Those reinforcements came under the leadership of Richomer, Gratian's *comes domesticorum* (i.e., the captain of the soldiers assigned to the imperial household). After joining forces with the east Roman taskforce under Traianus and Profuturus, Richomer fought a bloody battle with the Goths near the town of Ad Salices. The result was indecisive. Richomer returned west to seek further reinforcements, while Profuturus and Traianus withdrew to Marcianopolis, where they were subsequently reinforced by the *comes* Saturninus, whom Valens had sent ahead with a force of cavalry.[40] Despite these reinforcements, the Romans felt that they could not hold the passes through the Haemus range and so withdrew to the south of Thrace to await the arrival of Valens with the main Roman battle force, effectively abandoning most of the Balkans to Gothic raids.

In the meantime, Valens, who marched in person to Thrace, continued to appeal to Gratian for reinforcements, while his generals, during the campaigning season in 378, organized ambuscades with picked forces in preparation for a major confrontation with the Goths. That spring, Gratian set out with an army to assist his uncle, only to be delayed by an ad hoc campaign against a group of Alamanni. Gratian's delay prompted Valens to seek battle without western reinforcements and, on August 9, 378, a hot and dusty summer day, the east Roman field army marched out to meet the Goths near the city of Adrianople. The Romans were defeated and took massive casualties.

The size of Valens' army and that of the Goths at Adrianople is unknown.[41] Ammianus reports only that Valens "was leading many units that were neither contemptible nor lazy, especially because he had added to

[37] Isauria: Zosimos, *New History* 4.20.   [38] Ammianus, *Res gestae* 31.7.1.
[39] For the ranks of Profuturus and Traianus, see Appendix 1.
[40] Ammianus, *Res gestae* 31.7; for Saturninus' rank, see Appendix 1.
[41] We do not, as most recent scholarship has done, follow the estimates of Hoffmann, *Das spätrömische Bewegungsheer*, because we believe that his reconstructions of the Roman field armies rests on too

these many veterans."[42] This is, unfortunately, our most detailed report.[43] Ammianus' vagueness about the size of the Roman army at Adrianople, in turn, makes it difficult to quantify his claim that "it is agreed that scarcely one-third of the army escaped."[44] However, as we will see, the damage to Roman military manpower must have been severe, because for a generation afterward the east Roman army looked very different from its pre-378 form. Extensive also was the damage to the officer corps: two senior generals in Valens' entourage were killed in action, as were Traianus and Sebastianus; thirty-five tribunes, both many without specific assignments (*vacantes*) and many commanding units (*numeri*); the officials in charge of the imperial palace and stables; and most famously the emperor himself.[45] Despite these losses, the Roman high command survived Adrianople: Victor escaped the battle, while Iulius continued to serve in the east, where he responded to news of the disaster by organizing the massacre of Gothic soldiers by their Roman counterparts.[46] It was Victor who brought news of the battle to Gratian, who was at Sirmium.[47] This is Victor's final attested act in office and marks the end of a career spent in the shadow of two epochal failures of Roman arms, Julian's Persian expedition and the battle of Adrianople. He was still alive, and in retirement, in 380/1.[48]

Only those two men, Victor and Iulius, are explicitly attested as holding magisterial commands at the battle of Adrianople. Scholars have tried to add to their number, producing in some cases a whole college of *magistri* up to seven strong, most of whom fought at Adrianople. These other officers, who are not explicitly attested as *magistri* in the sources, are studied separately in Appendix 1, where we find that none of them were likely to have held that rank. Historians have attributed it to them in order to create a bridge between the two-*magistri* system that prevailed before 378 and the five-*magistri* system of the *Notitia*, which they believe was introduced by the next emperor, Theodosius I. They are enabled in this by the literary vagueness with which Ammianus sometimes describes their ranks, but this vagueness does not authorize the highly specific attributions that

---

much arbitrary guesswork. For our critique of Hoffmann's arguments, see Appendix 4. For a narrative based on Hoffmann, see Lenski, *Failure of Empire*, 334–341.

[42] Ammianus, *Res gestae* 31.12.1: *ducebatque multiplices copias nec contemnendas nec segnes, quippe etiam veteranos isdem iunxerat plurimos.*

[43] Less detailed: Zosimos, *New History* 4.24; Sozomenos, *Ecclesiastical History* 6.39–40; Sokrates, *Ecclesiastical History* 4.38.

[44] Ammianus, *Res gestae* 31.13.18: *Constatque vix tertiam evasisse exercitus partem.*

[45] Ammianus, *Res gestae* 31.13.18.

[46] Ammianus, *Res gestae* 31.16.8; Zosimos, *New History* 4.26.5–9.

[47] Zosimos, *New History* 4.24.3.   [48] Gregory of Nazianzos, *Letter* 134.

have been postulated, far less the assumption that a proto-*Notitia* system was in effect.

Even on its face, the proposed link between Adrianople and the *Notitia* system does not hold up to scrutiny. The armies described by the *Notitia* were formally established field armies with specific units and regional remits. By contrast, the forces Valens poured into the Balkans during the crisis were ad hoc deployments of units drawn from other theaters, such as Armenia, and the *comitatus*, which followed the emperor. These are not analogous structures and there is no reason to believe, even if we were inclined to accept the proliferation of *magistri*, that the command structure of 378 in any way anticipated or inspired the later system. There is one more problem. If we accept the inflated number of *magistri* whom scholars have imagined operating during this period, at least four of them are explicitly attested with Valens at Adrianople: Traianus, Sebastianus, Victor, and Saturninus. But there is no parallel in Roman history, before or after Adrianople, for four *magistri militum* being active at the same time in the presence of the emperor, much less at the same battle.

We find that the high command of the eastern empire was not characterized by radical innovation in the lead-up to Adrianople. Instead, it was marked by continuity with established practice. This conclusion extends the recent scholarly rehabilitation of Valens, whose reign has too often been judged in the shadow of the disaster at Adrianople.[49] Whatever his other mistakes, we do not find Valens scrambling in the years 376–378, multiplying generals without regard to their effect on the chain of command. Instead, we see an emperor responding to a major crisis as promptly as the logistics of ancient warfare and diplomacy allowed.

After Adrianople, the Romans ceded the field to the Goths and it would be years before they were able to successfully challenge them again in open battle. Instead, the Roman military played to its strengths and confronted the Goths from behind formidable walls and with the aid of advanced artillery, seeing as the Goths were incapable of conducting effective siege warfare. In this way, the Romans repulsed the Gothic attempt to take the city of Adrianople after the battle, while a later assault on Constantinople was defeated with the memorable participation of a recently arrived detachment of Saracen auxiliaries.[50]

---

[49] Lenski, *Failure of Empire*, began the rehabilitation.
[50] Adrianople: Ammianus, *Res gestae* 31.15. Constantinople: ibid. 31.16.3–7; Sokrates, *Ecclesiastical History* 5.1.

We cannot track in detail the political aftermath of Adrianople or how the Roman government responded to the disaster in the fall of 378. The narrative of Ammianus ends just after the battle and our subsequent sources do not give a clear account of what followed. All we can say for certain is that there followed a series of intrigues at Gratian's court that resulted in the return from Spanish exile of one Theodosius, the son of a general who had been executed for treason under murky circumstances in 375/6. Theodosius was sent to the Balkans to restore order and was made co-emperor in January 379, perhaps after a minor initial victory.[51]

Ammianus' account of Roman casualties at Adrianople suggests that Theodosius' immediate problem in 379 was manpower, and our other sources confirm this picture. The *Theodosian Code* contains a flurry of laws dated between 379 and 382, in which Theodosius addressed issues of recruitment, desertion, and the failure of the sons of veterans to enroll in the army, as was legally required.[52] The penalties involved could be harsh – estate managers were to be executed if deserters were found working under their supervision – but they were matched by the desperate measures that men took to avoid service, such as cutting off their own fingers to render themselves ineligible; these self-mutilations are even attested in the papyri.[53] Theodosius responded by drafting these men anyway.

These new recruits were poor replacements for the experienced *comitatenses* lost at Adrianople, and contemporaries expressed pessimism about the state of Roman arms: "the Goths have beaten us every time they have fought us. But we die well, as is fitting for noble men."[54] Recruits had always come overwhelmingly from the agricultural labor force, but now their numbers aroused comment, and court propagandists attempted to spin this in Theodosius' favor: "you [Theodosius] make farmers fearsome to barbarians."[55] The empire did not depend entirely on raw recruits, however, as Theodosius transferred existing units from the east, from the frontiers of Syria and from Egypt, to the Balkans.[56] He made good these transfers by sending back to those provinces new recruits from among

---

[51] Our most detailed account is unfortunately in Theodoretos, *Ecclesiastical History* 5.5. Scholars agree that this narrative cannot be accepted, but differ in their alternative reconstructions: Errington, "The Accession of Theodosius"; Sivan, "Was Theodosius I a Usurper?"; McLynn, "*Genere Hispanus*," 88–94; Omissi, *Emperors and Usurpers*, 255–263.

[52] Recruitment: *CTh* 7.13.8–11; desertion: ibid. 7.18.3 and 5; sons of soldiers: ibid. 7.22.9–11.

[53] *CTh* 7.13.10. Papyri: Zuckerman, "Two Reforms of the 370s," 115–116.

[54] Libanios, *Oration* 24.16: ἀλλὰ νῦν ὅσα ἐμαχέσαντο, τοσαῦτα νενικήκασι καλῶς μὲν ἡμῶν καὶ ὡς προσῆκεν ἄνδρας ἀγαθοὺς ἀποθνῃσκόντων.

[55] Themistius, *Oration* 14.181b: ποιεῖς δὲ ἤδη καὶ τοὺς γεωργοὺς φοβεροὺς τοῖς βαρβάροις.

[56] Syria: Libanios, *Oration* 24.48; Egypt: Zosimos, *New History* 4.30.

Gothic deserters. Ironically, the events of 376–378 had only increased Roman dependence on barbarian manpower, but that dependence coincided with a surge in anti-Gothic sentiment. During this period, Roman citizens lynched a Gothic commander, while Roman soldiers repeatedly and violently clashed with Gothic recruits.[57]

Despite these reinforcements, the east Romans were unable to openly confront the Goths on the field during this period. When Theodosius tried to do so in 380, using units brought from Egypt, his army was crushed and he himself barely escaped.[58] The emperor subsequently left the war to his subordinates and retired to Constantinople, where he sought another kind of victory by meddling in Church politics.

We can reconstruct only the broad outlines of the ensuing Gothic war. The Romans relied on ambush tactics, diplomacy, and small-scale battles designed to reestablish the Danube frontier.[59] That is, they were fighting a war of attrition that favored the resources and infrastructure of the empire. In 380/1, the western empire intervened by sending an army under the command of Bauto and Arbogast, which successfully drove the Goths out of Illyricum into Thrace and to the negotiating table. The result was a negotiated peace between an exhausted empire and an undefeated but harried force of Goths. The MM Saturninus, one of the officers who had survived Adrianople and had since been promoted, negotiated the treaty for the Romans. In return for this service, he received the consulship in 383 along with a panegyric that is one of our chief sources for the settlement of the war.[60]

The terms of the treaty of 382 can only be vaguely recovered, but their cumulative effect was to cede a portion of Roman territory to a semi-autonomous Gothic statelet.[61] This was a radical departure from established Roman policy and can only be understood as an admission by the emperors that the Roman military could not defeat the Goths after Adrianople. This explains some of the terms of the treaty, in particular the Gothic obligation to provide auxiliaries under their own commanders, and the ability of Goths to enroll in the Roman army as regular recruits. The Romans were playing for time to rebuild their forces. If they could

---

[57] Lynching: Libanios, *Orations* 19.22, 20.14; clashes: Zosimos, *New History* 4.30, 4.40.
[58] Zosimos, *New History* 4.31.
[59] Ambush: Zosimos, *New History* 4.25; diplomacy: ibid. 4.33–34; Danube: ibid. 4.34.5–6.
[60] Themistios, *Oration* 16.
[61] For the terms of the treaty, using all available sources, see Heather, *Goths and Romans*, 157–181. For an opposing reconstruction of the *foedus*: Halsall, *Barbarian Migrations*, 180–185.

metabolize Gothic military manpower and grant tax relief to their citizens in the meantime, all the better.[62]

We can discern little of the Roman high command or the organization of the Roman military in the era of Theodosius' Gothic wars. There is little indication that the *limitanei* remained in control of the Danube border, while the *comitatus* of the east appears to have been too badly mauled to resist Gothic depredations. Yet in the second half of the 380s, the Roman order can be seen reestablishing itself along traditional lines. By 386, frontier defense had been reestablished on the Danube. In that year, the general Promotus, either a *dux* or *comes rei militaris*, led a force of *limitanei* and river patrol craft to a significant victory against a Gothic group, the Greuthungi, who were trying to force a crossing. Theodosius celebrated a triumph for this victory and settled some of the survivors in Phrygia.[63] By 388, the eastern *comitatus* had likewise returned to its pre-Adrianople structure. In that year, Theodosius confronted the usurper Magnus Maximus (383–388), who had rebelled against Gratian in 383 and expelled Gratian's half-brother Valentinian II (375–392) from the west in 387. In this war, Theodosius' army was commanded by a *magister equitum*, the same Promotus who had proven himself on the Danube in 386, and a *magister peditum*, Timasius. The army was accompanied by the two *magistri* of the western empire, Arbogast and Richomer, the latter of whom had been among the survivors of Adrianople; obviously, these two western generals were not commanding western armies, which fought for the "usurper" Maximus.[64] Overall, then, this was a traditional fourth-century structure of command. Before setting out, however, Theodosius was forced to suppress a conspiracy among the Goths in his army, some of whom had allegedly been suborned by Maximus.[65] The Romans thus continued to rely on, and yet be suspicious of, Gothic manpower.

Theodosius spent the next three years in the west helping to establish Valentinian II on the throne. By the time that he returned to the east in 391, the situation in the Balkans had once again deteriorated. The origins of the troubles are unclear – Zosimos blames it on the Goths who had survived the purge of the army prior to the war with Maximus – and Theodosius'

---

[62] Tax relief: Pacatus, *Oration in Praise of Theodosius I*, in *Panegyrici Latini* 2.32.3.

[63] *Comes*: see Appendices 1–2. Battle: Zosimos, *New History* 4.35.1, 4.38–39; Claudian, *Panegyric on the Fourth Consulship of Honorius* 623–637; Triumph and date: *Consular History of Constantinople* s.a. 386. Phrygia: Heather, "The Anti-Scythian Tirade," 156–157.

[64] Timasius and Promotus: Zosimos, *New History* 4.45.2; Richomer and Arbogast: Philostorgios, *Ecclesiastical History* 10.8.

[65] Zosimos, *New History* 4.45.3.

returning army suffered a defeat. Once again, the emperor yielded command, this time to Promotus, and returned to Constantinople. It was in this context that Promotus died in battle and Stilicho rose to prominence.[66]

In the interval between the Gothic treaty of 382 and the civil war of 388, Theodosius had managed to negotiate a peace with the Persians, in 387. Tensions with Persia had been running high since the end of the reign of Constantine I in 337, and it is unclear what arrangements were negotiated by Victor prior to Valens' departure for Adrianople in 377. However, we know of no major military conflicts with Persia in the decade that followed Valens' departure, and, moreover, it appears that Theodosius stopped assigning *magistri* to the region after Iulius left office.[67] The treaty of 387 was built around the partition of Armenia and would initiate over a century of almost uninterrupted peace with Persia.[68] It is thus interesting that in the run-up to Theodosius' final civil war (against Eugenius in 394), he created the office of *magister utriusque militiae per Orientem* which is first attested, along with its first known occupant Addaeus, in 393.[69] Although not precisely the title found in the later *Notitia*, the post was consistently filled after Addaeus and its title quickly took on the standard form of *magister militum per Orientem* (MMO). There is even a law of 400 or 405 that discusses the command of the MMO as distinct.[70]

The MMO was the first of the regional commands attested by the *Notitia dignitatum* to come into being, and it is interesting that it did so in a region that was largely quiet by 393. This suggests that the office was formalized not out of pressing military need, but largely due to logistical realities. In 393, Theodosius was already preparing for his war with Eugenius, for which he would depart the following year. So far during his reign, he does not appear to have traveled east of Constantinople,[71] and yet, even with Persia quiescent, the region had perennial, low-level military needs, such as defense against raids. Oriens needed a ranking officer able to respond more quickly than the government in Constantinople. The wisdom of this approach was confirmed in 395/6, when Addaeus faced a Hunnic raid from his base in Edessa, though his response appears to

---

[66] Zosimos, *New History* 4.48–51; Stilicho: Claudian, *On the Consulship of Stilicho* 1.94–96, 1.102–103; *Against Rufinus* 1.316–317.
[67] See Appendix 2.   [68] Blockley, *East Roman Foreign Policy*, 42–44.
[69] *CTh* 16.8.9. We also find Gildo as MVM *per Africam* in 393 (*CTh* 9.7.9), but this position did not have a meaningful impact on the development of the eastern Roman high command and is anyway not part of the *Notitia*. It was an ad hoc creation, like most of the regional commands of those years. See Appendix 1 for MMOs after Addaeus.
[70] *CTh* 7.8.8.   [71] Seeck, *Regesten der Kaiser und Päpste*, 251–287.

have left much to be desired.[72] Unfortunately, we know nothing about the internal structure of this new office or the number and nature of the forces under its command.

Addaeus' title reflects a broader shift in military nomenclature that occurred during the late 380s. During this period, official use of the titles *magister equitum*, *magister peditum*, and *magister equitum et peditum* declined and the compound title *magistri utriusque militiae* (MVM) and the simplified form *magistri militum* (MM) gradually took their place. The office of MVM is first attested in the western empire by an inscription firmly dated to 370 and was interchangeable with *magister equitum et peditum*.[73] Senior commanders in the east are addressed as *magistri utriusque militiae* beginning with Hellebicus in 383.[74] This title reflected the joint composition of the forces that these generals commanded and suggests the increasing obsolescence of the distinction between the *equitum* and *peditum*. The final eastern *magister equitum* attested in the *Theodosian Code* is Timasius in 386,[75] after which all magisterial generals are addressed as MVM or MM. This was, however, a long process and it is possible that a pair of generals, Varanes and Arsacius, were serving as *magister equitum* and *magister peditum* as late as 409.[76] Given the limitations of our sources, it is impossible to know to what extent this overall titular shift corresponded to changes in military practice. *Magistri*, especially those not serving *in praesenti*, had led combined forces since the time of Constantius II, so the new title may simply have been a belated acknowledgment of the fact that infantry and cavalry commands were not practically separable, especially when detached from the *comitatus*. The acceleration of this process under Theodosius may also have been linked to his absence from all non-civil wars during his reign, requiring his field generals to command both types of forces.

When Theodosius marched west again in 394 to defeat the new usurper Eugenius and his military backer Arbogast, he took a large part of the eastern field army with him. Unfortunately, we do not know which armies, or units, these were or how large they were. The literary sources indicate that they contained large contingents of barbarian auxiliaries (or "federates"), a type of

---

[72] Pseudo-Joshua the Stylite, *Chronicle* 9; Greatrex and Greatrex, "The Hunnic Invasion"; for a full list of sources, see Greatrex and Lieu, *The Roman Eastern Frontier*, 17–19.

[73] MVM: *CIL* 3: 5670a (*Equitio comite et utriusquae militiae magistro*); interchangeable: *CIL* 3: 10596 (*Equitio viro clarissimo comite magistro equitum peditumque*).

[74] Hellebicus: *CTh* 9.39.1; other MVMs: ibid. 7.1.13 (Richomer), 12.1.128 (Abundantius), 7.4.18 (Abundantius, Stilicho, and others).

[75] *CTh* 4.17.5.   [76] See Appendix 3.

unit that would not have been part of the regular command structure to begin with (i.e., such units would not have been listed in the *Notitia*, regardless of when it was drawn up).[77] Zosimos reports that Theodosius appointed two MMs, Timasius and Stilicho, to lead his "Roman armies" (στρατόπεδα ρωμαϊκά), while command over the auxiliaries was given to the Goth Gaïnas, the Alan Saul, and Bacurius, a former Iberian king (i.e., from Georgia). These auxiliaries were mostly Goths, and a contingent of them fought under the command of the young Gothic warrior Alaric.[78] This heavy reliance on barbarian units in the eastern field army reflects the losses incurred at Adrianople (in 378) and the subsequent treaty with the Goths (in 382), while Theodosius' choice to place his barbarian allies in the front ranks at the battle of the Frigidus in 394, where they suffered appalling casualties, reflects the Romans' ongoing discomfort with this status quo and their desire to shift the balance between Roman and Gothic forces in the army.[79]

Theodosius remained in the west until his death in 395. He was the last emperor to rule both halves of the empire in their entirety, so his death marks the last point of common history between the military systems of east and west. His two generals, Timasius and Stilicho, whose specific offices are not identified in the sources, followed separate paths. Timasius returned to the east, where he fell from favor and was exiled in 396 as a result of the power struggles gripping the eastern court. Stilicho, meanwhile, remained in the west, where he pioneered a system of unified military control over the imperial administration that would characterize the politics of the western empire for the remainder of its existence.

Looking back from 395, we find that the history of the Roman military in the later fourth century was a story of continuity rather than radical innovation. The changes that followed the defeat of Adrianople did not involve any large-scale reimagining of the Roman command structure proper, but rather the coupling of the surviving Roman forces with semi-autonomous Gothic auxiliaries. There is no evidence that the *Notitia* system of three regional and two praesental Roman field armies was

---

[77] Barbarian auxiliaries in Theodosius' army: Zosimus, *New History* 4.57–58; Orosius, *History against the Pagans* 7.35.11–19; Sokrates, *Ecclesiastical History* 5.25; Sozomen, *Ecclesiastical History* 7.24; see Liebeschuetz, *Barbarians and Bishops*, 26 n. 9, 30–31, 33 n. 10.

[78] Generals: Zosimos, *New History* 4.57.2–3; Eunapios, *History* fr. 60; Gaïnas' background: Anonymous, *Funeral Oration for John Chrysostom* 47, 50–51; Sokrates, *Ecclesiastical History* 6.6; Sozomenos, *Ecclesiastical History* 8.4. Alaric: Zosimos, *New History* 5.5.4; Sokrates, *Ecclesiastical History* 7.10.1.

[79] Zosimos, *New History* 4.58.2; Orosius, *History against the Pagans* 7.35.19 (10,000 of them); compare Jordanes, *Getica* 28.145 (Theodosius took 20,000 Goths with him).

introduced by Theodosius I or his immediate successors. Although our sources are poor, whenever they do shine a light on the armies and generals of the eastern empire, we find these operating in the same mode established by the Constantinian dynasty. Thus, when Theodosius led his *comitatus* west in 388 and 394, his army was commanded by two *magistri* and, at least in 388, we know that these included one *magister equitum* and one *magister peditum*. The distinction between the *comitatenses* and *limitanei* continued to be maintained, with local frontier forces responsible for river defense in 386, just as they had been in 376. We find no conclusive evidence for the supposed proliferation of *magistri* that is attributed by scholars to Valens and Theodosius (see p. 20 for the passage in Zosimos).

Our survey has focused on generals rather than armies because our sources preserve much more evidence about offices than they do about the size and nature of the imperial field armies. How many field armies did the eastern empire have in the fourth century? If we define a field army by the standards of the *Notitia* (and the attested practice of the later fifth century) as about 20,000 men,[80] it is unlikely that the fourth-century eastern empire had more than two such armies, matching the two *magistri* who commanded them. Put differently, the military structure of the Tetrarchy still remained in force. Moreover, these two armies would probably not have operated at full strength, as units from them were likely dispatched to the provinces on special assignment or placed under the command of the *magistri* who were occasionally posted to Illyricum or Oriens (Iovinus, Lupicinus), where they were joined by upgraded *limitanei* forces (sometimes called *pseudo-comitatenses*). Thus, if Valens marched to Adrianople with the equivalent of one and a half field armies, the ensuing battle caused the destruction of one field army equivalent (two-thirds, as Ammianus says). These losses required Theodosius to supplement the remainder (possibly still divided formally between two armies) with barbarian auxiliaries. Of all eastern emperors, Theodosius was the least likely to have been responsible for creating the three regional and two praesental armies that are documented in the *Notitia*, requiring 100,000 Roman soldiers in total. He simply did not have the resources, and for years after his death, as we will see, the eastern empire relied on a mix of depleted Roman and unruly barbarian forces. Nor is there any evidence that regional *magistri* were created for Illyricum or Thrace during this period, whether on a permanent or temporary basis, though a regular command for Oriens was established in about 390.[81] In sum, there is no way to

---

[80] See p. ix.   [81] See Appendices 1–2.

reconcile what we find in the sources for the reign of Theodosius with the military organization described by the *Notitia*.

This last point is important because scholars have often placed great weight on a passing polemical comment by the later pagan historian Zosimos about the high command under Theodosius, an emperor whom he hated on largely religious grounds:

> [Theodosius] created more commanders of the soldiers than there were before. Although previously one man had been the cavalry commander and one man had been placed in charge of the infantry, he distributed these offices to more than five men, and in this way he burdened the public finances with the greater cost of their supplies.[82]

Scholars have traditionally understood this passage as proving the establishment of the regional commands listed by the *Notitia*. But even on the face of it, Zosimos does not claim that Theodosius appointed five generals, as in the *Notitia*, but "more than five." In fact, Zosimos is being both rhetorical and polemical.

Zosimos' digression is not so much about the command structure of the Roman military as the proliferation of magisterial offices (ἀρχαί) and the ensuing financial cost. In other words, the issue is not that there were too many generals in the field, but that there were too many generals drawing a salary. Understood in this way, Zosimos' comment can easily be reconciled with our available evidence, but at the cost of its offering any support for the implementation of the *Notitia* system under Theodosius. For example, in 388 we know of at least five active *magistri* in the eastern empire: Timasius and Promotus, who were *in praesenti* under Theodosius himself (we use the term descriptively, not in a technical sense); Richomer and Arbogast, who were *in praesenti* for the fugitive Valentinian II; and Hellebicus, who was returning from an investigation in Antioch. It is also possible that men such as Saturninus, who is reported to have been continually influential at court throughout Theodosius' reign, continued to enjoy the benefits associated with their former rank as *magistri*.[83] It would not be surprising if all of these men received salaries appropriate to their rank. Thus, we can easily explain Zosimos' comments without recourse to the eastern *Notitia*. Moreover, a similar situation occurred

---

[82] Zosimos, *New History* 4.27.1–2: τοὺς δὲ τῶν στρατιωτικῶν ἡγουμένους πλείονας ἢ πρότερον εἰργάσατο. Ἑνὸς γὰρ ὄντος ἱππάρχου καὶ ἐπὶ τῶν πεζῶν ἑνὸς τεταγμένου, πλείοσιν ἢ πέντε ταύτας διένειμε τὰς ἀρχάς, τούτῳ τε καὶ τὸ δημόσιον σιτήσεσιν ἐβάρυνε ἀρχάς, τούτῳ τε καὶ τὸ δημόσιον σιτήσεσιν ἐβάρυνε πλείοσιν.

[83] Zosimos, *New History* 5.9.3.

about 393, when Richomer was once again in the east, Timasius and Stilicho were assigned to the army that Theodosius would take west, and Abundantius and Addaeus were also in office, the latter in Oriens.[84] When added to the proliferation of honorary appointments attested during this period, Zosimos' complaint makes perfect sense and accurately reflects the shifting nomenclature of generals, but offers no insight into the formal organization of the Roman high command.[85] Zosimos is polemically comparing the minimum number of active generals under Theodosius' predecessors with the maximum number of titleholders under that emperor.

Yet despite the broad continuity we observe during this period, our sources preserve evidence for three major innovations in the reign of Theodosius. The least important of these is the changing nomenclature of magisterial commands, which by 395 were generally called MVM or MM rather than by the branch-specific designations found in earlier periods. It is important to note that these offices were qualitatively different from those of the same name found in the west after 395. In the west, the MVM became a supreme commander-in-chief, as demonstrated by the career of Stilicho and the sequence of generalissimos who followed him as the effective heads of state, often acting behind weak emperors. In the east, however, these commands were more numerous and under civilian control.[86]

Theodosius' second innovation was the creation of a formal command for Oriens. Although emperors had been appointing generals to ad hoc commands in the region since at least the reign of Jovian, it was Theodosius who gave this office its first official form and, in so doing, established the template for the regional commands that are characteristic of the (much later) *Notitia* system. While it is inaccurate to claim Theodosius as the father of the *Notitia* system, it would be fair to understand him as its grandfather.

The final innovation of Theodosius' reign was a product of necessity rather than policy: his dependence on barbarian manpower. To a large extent, this was not Theodosius' fault. He inherited a shattered army in an empire that lacked the infrastructure necessary for the rapid, mass mobilization that had characterized the Roman military in the

---

[84] For these appointments, see Appendix 1. Admittedly, we cannot be certain that Stilicho was made MVM prior to Richomer's death in 393; for the date, see *PLRE* I, 764 (Richomeres).

[85] Honorary appointments: *CTh* 8.5.44.

[86] Numerous: *CTh* 7.4.18; civilian control: Zosimos, *New History* 5.9. See also Chapter 2.

Republican period. The eastern empire of the fourth century was never going to recover quickly from a defeat such as Adrianople. In response to this reality, Theodosius temporized, fighting a war of attrition, seeking political settlements, and finding opportunities to co-opt and erode the military capacity of the Goths. It was a sound strategy, one that played to the structural advantages of the Roman state. And it ultimately worked, as least for the east. It also, however, established the dynamics that would define the next phase of the eastern Roman military, which was marked by under-militarization on the Roman side and by violent, ethnically inflected tensions between the Roman civilian administration and the Gothic military forces that it ostensibly commanded.

CHAPTER 2

The Late Emergence of the Eastern Notitia *System (395–450)*

A nearly unanimous consensus among scholars dates the eastern portion of the *Notitia dignitatum* to about 395, give or take a few years. This has had dramatic consequences for our understanding of the history of east Roman military structures, though those consequences are somewhat obscured in the scholarship. It is helpful here to lay out the implications if we assume that the *Notitia* is a snapshot of the eastern command structure in 395, or 401 at the latest. First, we suddenly find five "named" generals and armies that formed specific regional commands, namely for Illyricum (under the *magister militum per Illyricum* or MMI), Thrace (under the *magister militum per Thracias* or *per Thraciam* or MMT), the praesentals I and II (under the two *magistri militum praesentalis* I and II, or MMP), and Oriens (under the *magister militum per Orientem* or MMO). Thus, the flexible, modular, and mobile field armies of the fourth century acquired a more settled distribution and posting to their respective regions. Second, the *Notitia* implies that these Roman armies (not including barbarian auxiliaries) were each about 20,000 men strong.

Thus, accepting the *Notitia* as an accurate guide to the organization of the army at the turn of the century requires us to suppose a radical reconfiguration took place in the twenty-two years between the battle of Adrianople, where Ammianus' account ends, and about 401, even though none of the specific armies and generals that are listed above are attested in all the other sources for that period, except for the MMO. Moreover, for reasons that remain unexplained, the *Notitia* reflected a decision (presumably made by Theodosius I or his closest advisors) to organize the military commands of the eastern and western empires in drastically different ways: first, the west retained the old system of division between MM *peditum* (infantry) and *equitum* (cavalry), whereas the east dropped it; and, second, the west invested supreme authority in the hands of the MMP *peditum*, supported by an MMP *equitum* and an MM for Gaul, whereas the east divided military power among five seemingly equivalent, regional MMs.

No explanation has been given for this huge discrepancy that, nevertheless, is supposed to have originated in a single, coherent Theodosian program.

As we have seen, historians soften the revolutionary nature of the *Notitia*'s reforms by trying to fit the events and prosopography of the years before 395 into the mold provided by the *Notitia*, to make it seem as though the Roman army was already operating according to the *Notitia*'s categories. That is, they impose various elements of the *Notitia* system onto the sources for earlier periods so that the reforms indicated in the document seem less radical. Known east Roman generals are pressed into being MMIs, MMTs, or MMPs even though the sources call them only MMs with no regional designation. This is done both in the *PLRE* and in narrative reconstructions. This practice stems from an assumption that the titles in the *Notitia* were not invented for and by that document in about 395 but were part of standing practice, even though they are not attested in any other source. The surviving laws of the fourth and early fifth centuries have headings that accurately name the titles of the officials to whom the laws are addressed, but these named regional commands do not appear in those titles. This results in a lot of aimless hand-wringing about who was MMP and who MMT at a time when in reality there were only MMs.[1] Here we avoid the temptation of fitting the historical facts into the model provided by the *Notitia* or assuming in advance that we know its date. Absent the framework of the *Notitia*, the sources present a history for the field armies and their generals that is radically different from that found in modern scholarship.

In fact, the evidence does not confirm the traditional narrative on any level. First, the titles for generals in the *Notitia* are not used until the 440s (with specific exceptions, such as Oriens). Second, there is no evidence for regional field armies and commands until the second half of the fifth century (again, excepting Oriens). And third, the history of the eastern empire after 395 – the focus of this chapter – disproves the notion that it had five Roman field armies of 20,000 men apiece, or even that it sought to create them in accordance with the *Notitia* blueprint as soon as the troubles of the years 395–400 were over. Thus, instead of dating the eastern *Notitia* to 395 and allowing its shadow to fall backward over the later part of the fourth century and forward over the early fifth century, the evidence compels us to situate that document in the 440s and allow its shadow to fall only on the second half of the fifth century. It is only in the 440s that

---

[1] For example, see the *PLRE* I on Stilicho, Abundantius, and Timasius. None of these titles is attested for any of these men.

the eastern *Notitia*, contemporary laws, and the narrative sources actually align.

Apart from the MMO, the other named positions (MMI, MMT, and the MMPs) are not mentioned until the 440s (with one specific ad hoc exception, discussed later). The fact that the laws and the literary texts consistently mention the MMO and not the other offices strengthens the value of their negative testimony for the other "named" offices. In other words, we need not worry that the compilers of the *Theodosian Code* (in the late 430s) and the *Justinianic Code* (in the early 530s) stripped from the headings of the laws the named commands of all the generals, leaving them all as generic MMs, but failed to do so only in the case of the MMO. Instead, the headings reflect a consistent reality, namely that there was an MMO from an early date, but no other regular named commands before the 440s. Until then, the fourth-century system of ad hoc flexible commands and appointments of MMs or MVMs continued. Moreover, the military history of the years 395–441 undermines the notion that Constantinople had at its disposal the field armies that are listed in the *Notitia*, which, as we shall demonstrate, it did have at its disposal after the 440s.

Absent the evidence of the *Notitia*, these broad continuities are precisely what we would expect to see in the period after 395. The default historical assumption must always be for continuity with the evidentiary burden falling on those arguing for change. The more drastic the change, the higher the burden of evidence. This is in part why scholars have sought evidence for a proto-*Notitia* system in the lead-up to Adrianople: continuity would lower the burden of evidence for a poorly documented yet allegedly epochal shift in Roman military structures. We belabor this point here because scholars who have internalized the accepted narratives of this period may unconsciously reverse this burden and argue that we cannot conclusively prove that the *Notitia* system was *not* in effect or that we are arguing from silence. However, given the shortcomings of the *Notitia* as evidence for its own reforms, the burden of proof rests on those advocating for its implementation around 395. It is enough for us to demonstrate that a narrative of continuity fits the available evidence, which it does, much better in fact than the standard narrative.

When Theodosius I marched west in 394 to defeat his rival Eugenius (and Eugenius' military puppet-master, the MM Arbogast), he took a large part of the eastern field army (or armies) with him. Unfortunately, we do not know which armies (or units) or how large they were. The literary sources indicate that they contained large contingents of barbarian auxiliaries (federates),[2] a type of unit that would not have been part of the regular command structure to begin with (i.e., such units would not have been listed in the *Notitia*, regardless of when it was drawn up). Theodosius died in Milan in January 395. Only a few months later, the eastern empire's Gothic auxiliary units under Alaric rebelled in the Balkans and proceeded to ravage Macedonia and Thessaly. Constantinople apparently had no army to send against them. The MM Stilicho, one of Theodosius' right-hand men and now the head of Honorius' government in the west, marched to Illyricum with the combined western and eastern field armies but, for reasons that we need not investigate here, he withdrew before engaging with the rebellious Goths and sent the eastern army on to Constantinople; this eastern army had just defeated its western counterpart at the Frigidus. A hostile source, Zosimos, says that Stilicho kept the better units for himself and returned the worse ones to Constantinople, though it is not clear how this could actually have been done.[3] Be that as it may, we do not know the identity and size of the units that were returned any more than we know those of the eastern units that had marched west with Theodosius in the first place, apart from the fact that they contained a large barbarian component.

Alaric and his Goths continued to ravage Greece for two years. In 397, the court of Arcadius reached a deal with him, perhaps appointing him as MM, which enabled him to settle his men in Illyricum. There is no question of Alaric being appointed MMI, as that office did not exist yet and is nowhere attested before the 440s. (Efforts to reconstruct the history of that office in this period are therefore entirely moot, as it is never actually attested.[4]) During the two years when Alaric was on the rampage, Constantinople sent no forces against him, despite the return of the eastern field army in 395. It was only Stilicho from the west who made some effort to contain him, unsuccessfully. It is therefore unlikely that the eastern empire had at its disposal four field armies in the vicinity at this time (namely for Illyricum, Thrace, and two praesentals). There was likely only one field army, possibly under strength, along with smaller units scattered in the Balkans and Oriens. The Goths that Alaric himself was leading had

[2] See p. 18.
[3] Zosimos, *New History* 5.4.2, 5.7.3–6; for the return of the eastern armies, see also Claudian, *Against Rufinus* 2.101–292 (their descriptions here, as in his other poems, are ethnographically colorful, not militarily precise); Philostorgios, *Ecclesiastical History* 11.3; Marcellinus Comes, *Chronicle* s.a. 395.5; and other sources; modern reconstructions in Cameron, *Claudian*, 164–168; Heather, *Goths and Romans*, 201–205.
[4] *Pace* Cameron and Long, *Barbarians and Politics*, 7.

probably formed a large part of the forces that Theodosius had led west in 394 (indeed, he had opened his attack by sending them in first, at the battle of the Frigidus). What with the losses in the war and Stilicho's alleged chicaneries in "withholding the best units," Constantinople does not appear to have had any sizable forces at its disposal, far less the structure reflected in the *Notitia*. In the context of the power struggle between Stilicho and the eastern court, the latter had an incentive to defeat Alaric in order to remove Stilicho's pretext for military intervention in the east. If significant armies of any sort existed, we expect Constantinople to have used them in this crisis. Instead, their existence is never mentioned. All we hear about are Alaric's forces and the eastern armies that had gone west in 394 and were now returned by Stilicho.

In 395, an army of Huns crossed the Caucasus and launched a devastating series of raids into the Roman and Persian empires. We have only scanty notices about this on the Roman side, but there appears to have been no serious reaction to the invasion on the part of the Roman army. This was when Stilicho still had the eastern field armies with him, and it appears that the MMO (Addaeus) was unable or unwilling to mount an effective resistance, suggesting that he did not command significant military forces. In fact, his men are said to have been mostly Gothic auxiliaries (though the sources for this specific claim are poor).[5] In 397 or 398, after Alaric had been pacified by the eastern court by the grant of an MM title, the most powerful individual at the court, the eunuch chamberlain Eutropius, personally led an army to the east against another group of Huns who had invaded Asia Minor, and he scored some kind of victory against them. The fact that a chamberlain marched against them does not mean, of course, that the court was short on generals, but rather that Eutropius wanted the credit and perhaps feared empowering a potential rival. Unfortunately, our main account of this expedition occurs in a poetic invective against Eutropius by the Latin poet Claudian, and its genre and poetic language prevent us from extracting reliable information from it about the eastern command structure or its armies. Presumably, Eutropius used the field armies returned by Stilicho in 395, at least in part.[6] Our sources do not explain why the Romans took the field against the Huns in 397/8 but not against Alaric. It may be telling that Eutropius went east only after Alaric had accepted terms. Constantinople evidently did not have the

---

[5] The sources are collected and studied by Greatrex and Greatrex, "The Hunnic Invasion"; Trombley and Watt, *The Chronicle of Pseudo-Joshua the Stylite*, 10 n. 40.

[6] Claudian, *Against Eutropius* 1.234–282, 2(pr).55–56; Liebeschuetz, *Barbarians and Bishops*, 99–100.

resources or confidence to deal with both enemies simultaneously, or even just Alaric.

The next crisis faced by the eastern court was the complicated Gaïnas affair, in 399–400. To summarize, a Romano-Gothic officer named Tribigild rebelled in Phrygia in 399 with an army of federate Goths. The court sent against him the military officer Leo (with an unspecified rank), but Tribigild defeated Leo, even though Tribigild himself had just been defeated by local defense forces in Pamphylia. The court then sent Gaïnas to suppress Tribigild. Gaïnas was also of Gothic origin and related to Tribigild. He and his mostly Gothic army joined forces with Tribigild and marched on the capital, demanding the dismissal of the eunuch Eutropius. This was granted, and Gaïnas was appointed MM. He introduced more than 7,000 of his Gothic soldiers into Constantinople and tried to bully the court, whereupon, in 400, the populace of the City rose up and slaughtered his army in what can only be described as an ethnic pogrom.[7] Gaïnas' other forces were defeated by the MMO Fravitta, another Romano-Gothic officer who was brought up from the east in haste for that purpose. Gaïnas was killed by some Huns as he fled across the Danube.[8]

As we argue in Appendix 3, none of these men were formally MMPs, nor were they called that. In fact, it does not appear that any of them save Fravitta and, after his return to Constantinople, Gaïnas held the rank of MM at all.[9] But were Leo and Gaïnas commanding the praesental field armies, as those are listed in the *Notitia*? They do seem to have been commanding forces based around Constantinople. But the events are impossible to reconcile with the existence of such armies, certainly not any that were enrolled to the notional strength of 20,000 men. Zosimos, our most detailed narrative, emphasizes that Tribigild commanded barbarian and not Roman soldiers.[10] In order to threaten a full praesental army, if that is what Leo commanded, Tribigild would have had to be leading an army of roughly comparable size, that is roughly 20,000 men. But even if

---

[7] 7,000: Zosimos, *New History* 5.19.4.

[8] The episode has been studied many times. The main sources are cited by the *PLRE* I, 379–380 (Gaïnas) and *PLRE* II, 661–662 (Leo 2) and 1125–1126 (Tribigildus). The most detailed study that is based on the sources is Liebeschuetz, *Barbarians and Bishops*. Cameron and Long, *Barbarians and Politics*, correct some of the interpretive distortions in Liebeschuetz's account (such as the existence of anti-barbarian "parties" in Constantinople), but too easily dismiss the testimony of the sources about Gaïnas' actions in order to push their own interpretation.

[9] Liebeschuetz, *Barbarians and Bishops*, 101–102.

[10] Zosimos, *New History* 5.13.2; additional sources for that claim: Liebeschuetz, *Barbarians and Bishops*, 100.

Leo's army was under strength, it is hard to imagine that a barbarian army equivalent in size to a Roman field army was operating in Asia Minor under a barbarian general in 399. Moreover, at the lowest point of his rebellion, following his defeat by local defense forces in Pamphylia, Zosimos reports that Tribigild's followers amounted to only three hundred men.[11] Zosimos attributes Tribigild's defeat of Leo to the insinuation into Leo's army of barbarian soldiers sent by Gaïnas who overran the country and attacked the Roman forces, while the western poet Claudian reports that Leo was caught in an ambush.[12] This narrative is unintelligible if we assume that Leo's allegedly praesental armies were anywhere near their notional strength. Leo's defeat presents another problem. If a full field army were destroyed or mauled in a rebellion, we could reasonably expect that one of our sources would mention it. As for Gaïnas' army, that too appears to have consisted entirely of federate barbarian forces.[13]

The overwhelming evidence therefore indicates that Leo and Gaïnas were campaigning with relatively small armies. In fact, the entire affair, especially the Roman reliance on barbarian units under Gaïnas' command, makes more sense if we assume that Tribigild's army was relatively small, but caught the court off-guard, requiring the rapid mustering of whatever forces were at hand or could be spared from other commands. This explains how Tribigild could be defeated by a local militia in Pamphylia,[14] and strongly suggests that the *Notitia* system of field armies did not yet exist. In the end, the court had to bring up the MMO in order to deal with the situation. Put differently, the revolt of Gaïnas could not have played out in the way that is described by our sources if the court had three armies of 20,000 men in the vicinity to call upon (i.e., of Thrace and praesentals I and II). Clearly, neither the command structure nor the numbers reflected in the *Notitia* yet existed.[15] The episode suggests that the armies of the eastern empire at this time consisted overwhelmingly of barbarian federate auxiliaries. Only the forces led by Leo are called "Roman" in contrast to Gaïnas' barbarians.[16]

This extreme reliance on barbarian soldiers in the generation after the treaty of 382 elicited considerable pushback from "patriotic" Roman

---

[11] Zosimos, *New History* 5.16.

[12] Zosimos, *New History* 5.17.2; Claudian, *Against Eutropius* 2.432–473.

[13] Sources in Liebeschuetz, *Barbarians and Bishops*, 37, 102.   [14] Zosimos, *New History* 5.15–16.

[15] The reliance on barbarian soldiers and the gap between what the narrative reveals and the norms of the *Notitia* is central to the analysis of Liebeschuetz, *Barbarians and Bishops*, 34–55, but he (along with almost everyone else) does not question the early dating of the *Notitia* nor realize that its top military ranks are not attested in this period.

[16] For example, Zosimos, *New History* 5.17.1, 5.18.1, 5.19.1, among other sources.

authors at this time, who argued that the empire should be recruiting its soldiers among its own people, who were raised within and loyal to the Roman polity. Following the events of 399–400, Constantinople would gradually adopt precisely such a policy, refuting the belief of many modern historians that there was now no alternative to barbarian recruitment.[17] But the entire controversy would not have happened at all had the field armies of the eastern empire around AD 400 already consisted of mostly regular Roman units, as called for in the *Notitia*.

Assuming the existence of the *Notitia* structure at this time, as many historians and the *PLRE* do, can lead to far-reaching distortions of these events. One study, for example, which wants to downplay the role of ethnicity, pushes aside the clear and consistent evidence of the sources that Gaïnas' soldiers were barbarian federates and argues instead that they must have been Roman because he was the "praesental" general and thus in command of Roman armies. But neither that title nor those Roman armies are attested: they are introduced via the *Notitia* paradigm. Thus, the role of ethnic conflict in the events is suppressed, when in fact it was central to the Roman understanding of the entire episode.[18] Gaïnas did gain command over some Roman soldiers when he was made MM after strong-arming the court with his mostly barbarian army, but, when he later fled to the Danube, he executed the few Roman soldiers who had stuck with him, and crossed the river with only his barbarian followers.[19] Those followers were the survivors of the ethnic pogrom of 400. Ethnicity had life-or-death implications in these conflicts.

The years 401–440 were the most peaceful in the history of the eastern empire. The empire was governed by a competent group of mostly civilian officials in Constantinople, under two emperors who were wise enough to keep out of the way and not have strong opinions about governance: Arcadius (395–408) and his son Theodosius II (408–450). Military threats were minor or distant. In the first decade of the century, Alaric was occasionally based in northwestern Illyricum but was preoccupied with the western empire, where he eventually sacked Rome in 410. During much of this decade a state of cold war existed between the western and the eastern courts, stemming largely from Stilicho's ambitions, but this ended when he was murdered in 408. In 410, Constantinople sent an army of 4,000 to guard Arcadius' brother, the emperor Honorius (395–423), in

---

[17] Kaldellis, "Classicism, Barbarism, and Warfare."
[18] Cameron and Long, *Barbarians and Politics*, 202–209.   [19] Zosimos, *New History* 5.21.6.

Ravenna. We do not know which units these were, though, inevitably, at least one scholar has tried to identify them on the basis of the *Notitia*.[20]

The praetorian prefect Anthemius was in charge of the administration for many years during this period, and it was he who initiated the construction of the Theodosian walls of Constantinople, a project that lasted nine years (404–413).[21] This expanded the City, doubling its area, and further protected it against the likes of Alaric, as all could see how he was threatening Rome in the west. Judging from the position of the Golden Gate built by Theodosius I, the construction of the Theodosian walls was possibly planned as early as his reign,[22] but postponed because of the troubles and political instability of the years 395–400.

In 409, a Hun named Uldis, the one who had killed Gaïnas, crossed the Danube and raided Thrace. No Roman army came out to confront him, but the commander of the forces in Thrace (ὁ ὕπαρχος τῶν Θρᾳκίων στρατευμάτων) tried to open peace talks with him. Uldis refused, whereupon Constantinople bribed many of his followers to desert him and he fled. A tribe following him, the Sciri, were taken captive by the Roman forces and dispersed as agricultural laborers.[23] It might be tempting to see this commander of the Roman forces in Thrace as an MMT, but it does not appear that he led a field army with which to meet the enemy, as did the confirmed MMTs of the later fifth and sixth centuries, who routinely led field armies out to confront invaders such as Uldis. Moreover, in the Greek military argot of the period, ὕπαρχος is never used to refer to an MM (those terms are *strategos* or *stratelates*). *Hyparchos* literally refers to a subordinate officer. In a technical sense in this period, it was used to translate Latin *praefectus* and was used most commonly for the praetorian prefects and prefects of Constantinople. But, as it happens, there were also military prefects who commanded units of the empire's border soldiers, the *limitanei*, and it is likely one of these who made the overtures to Uldis.[24] Thrace certainly had defense forces, but they do not yet appear to include a dedicated field army. Under the *duces* of Scythia, Moesia Prima, and Moesia Secunda, the border provinces that were precisely in question in

[20] Sozomenos, *Ecclesiastical History* 9.8.6 (4,000); Zosimos, *New History* 6.8.2 (the number of soldiers, 40,000, is obviously wrong here); Prokopios, *Wars* 3.2.36 ("a great number"). Identification (conjectural): Hoffmann, *Das spätrömische Bewegungsheer*, vol. 1, 46–48.

[21] Nine years: see the inscription in Lebek, "Die Landmauer von Konstantinopel." Anthemios: Rendina, *La prefettura di Antemio*.

[22] Bardill, "The Golden Gate."

[23] Sozomenos, *Ecclesiastical History* 9.5; *CTh* 5.6.3. Uldis is *PLRE* II, 1180 (Vldin).

[24] Military prefects: Jones, *Later Roman Empire*, 640; all *hyparchoi* (including military): Mason, *Greek Terms for Roman Institutions*, 13, 95, 155.

this episode, the *Notitia* lists a number of military *praefecti* who commanded legions of *limitanei*.[25] The Uldis episode, therefore, both in its narrative and prosopographical aspects, suggests that the field-army command of Thrace, under an MMT, did not yet exist, only a system of *limitanei* whose command structure anticipated that described in the *Notitia*.

Uldis' invasion was perhaps a minor incident, but the potential for trouble coming from north of the Danube and the fact that Alaric was still on the loose prompted Anthemius to take strong defensive measures. A set of interlinked laws from either 407 or 413 provided for the fortification of cities in Illyricum and their provisioning in the wake of Alaric's depredations. Significantly, these laws were issued to the praetorian prefect of Illyricum,[26] as no designated general for that region (viz., an MMI) is yet attested.

Now, one of the fundamental problems in studies that assume a functioning *Notitia* system is the role of arguments from silence. As a general rule, we cannot argue that something, such as a military command, did not exist simply because our sources do not mention it, especially when there is a positive reason to think it existed, such as the *Notitia*. Our ancient sources are simply too limited for historians to expect consistent attestation of all but the most basic features of the ancient world. Yet there must be limits to our credulity, especially when the positive evidence is weak or suspect. In our case, we have a complete silence regarding the MMI and MMPs for over forty years of east Roman history after the *Notitia* was supposed to have been produced, a period during which we can reasonably expect them to have been active at several points (Alaric, Tribigild and Gaïnas, Uldis). This is perhaps too long a gap to be explained even by the vagaries of our ancient sources, especially when it coincides with a period when the laws in the *Theodosian Code* divulge the titles of many high officials.

The period 395–440s would be entirely lacking in MMTs too but for one solitary case. In 412, we have the first reference to a *magister militum per Thracias*, though there would not be another until the 440s. This solitary attestation occurs in a law issued to the MMT Constans, instructing him to carry out a major reorganization of the Danube fleet and river defenses, roughly the region from where Uldis had so recently crossed.[27] It is likely no accident that this first known MMT (or "proto-MMT") appears in connection with a major defensive reform or that he is the only MMT

---

[25] *ND Or.* 39–41.   [26] *CTh* 11.17.4 and 15.1.49, 12.1.177; *CJ* 10.49.1.   [27] *CTh* 7.17.1 (412 AD).

attested for the entire period of the long peace, 401–441. In other words, we propose that this was not a routine posting, known through a law on routine matters, but an exceptional command with a specific, goal-oriented remit, which is specifically defined by the law in question. Moreover, there is as yet no evidence for a "field army of Thrace" resembling that laid out in the *Notitia*. The law in question deals only with the Danube fleet, and it is possible that Constans' was still only an ad hoc appointment to the diocese of Thrace, charged with organizing river defenses, rather than commanding or creating a putative field army of Thrace. Even if he did command an army, there is no reason to see Constans' appointment as fundamentally different from the ad hoc regional commands that had been common since the reign of Julian. Constans was to Thrace was Lupicinus had been to Oriens: an exceptional posting within an evolving system that would only later be regularized when circumstances changed.

Oriens was the first to be regularized. It was a discrete command far from the capital and the other Balkan armies. It faced a major potential enemy (Persia), a politically stable entity with a long history of war against Rome. (In this period there was only one brief war between the two empires, in 420–422.[28]) Given the distance from Constantinople, the size of the border region, and the consistency of the threat from Persia, it made sense for the Roman military establishment to have a specific designated command for that potential front. As we noted, the MMO appears to have been in place from the 390s.

The continued demilitarization of the rest of the empire is reflected in the course of this brief Persian war in 420–422. In order to prosecute the war, the high command moved many units from the Balkans to the eastern front. This left the Balkan provinces exposed to an army of Huns that raided as far as Thrace in 422.[29] We do not hear of the field armies of the MMT, MMP I, and MMP II during those events. Thus nothing about the military history of this period suggests that those named commands, or the armies listed under them in the *Notitia*, existed, at least not at anything resembling their paper strength in the *Notitia*.

Apart from Constans, all we find during this period are "generic" MMs executing a wide range of functions on the court's behalf, including diplomatic, political, legal, and even ecclesiastical duties. The *PLRE* and other scholars insist on pressing these MMs into the named commands

---

[28] Greatrex and Lieu, *The Roman Eastern Frontier*, 36–43.
[29] Croke, "Evidence for the Hun Invasion"; soldiers transferred to the east: Theophanes, *Chronographia* a.m. 5943, p. 104 (a *numerus* from Greece sent to the east).

(i.e., MMP, MMT, MMI), on the assumption that they were operating within the system laid out in the *Notitia*, but this, we propose, is an anachronism. During the long peace, the vast majority of these generals – in fact, all but Constans and the MMOs – were generic MMs, assigned to whatever function the court wanted. An example of the modern bias is Macedonius, an MM attested in a law of 423. The *PLRE* cannot make him MMO because that position is known to have been held by someone else at that time, and so it decides that he must have been either MMI or MMT, even though the law deals with soldiers' legal rights generally and is not specifically about those regions. He is accordingly placed in the fasti of *both* the MMIs and MMTs, with a question mark in both cases. In reality, Macedonius was just an MM-at-large, like most of his colleagues during this period (and during the fourth century).[30]

In fact, a law of 413 makes clear that the court was still sending out *comites* to carry out military functions "to any province or provinces for their defense" and that other men could also be sent out to "act in the place of the *illustres* masters of soldiers"; in other words, these were non-MMs who functioned as if they were real MMs.[31] An actual case of this is attested in 354 AD,[32] which means that the early fifth century was still adhering to the ad hoc approach of the fourth, not to the formalized one of the *Notitia*. The approach was so ad hoc that the court had to issue a law in 441 to define the relative court status of all its various generals.[33] Significantly, that law does not mention the named regional commands (MMI, MMT, MMP I and II, MMO). The law requires further discussion because it refutes the pervasive tendency in the scholarship to press generals named in the sources only as MMs into one of the regional commands known from the *Notitia*. In fact, it definitively severs the link between military office and the command over armies with broad implications for how we reconstruct the history of the late Roman military.

*

There is a bias in the scholarship in favor of assigning attested generals (MMs or MVMs) to the specific regional commands listed in the *Notitia* and against leaving them as undesignated "generic MMs at large" (if you will). For instance, whenever an MM is attested as being at Constantinople, there

---

[30] Macedonius 4 in *PLRE* II, 697, 1291–1292, based on *CJ* 3.21.2.
[31] *eos, qui vicem illustrium virorum magistrorum militum susceperint peragendam*: *CJ* 12.12.2 = *CTh* 6.14.3.
[32] Ammianus Marcellinus, *Res gestae* 14.11.5, 15.13.3 (*pro magistro equitum agente … militem regens*).
[33] *CJ* 12.8.2, discussed later in the chapter.

is a bias toward presuming that he was an MMP, even though we know that many generals were present at the court of Constantinople at any given time on business (or simply because they were senators, with no military responsibilities despite their military titles). Despite this bias, the fasti of the *PLRE* II and III name many generic MMs who were not posted to one of the regional commands, effectively admitting that such generals were common. To pick a random case, one Stephanus is addressed in a law of Anastasius (who ruled in 491–518) simply as *magister militum*.[34] Some of these cases, we suspect, are listed as generic MMs in the fasti of the *PLRE* only because the regional commands in the areas where they appear are known to have been occupied by someone else at the same time, as we saw in the case of Macedonius.

In fact, the situation with generals at the Constantinopolitan court was even more complex, as revealed by the aforementioned law of Theodosius II of 441 that tried to sort out their relative ranks *right before* the creation of the regional command system of the *Notitia*.[35] These gradations of rank (corresponding to fundamental differences in the manner in which one held office) are known and can be reconstructed from other evidence, especially inscriptions and narrative texts, but this law conveniently lays them out, for it tried to clear up the confusion caused by different kinds of generals jostling for status at the court.

This law of Theodosius II attempts to sort out the relative ranking of men who held *illustris* senatorial rank by virtue of their office. This applied to all offices that conferred *illustris* rank and not just to generals, but we will focus on generals. Theodosius II establishes the hierarchy they will have at his court, from higher to lower. First are those who have actually exercised the functions of the office in question, whom he calls *administrationes*. Second are the *vacantes*, or "titular" officeholders, who received the belt of office while at the court. *Vacans* meant that one held the title associated with the position but did not exercise its functions (although, as we will see, *vacantes* were sometimes, and possibly often, men who were qualified to exercise those functions, and did so). Third were those to whom the belt of office was mailed because they were not present at the court (presumably these were *vacantes* too, although they are not explicitly called that here). Fourth were those who held a position in a purely honorary way (*honorarii*) and who, while present at the court, received a codicil but not a belt of office. Fifth were those to whom the insignia of office were mailed;

---

[34] *CJ* 7.51.6: Stephanus II in *PLRE* II, 1030, known only from this law.
[35] *CJ* 12.8.2 of AD 441; compare Jones, *Later Roman Empire*, 535.

presumably they, too, were *honorarii*, and they, too, did not receive the belt of office. Theodosius II ranks the *administrationes* higher than the *vacantes*, and the latter higher than the *honorarii*. All these men could potentially be called "generals" in any given type of source.

Now, the lower end of each category could overlap with the upper end of the next. For example, Theodosius notes that some *magistri militum vacantes* were given actual military commands. He names the *vacans* MM Germanus, who, in 440 or 441, was sent to Sicily in an abortive campaign against the Vandals in North Africa, and also one Pentadius, who, while *vacans*, exercised the function of praetorian prefect on that same expedition (i.e., he organized its logistics and finances).[36] These two men and others like them, the emperor says, count as *administrationes* even though they had held their position only as *vacantes* at the time. We also know of military *tribuni vacantes* in the fourth century who carried out special operations, so some *vacantes* were perhaps officers with a titular rank waiting to be activated.[37] Thus, some or many of the *vacantes* MMs hanging around the court were military men who could potentially be entrusted with campaigns. But other *vacantes* held office in a way that was little different from the *honorarii* ranked below them.

Honorarii must be distinguished from *honorati*. The latter were all current or former holders of high office. *Honorarii* were a special subcategory, men who, for the most part, had no experience in the formal domain of their office but who were awarded it (along with its social and financial perks) as a way for the regime to reward them and create cadres of loyalists. They were treated by the court *as if* they had once held it, even though they had nothing to do with its actual business. In 450–455, *honorarii* are said to have attained their rank "without having acted (*sine actu*)."[38] In the 480s, the emperor Zeno called them men "who without having done any administration (*sine administratione*)" have been awarded with honorary codicils and so occupy a high rank and "appear to have carried out what in fact they have not carried out."[39] Thus, for example, city councilors could be given the honorary rank of *comes*, and professors of Greek and Latin in Constantinople could, upon retirement, be given the honorary rank of ex-*vicarius*.[40] Honorary offices were one way to reach *illustris* rank.[41] In 439, there was a fear that Jews might be

---

[36] For the expedition, see pp. 40–41. For Germanus 3 and Pentadius 2, see *PLRE* II, 505, 858, respectively.
[37] Jones, *Later Roman Empire*, 640.   [38] *CJ* 12.40.10.6 (issued at Rome).
[39] *CJ* 3.24.3.2 (issued at Constantinople).   [40] *CJ* 10.32.47 (395 AD) and *CJ* 12.15.1 (425 AD).
[41] *CJ* 1.3.21 (issued at Constantinople in 442 AD).

illicitly attaining high rank this way.[42] As there was no requirement that *honorarii* specifically disclose that their office was not administrative in, say, their private correspondence, there is always a possibility that some "generals" have snuck into our fasti who had nothing to do with the military establishment. But they would be unlikely to show up in narrative sources about war and politics.

Draft formularies of appointment (*codicils*) to *vacans* positions survive in the *Variae* of Cassiodorus, a Roman official in the service of the Ostrogothic kings of Italy in the early sixth century. They note that such appointments do not confer "real power" but only honor; that they carry "influence" but not administrative authority. One of them is awarded to a child, to honor his father (and keep him loyal to the regime). Thus, it appears that by this date, and in Gothic Italy, *vacans* positions had effectively become what *honorarius* positions were in fifth-century Constantinople.[43]

Therefore, in 441 in Constantinople we observe the following hierarchy of MMs:

1. MM *administrationes* (not yet linked to specific regional commands, apart from Oriens, which is not mentioned in the law)
2. MM *vacantes*, counting as *administrationes* due to a military assignment
3. MM *vacantes*, essentially honorific, though perhaps kept as a reserve officer corp
4. MM *honorarii*, purely honorific

Thus, we must not assume that an MM present at the court must have been an MMP, even if in a generic sense he was *in praesenti* (at the court). The court was crawling with MMs of various kinds.

Additionally, we cannot assume that the existence of a general implies the existence of an army for him to command, even when we have positive evidence for a named command. This law makes clear that the office and function of the *magistri* were not linked in the way modern scholars have generally assumed. It is an honest mistake, but this law is explicit: holding the rank of general did not mean that one also commanded armies.

To conclude, the law of 441 refutes the assumption that MMs or MVMs present at the court in this period must have been MMPs. That is our main interest in this law. The fact that it fails to mention any of the regional

---

[42] *CJ* 1.9.18 (issued at Constantinople in 439 AD).
[43] Cassiodorus, *Variae* 6.10.3, 6.11.2, 215 (trans. Bjornlie, pp. 259–262, and 91–92, respectively).

commands is also consistent with our overall argument for the late evolution of the *Notitia* system but is not decisive proof for it. The logic of the law does not require it to mention the regional commands (it does not mention the MMOs, who we know existed at this time). Our overall argument for the late evolution of that system is instead based on its absence from all the empirical evidence for the period before the mid-440s.

*

The absence of named regional MMs for the period 401–441 – including from the law of 441 – is no accident of the sources. Though this absence is not conclusive proof that these offices did not exist, this happens to be an exceptionally well-documented period for court officials, given the compilation of the *Theodosian Code* in 438, which privileged recent laws issued by the regime of Theodosius II, and the extensive registry of high officials that we can access through the Church Council of Ephesus I (431) and its aftermath.[44] In all this documentation, there is only one MMT (Constans in 412) and no MMIs or MMPs.

Moreover, we have no references to their corresponding field armies. This is perhaps less surprising, as the sources are more likely to mention a prominent general by name or office than they are to specify the exact armies that he was commanding, if any. Yet the scholarship has "invented" those regional armies for this period through the following set of assumptions: first, MMs are pressed into being MMIs, MMTs, or MMPs, and then the regional armies of those generals are assumed to exist along with the officers who commanded them. In this way, the history of the regional field armies (including the praesental armies) has been filled up and stretched from 395 to 630. That is why it is important to insist that most of the generals who we know before the 440s were "generic" MMs and that the regional armies come fully into existence only after the 440s.

In the decades after 395, the eastern empire was relatively demilitarized in comparison with what came after. We have seen that Constantinople had few armies with which to face the challenges of 395–400 (Alaric, Tribigild, Gaïnas), and we do not find evidence for the existence of multiple field armies in the decades after that, though our narrative will show that there was a gradual buildup before the 440s. This approach made sense. Constantinople was at peace with Persia, and an MMO, leading forces of unknown size, was deemed sufficient to

---

[44] Matthews, *Laying Down the Law*; Millar, *A Greek Roman Empire*.

defend the east (unlike the fourth century, when the eastern border frequently required the attention of the emperor in person with his field armies). Moreover, until the buildup of Hunnic power under Attila, there was also no enemy north of the Danube that could do more than raid the Roman empire, and the *limitanei* usually dealt with those threats. Finally, Constantinople was now in the hands of civilian politicians and administrators, who had learned from the Gaïnas episode and also from what was unfolding in the west that the single greatest threat to their position were their own generals, especially barbarian types leading mostly barbarian soldiers. After 400, Constantinople had a political incentive to keep the armies small and no strong military incentive to build them up.

This is not to say that the eastern empire was completely demilitarized. Many of the individual units that later made up the field armies and that are itemized in the *Notitia* were likely in existence at this time (several are attested in Ammianus). That Constantinople was replenishing its military strength during the period is evident from its war with Persia in the 420s and the aid it began to send to the west starting in that same decade, but in the absence of active military pressure there was no impetus for remilitarization on the scale of the *Notitia*.

In 424–425, the eastern empire had armies to send to Italy to depose the "usurper" Ioannes and install the child emperor Valentinian III on the western throne. We have only brief accounts of this war, and one of them features an angel. It appears that Constantinople deployed two field armies, one under Ardaburius, the hero of the Persian war of 420–422 and his son Aspar, and the other under the otherwise unknown Candidianus, a general whose exact title or command (if there was one) is not specified. The size of the military forces that each side deployed is also unknown. Ardaburius explicitly held the title MVM and, as he was heading toward Aquileia, he divided his force into two, taking the main army and fleet with him into the Adriatic and giving command of the cavalry to his son Aspar. He was then blown off course and captured by Ioannes' forces, but Aspar arrived with the cavalry to save the day. (Candidianus meanwhile invaded north Italy with great success, but the surviving narratives focus on the Ardaburii.) Thus, it seems that the command structure in this war consisted of an MVM who assigned his cavalry to Aspar, who was presumably a *magister equitum* or at least replicated the functions of one (it is also possible that this was an arrangement of strategic convenience – seeing as Ardaburius was about to take to the sea – that was unrelated to Aspar's rank and title). Candidianus led the second invasion army, presumably as an

MM or MVM. This, then, was still the fourth-century command structure, not that of the *Notitia*.[45]

In 431, Constantinople sent "a large army" under Aspar to North Africa to help the western empire cope with the Vandal invasion. Aspar was now a general (*strategos*) in his own right. We are not given exact numbers for the force that he led, but he was up against the Vandals, who had crossed over from Spain in 429 and could probably field about 15,000 men, the equivalent of a Roman field army, representing a migrating population of around 80,000 people. Aspar was assisted locally by the western commander, Bonifatius, though they were defeated by the Vandals. It is likely, then, that Aspar and Bonifatius led a combined force of roughly the same scale as the Vandal army, though we do not know what portion of it each of the two generals contributed. Presumably Aspar brought most of it, an equivalent of half of one of the later field armies of the *Notitia*.[46]

Before he departed from North Africa in 434, Aspar concluded a treaty with the Vandals and their king Gaizeric that safeguarded Carthage and its province, Proconsularis, for the Romans, though the treaty held for only five years. In 439, Gaizeric broke the treaty and conquered Carthage. Constantinople, following its policy of solidarity with the western empire, sent "a large fleet" that reached as far as Sicily before it was recalled. Later sources tell us that the fleet contained 1,100 or 1,170 ships but we cannot rely on this obviously inflated number from an eighth-century source to extrapolate the size of the forces that they carried. The generals in command are variously reported as three (Areobindus, Ansila, and Germanus) or five (those three plus Inobindus and Arintheus). Their precise titles on this expedition are not given in the sources, except for Germanus, who was an MM *vacans*.[47] There is no reason to believe that they held the named commands of the *Notitia* (MMI, MMT, MMP, or MMO – when Belisarius was sent to conquer North Africa in 533 he held the position of MMO). Moreover, we cannot calculate how many field armies were

---

[45] Olympiodoros, *History* fr. 43.1: Ardaburius as MVM (explicitly so called); ibid. fr. 43.2 = Philostorgios, *Ecclesiastical History* 12.13–14: Aspar took over the cavalry; Sokrates, *Ecclesiastical History* 7.23 (including the angel); for the context, see Matthews, *Western Aristocracies and Imperial Court*, 378–381.

[46] Prokopios, *Wars* 3.3.35 ("large army" and *strategos*); largely repeated by Theophanes, *Chronographia* a.m. 5931, p. 95. 80,000 Vandals: Victor of Vita, *History of the Vandal Persecution* 1.2; and Prokopios, *Wars* 3.5.18–19 (the same number, but all warriors, which is almost certainly a mistake); for the numbers involved here, see Heather, *Empires and Barbarians*, 175–177.

[47] Prosper Tiro, *Chronicle* s.aa. 441 and 442, pp. 478–479 ("large fleet" and three generals); Theophanes, *Chronographia* a.m. 5942, pp. 101–102 (garbled chronology; 1,100 ships and five generals); Nikephoros Xanthopoulos, *Ecclesiastical History* 14.57 (1,170 ships; names only Areobindus and Germanus). Germanus as *vacans*: *CJ* 12.8.2; for the meaning of *vacans*, see p. 35.

conveyed by this large fleet. If we assume on the higher end that it was two, then, to calculate the total mobile forces of the eastern empire at this time we need to add the army of the MMO (though parts of it may have been sent west with the fleet) and whatever reserves stayed behind. The latter were likely skeletal, which is why the fleet was recalled quickly when Attila the Hun invaded the Balkans in 441.

However, if we try to imagine these events assuming that the *Notitia* system was in effect in 441, then this episode becomes unintelligible. Even if we take a maximalist view and assign two field armies, or almost 40,000 men, to the expeditionary force, Constantinople should still have had roughly 60,000 soldiers at its disposal when Attila invaded, including at least 40,000 in or near the Balkans. Even that number assumes that none of the units assigned to the North African expedition were drawn from the army of Oriens. Moreover, these 40,000 soldiers would not include *limitanei*, so the effective number of available soldiers is pushed even higher. These forces should have been deemed sufficient to confront Attila without the need to recall the expedition. Even if the threat posed by Attila required the recall of some expeditionary forces, as many as 20,000, or a full field army, could have been recalled while still maintaining a numerical advantage against the Vandals. That is, if the *Notitia* system was in place in 441, the Romans should have been able to direct 60,000 field army soldiers against Attila, a force equal to the army Julian used to invade Persia, while still sending a force of 20,000 against the Vandals. It is impossible to reconcile Roman armies on this scale with the evidence of the sources and the course of events.

In order to preserve the traditional dating of the *Notitia* system, then, we must either imagine that it had fallen into desuetude less than fifty years after it was allegedly put into effect while simultaneously failing to leave direct evidence of its existence – or that the system simply did not exist. The available evidence favors the latter interpretation. When Attila invaded in 441, the *Notitia* armies were not in place to oppose him.

Instead, the strategic configuration changed during the 440s in response to – or in preparation for – the major attacks of Attila the Hun. Constantinople had been watching the growth of Hunnic power north of the Danube for decades, no doubt with growing apprehension. Back in 422, the court had agreed to pay 350 lbs of gold annually (= 25,200 *solidi*) to the Huns to keep them at bay. This was protection money pure and simple. That sum had subsequently, in the 430s, been doubled to 700 lbs of gold.[48]

---

[48] Priskos, *History* fr. 2; see Croke, "Evidence for the Hun Invasion."

This was not a trivial sum, which suggests that Constantinople was taking the Huns seriously, perhaps seriously enough to have also initiated a program of remilitarization in the Balkans that would culminate in the *Notitia* structure of two designated Balkan field armies (Illyricum and Thrace) backed by the two praesental armies, which, as we will see, may have functioned as reserves.

Attila's invasions were massive, swift, and caused appalling amounts of destruction to both cities and the Roman armies. The imperial establishment was "gripped with overwhelming fear."[49] A contemporary author lamented that "there was so much bloodshed, it was not possible to count the dead. Even the monks wanted to escape to Jerusalem, and the Huns almost captured Constantinople ... They so devastated Thrace that it will never recover."[50] Specifically, in 441–442 Attila raided Illyricum in a surprise attack, taking Singidunum, Viminacium, and the major city of Naissus, which he destroyed. The Roman response was led by Aspar as MM, who arranged a peace (likely through greater subsidies to the Huns, possibly up to 1,000 lbs of gold per year = 72,000 *solidi*).[51] The days of relative demilitarization were over. In 443, the court issued a law to strengthen the border defenses: *duces* were to ensure that units were up to their full complement and that soldiers were properly trained, a tacit admission that this had not been true before, and the *magister officiorum* was to report every year on the state of the army and river patrols.[52]

In late 446, Attila invaded again along the Danube, capturing many cities and forts. We lack a coherent narrative and have only scraps of information from fragmentary sources. We hear of one Theodulus, the "general in command of the regiments in Thrace" (ὁ τῶν στρατιωτικῶν κατὰ τὸ Θράκιον ταγμάτων ἡγούμενος), based at Odessus. This is likely a reference to the office of MMT, and Odessus was where some MMTs were headquartered in the sixth century.[53] In the following year, 447, Attila defeated and killed Arnegisclus, who is specifically called the *magister militum Mysiae* in a Latin source (Mysia is only an archaizing term for Thrace) and the στρατηλάτης Θράκης ("general of Thrace") in a Greek

---

[49] Priskos, *History* fr. 9.3.   [50] Kallinikos, *Life of Hypatios* 52.
[51] Marcellinus Comes, *Chronicle* s.aa. 441.1, and 442; Priskos, *History* fr. 6 for Viminacium and Naissus; 11.2.50–55 for bones at Naissus. The increased subsidy is inferred from the years that were unpaid in 447: ibid. fr. 9.3.4–5; for the chronology of the war, see Maenchen-Helfen, *The World of the Huns*, 108–125.
[52] Theodosius II, *Novel* 24.
[53] Priskos, *History* fr. 9.3.59–60, also 9.2 for Odessus; for Odessus, see also the rebellion of Vitalianus in Chapter 4. The dating of the second Hun war in Maenchen-Helfen, *The World of the Huns*, 119, is to be preferred over that in the *PLRE* II, 1105–1106.

source. Arnegisclus was certainly an MMT, and he had set out to face Attila from the nearby city of Marcianopolis. After defeating him, Attila captured Marcianopolis and pressed on to Constantinople.[54] It would appear, then, that this is the moment at which the court began to appoint a regular succession of generals with a specific responsibility for Thrace, that is MMTs. Arnegisclus had replaced Theodulus, giving us two men in that post in the course of a year (446/7). The emperor then sent out the generals Aspar, Areobindus, and Argagisclus (Arnegisclus?), but Attila defeated them in southern Thrace. We are not told what specific commands these generals held, if any (they may have been generic MMs).[55] After that, the Romans quickly came to terms, agreeing to a massive tribute payment to Attila – 2,100 lbs of gold per year with a back payment of 6,000 lbs for unpaid years – and ceding a long and wide strip of territory along the Danube, extending from Pannonia to northern Thrace.[56]

In the course of this war with the Huns, then, we have two securely attested MMTs, and in 449 we have the first securely attested MMI, Agintheus, a man also said to have been dealing with the mess that was left behind by Attila. He is called "in command of the Illyrian armies (τὸν ἐν Ἰλλυριοῖς ταγμάτων ἡγούμενον)."[57] We might be tempted to treat Agintheus as a *dux* who commanded the *limitanei* of Illyricum, but these two offices (MMT and MMI) are fairly regularly attested after that, so it is more likely that he is the first-attested MMI. Moreover, the first-confirmed MMPs are one Apollonius in 443 or shortly after, who went on an embassy to Attila in 451, and Anatolius, who went on an embassy to Attila in 450, but may have held the position of MMP before that.[58] It is from now on that we get a more or less regular (or at least periodic) attestation of the MMP commands too. In fact, the official category *praesentales* (for both generals and armies) comes into being only in the 440s, quite suddenly and simultaneously in the laws, in the narrative sources, and (as we propose) in the *Notitia*. This was no accident: before the 440s we have only ad hoc MMs at the court, whereas after Attila we begin to see the structure of the *Notitia* in place. This means that the eastern *Notitia* reflected a command structure that emerged in the 440s, marking a pivot between the earlier,

[54] Arnegisclus: Jordanes, *Romana* 331 (*Mysiae*) and *Chronicon Paschale* s.a. 447 (p. 586) respectively; *PLRE* II, 151 (Arnegisclus). Marcellinus Comes, *Chronicle* s.a. 447.5 calls him only an MM.
[55] Theophanes, *Chronographia* a.m. 5942, pp. 101–102 (chronologically garbled).
[56] Payments: Priskos, *History* fr. 9.3.
[57] Agintheus: Priskos, *History* fr. 11.2.56; *PLRE* II, 34 (Agintheus).
[58] Apollonius: *CJ* 1.46.3 (called only MM) and 12.54.4 (*Apollonio magistro militum praesentali*); *PLRE* II, 121 (Apollonius 3); Anatolius: Priskos, *History* fr. 15.3.4–5: τῶν ἀμφὶ βασιλέα ἄρχοντα τελῶν; *PLRE* II, 85 (Anatolius 10).

relatively demilitarized period and the much more militarily active second half of the fifth century, when field armies and their "named" MM commands are amply and consistently attested. It is also no accident, we propose, that all the generals holding the new "named" commands in this decade were involved directly in the crisis caused by Attila.

This is unlikely to be a bias in our surviving evidence. The 440s are perhaps the most poorly documented period in the history of the eastern field armies. The fact that we can nevertheless observe the sudden emergence of these *Notitia* structures in our sources is powerfully suggestive, especially when compared to the complete absence of similar evidence for the much more fully document period from 401–438. We should therefore understand this change in titles to reflect a new formalization of the command structure.

It may have been the new strategic challenge posed by the Huns that prompted the construction of the initial version of the Thracian Long Walls, which is usually attributed to the later emperor Anastasius (491–518), but may have only been restored or rebuilt by him.[59] An earlier date would explain why the future emperor Leo was summoned from a praesental unit stationed in Selymbria, the southern anchor of the wall, to become emperor in 457.[60]

But what about the armies themselves? Unfortunately, our poor sources for the Roman response to Attila's invasions do not provide us with evidence about the size and composition of the armies that tried to resist him. Some, perhaps most, of the units listed in the *Notitia* predated the reform of the system in the 440s. We are not saying that they were all newly created to accompany the restructuring reflected in that document. What we are arguing is that those preexisting units had been operating well below their paper strength in the period of peace before the 440s, as the law of 443 explicitly acknowledges, or that they were empty shells, and that now, to face the crisis, they were revived and reshuffled in ways that we cannot reconstruct in order to implement the new system reflected in the *Notitia*.

There is one sign, however, that some or many of the units listed in the *Notitia* were newly created by Theodosius II, and this is that the eastern *Notitia* lists many units named after Theodosius and a small number named after Arcadius and Honorius, whereas the western *Notitia* lists no units named after Arcadius and Theodosius and many named after

---

[59] Dated to the 440s by Whitby, "The Long Walls," *contra* Croke, "The Date of the 'Anastasian Long Wall'." Crow and Ricci, "Investigating the Hinterland of Constantinople," 239, support Croke's date, but without providing evidence or arguments against Whitby's.

[60] See Chapter 3.

Honorius. It is more likely, we propose, that the Theodosius in question was the second of his name and not the first, as is usually assumed. If it had been the first, given that he was in command of the entire empire at two points in his career (after 388 and again in late 394), and the fact that the combined field armies of east and west were in the hands of his general Stilicho in 395, who allegedly kept some of the better eastern units for the west, then we would expect some units named after Theodosius I and even Arcadius to be present later in the west when its *Notitia* was drawn up. But we find no such units, and instead we find only units named after Honorius. This suggests that at least some of the eastern units that were named after members of the Theodosian dynasty were created after 395 and that many of the eastern Theodosian units were created by Theodosius II (even if they were named in honor of his grandfather Theodosius I). Even the units named for Arcadius may have been raised under Theodosius II, as he was apparently keen to promote his father's legacy, not least by finishing his column and adorning it with a statue.[61] There is also a question of scale, as there are fourteen field army units named for Theodosius (as well as six units of *limitanei*). That is a huge number of new units to ascribe to the apparently understaffed military led by Theodosius I and Arcadius, both of whom relied, to a greater degree than any emperor before or after, on barbarian auxiliaries. If this reconstruction is correct, then the *Notitia* reflects a major process of unit creation under Theodosius II, which is what we would expect from the period of crisis in the 440s following so many decades of relative demilitarization.

What we have in the *Notitia*, therefore, is a bureaucratic snapshot of a newly devised framework for the command structure that we observe in motion in the years 450–506. Because this document (on the eastern side) has been dated universally to a much earlier period, this major restructuring and upgrade of the east Roman army in the 440s forms no part of our historical knowledge to date. For example, estimates of the cost (in gold coins) of the army of Theodosius II assume that the court had to pay for the full military complement specified in the *Notitia* for the entire duration of the reign.[62] It is understandable that historians have missed this reorganization, as the *Notitia* has traditionally been dated to the end of the fourth century. Moreover, the sources for the 440s are probably worse than for any other decade of the fifth century. Theodosius II had issued his *Code* in the late 430s and so for the laws of the 440s we have to rely on the much

---

[61] *Paschale Chronicle* s.a. 421, p. 579.
[62] Treadgold, "Paying the Army in the Theodosian Period," 308–309.

later *Justinianic Code*. The narrative sources for the 440s are also abysmally bad. And yet, despite these limitations, we have for the 440s – and for the first time in east Roman history – explicit attestations for the top offices called for by the *Notitia*. All the evidence that we have aligns with a creation of the *Notitia* system in the 440s, with one element of it being earlier (MMO) and one (MMT) having been tried out only once (in 412) for the purpose (as far as we can tell) of a one-time reform.

As the 440s are so poorly documented, we lack explicit evidence that a reorganization of the military took place at that time, or in the period leading up to it. Of course, the same is true of the 390s, when scholarship has traditionally placed the *Notitia*, and proponents of either date can cite the *Notitia* itself as being that otherwise missing evidence. However, this would not be the only major structural reform to occur under Theodosius II that has left scarcely a trace in the extant sources. At some point during his reign, the ancient athletic and artistic guilds were folded into two pan-imperial guilds, the Blues and the Greens, which became responsible for entertainments and for leading acclamations in the major cities. We know that this reform took place because of the appearance of the new relevant institutions, titles, and behaviors,[63] a parallel to the argument that we are making here for the field armies. The compilation of the *Theodosian Code* at the end of the 430s is another major project that we would barely know about from evidence external to the *Theodosian Code* itself. We thus need to add a major military overhaul to the initiatives of the regime of Theodosius II.

Our argument for a revamping of the military structure in the 440s fits the totality of the evidence much better than do the 390s, a date that was chosen by past scholarship for shaky and largely a priori reasons. Moreover, it may explain better what happened next. Specifically, a putative reorganization and beefing-up of the east Roman military in the wake of Attila's first attacks (in 441 and 447) might explain the confidence shown by the emperor Marcian (450–457) in defying Attila. In 451, Attila attacked Gaul and was defeated, at Châlons, by the western general Aetius and his Visigothic allies. In 452, Attila invaded Italy. Marcian not only refused to send the pledged tribute, he also sent soldiers to help Aetius defend Italy and another army to attack Hunnic settlements behind enemy lines, a risky provocation. Unfortunately, we know of these actions solely from a concise

---

[63] The creation of this institution requires further study. For now, see Roueché, *Performers and Partisans at Aphrodisias*, 44–47, 58–60 (arguing for a more bottom-up development); Liebeschuetz, *Decline and Fall of the Roman City*, 205–210.

western chronicle, so we can say nothing more about the armies involved.[64] Marcian could have let the western empire face the storm on its own, but instead he stuck his neck out by way of a direct cross-border action against the Huns. The Scourge of God threatened reprisals, but he hemorrhaged to death on his wedding night and his vast empire disintegrated quickly.[65] Marcian's provocation may have been foolhardy, or it may have rested on his confidence in a revamped east Roman army.

If our argument holds, we should regard the 440s as a major turning point in the history of the eastern empire. It inaugurated a new phase of the Roman army that lasted until the later fifth century. In this period of about fifty or sixty years, we find that the *Notitia* system was actually in effect, as reflected in both laws and narrative sources, as it was not before the 440s. After that period, however, the empire's military structure began to evolve again. Just as we should not project it back onto the early fifth century, so, too, we should not project it onto the sixth. The era of the *Notitia*, to which we will now turn, was thus a discrete and rather short-lived phase in the evolution of the Roman military during late antiquity rather than its default setting.

---

[64] 452 campaign: Hydatius, *Chronicle* s.a. 452: *missis etiam per Marcianum principem Aetio duce caeduntur auxiliis; pariterque in sedibus suis et coelestibus plagis, et per Marciani subiguntur exercitum: et ita subacti, pace facta cum Romanis proprias universi repetunt sedes, ad quas rex eorum Attila mox reversus interiit.* Marcian's refusal to pay: Priskos, *History* fr. 24.2, known from Theophanes, *Chronographia* a.m. 5946, p. 108.

[65] Attila's threat: Priskos, *History* fr. 24.2, known from Theophanes, *Chronographia* a.m. 5946, p. 108; disintegration: Jordanes, *Getica* 259–266.

CHAPTER 3

The "Classic" Phase of the Eastern Field Armies (450–506)

The threat of Attila and the devastation of his invasions prompted Constantinople to design and deploy a new, five-army military system. The Balkans were defended by two field armies under the MMI and MMT along with the units of *limitanei* stationed along the border. This is the "classic" system described by the *Notitia dignitatum* that scholars have long taken as the default template for the east Roman military from the late fourth through to the seventh centuries. As we will see, however, this system was in place for just over fifty years before it, too, began to be disassembled, or rather changed to meet new challenges and promote a different set of imperial ambitions. Just as it had come into existence in response to specific circumstances, rather than as part of a coherent "grand strategy," it was broken up as circumstances changed and the balance of military threat shifted from the Danube to the Euphrates.

Leo I (457–474) was the first and only known praesental officer below the level of general to become emperor. A native of Thrace and ethnic Bessian, he was serving as tribune (i.e., commander) of the *Mattiarii*, a praesental unit according to the *Notitia*, which gives the *seniores* of that unit to the MMP II and the *iuniores* to the MMP I.[1] Leo's was a storied if not glorious unit. The *Mattiarii* had participated in Julian's Persian expedition in 363 and then fought in the battle of Adrianople in 378,[2] so they had been among the main units in the imperial presence during the fourth century. They were thus "proto-praesental soldiers" long before the specific configuration that is recorded in the *Notitia* came into effect. Leo was, moreover, summoned to the capital from Selymbria in Thrace, giving us precious information about where this unit was based.[3]

---

[1] Konstantinos VII, *Book of Ceremonies* 1.100 (eds. Dagron and Flusin, vol. 2, 406 = 1.91 in the Bonn ed.): κόμης ὢν καὶ τριβοῦνος τῶν ματτιαρίων; see also *ND Or.* 5.47, 6.42. For his career, see *PLRE* II, 663–664 (Leo 6).

[2] Ammianus Marcellinus, *Res gestae* 21.13.16, 31.13.8; Zosimos, *New History* 3.22.2.

[3] Kandidos, *History* fr. 1 (= Photios, *Bibliotheca* 92).

We briefly lose track of the praesental armies and their generals, excepting the obscure Lucius, between the Hunnic invasion of 448 and Leo's accession in 457.[4] Attila was at first preoccupied in the west, and then he died in 453. The resulting power vacuum in the north produced some minor incursions into east Roman territory by groups previously under the control of the Huns, but none of these appears to have been large or reached close to Constantinople. They were successfully repelled by Roman forces, but we are not told exactly by what units, except in one case: Dengizich, the son of Attila, was defeated and killed by the MMT Anagastes in 468.[5] However, tensions began to mount during Leo's reign as two rival groups of Goths established themselves in Pannonia and Thrace, setting the stage for the struggle between their leaders, Theoderic Strabo and Theoderic the Amal, in the 470s. Nevertheless, the Romans still found the Danube frontier manageable through the 460s.[6] It is during this period that the future emperor Zeno became MMP (if, indeed, he held the position at all – the matter is unclear) and may have dispatched praesental soldiers to suppress bandits in Isauria.[7]

In 468, Leo felt secure enough on the Balkan frontier, or desperate enough about the situation in the west, to launch his catastrophic expedition to North Africa under the command of his brother-in-law, the future usurper Basiliscus. The failure of this expedition accelerated the power struggle between Leo and the long-serving general Aspar, resulting in Aspar's assassination in 471. (The careers of all these men, who have been proposed as MMPs in this period or really did hold that office, are discussed in detail in Appendix 3.) The murder of Aspar in turn kicked off a rebellion among the Thracian Goths under the leadership of Theoderic Strabo, who was related to Aspar by marriage. It was in this context that Strabo attacked Philippi and Arkadiopolis, earning his first appointment as MMP, which temporarily appeased him.[8] There is no reason, however, to think that Strabo physically took command of the praesental armies. It is unlikely that Leo, having just escaped from under Aspar's thumb, would hand over to Strabo the control of a Roman field army charged with the defense of Constantinople, especially in light of the

---

[4] For Lucius, see Appendix 3.
[5] For example, Jordanes, *Romana* 336; Sidonius Apollinaris, *Carmina* 2.224–298 (= *Panegyric for Anthemius*); Dengizich (Attila's son): Marcellinus Comes, *Chronicle* s.a. 469; *Paschal Chronicle* s. a. 468.
[6] Heather, *Goths and Romans*, 242–256.
[7] Ioannes of Antioch, *History* fr. 229; for the MMPs of this period, see Appendix 3.
[8] Malchos, *History* fr. 2; see also Appendix 3.

Goth's weak bargaining position. Moreover, there are no reports of Roman soldiers serving under Strabo during any of his stints as MMP and we find him instead leading only Gothic forces. We should therefore understand his praesental appointment as a court title designed to boost his prestige and disguise Roman tribute as military pay, a practice dating back at least to the time of Attila, if not Alaric.[9] Even in this "classic" phase, then, holding office and commanding the forces nominally under it did not always go hand-in-hand. This observation has two critical corollaries. First, we cannot take the attestation of an MMP as evidence for the presence, or even existence, of praesental armies. Second, we must be open to the possibility that MMPs who are not attested in command of such forces held an honorary rank.

Shortly after Leo came to an arrangement with Strabo, most likely in 472, the emperor promulgated a law regulating which imperial bureaux were authorized to issue official letters of appointment for the staffs of various offices. Addressed to the praetorian prefect of Oriens Erythrius, it divides people in imperial service into three categories for the purposes of this kind of paperwork: palatine officials and functionaries; the civilian administration (i.e., those under the praetorian prefects); and military officials, janitors, and doorkeepers. Each of these three categories is to receive its certificates from a different bureau. The first military officials mentioned in the third category are the MMPs, indicating their higher prestige, followed by the MMO and MMI; oddly the MMT is missing from the law.[10]

Strabo's first stint as MMP did not last long enough for him to take any meaningful action. The year after his appointment, Leo died, followed shortly by his grandson Leo II, which brought Zeno, Leo II's father, to the throne.[11] Zeno had been a devoted enemy of Aspar, and Strabo appears to have expected trouble from the new regime, leading him to kidnap and murder the MMT Heraclius in 474 before breaking into open revolt.[12] It is unclear what, if anything, Strabo's revolt accomplished and it was soon eclipsed by Basiliscus' coup, which drove Zeno from Constantinople in the winter of 474/5. As discussed in Appendix 3, it appears that Strabo came to terms with Basiliscus, but there is no sign that he resumed his former praesental command.

The usurpation of Basiliscus brought to prominence his nephew Armatus, who was made MMP in 475 and sent in 476 to confront Zeno,

[9] Priskos, *History* fr. 11.2.623.   [10] *CJ* 12.59.10.   [11] Croke, "The Imperial Reigns of Leo II."   [12] Malchos, *History* fr. 6.2; *PLRE* II, 541–542 (Heraclius 4).

who was coming up from Isauria. Armatus' office is explicitly attested by the chronicler Malalas, who also reports that Armatus was sent against Zeno with all the units from Thrace, Constantinople, and the palace, which is likely all the units that Basiliscus had available.[13] This army, led by the MMP himself, is likely to have included praesental units as there were no other armies stationed between Isauria and Constantinople, and the units of the city and palace would have been too small to form the core of Armatus' force. Moreover, it is unlikely that Basiliscus would have been desperate enough to completely empty Constantinople of soldiers or to significantly deplete the armies of the MMT, which would effectively have surrendered Thrace to Strabo.[14] It is likely that the "units from Thrace" were praesentals and not from the Thracian field army, but a combination is possible.

Armatus promptly betrayed Basiliscus and facilitated Zeno's return to power in 476, in exchange for a lifetime appointment as the senior MMP and the appointment of his son as Caesar (a high but honorary court rank). After Zeno regained the throne, however, he had Armatus murdered and ordained his son as a priest. Zeno also came to an arrangement with Theoderic the Amal, likely giving the Goth an honorary post as MMP by 477 (discussed in Appendix 3). In that same year, Strabo attempted to reconcile with Zeno and, in response, Zeno "summoned as quickly as possible all the units – as many as were in the direction of the Pontus and throughout Asia and as many as had been assigned to the eastern divisions – and a large multitude was present from every part."[15] This description by the excellent historian Malchos divides the mustered units into two indefinite relative clauses and distinguishes between units from Asia and the east (Ἑῷα). Ἑῷα and its related adjectives were standard ways of describing the prefecture of Oriens and the office of the MMO, which indicates that the units stationed "throughout Asia" were likely units from Asia Minor. The reference to units in the direction of Pontus in the same clause as the units from Asia suggests that Malchos understood there to be some connection between these forces. The only units that might fit this description would

[13] Armatus as MMP: *PLRE* II, 148–149; his forces against Zeno: Malalas, *Chronicle* 15.5.
[14] Though this was perhaps the force behind Zeno's later accusation that Strabo convinced Basiliscus to "get his own soldiers out of the way" (ἐκποδὼν ποιήσασθαι) and rely only on Strabo's own Goths: Malchos, *History* fr. 15. Heather and Blockley suggest that this refers to the replacement of the Isaurian palace guard by Goths: Heather, *Goths and Romans*, 274; Blockley, *Fragmentary Classicising Historians*, vol. 2, 423 n. 26. But it may refer specifically to this episode of civil war in 475.
[15] Reconciliation: Malchos, *History* fr. 15; quotation: fr. 18.1: ὅσα τε πρὸς τῷ Πόντῳ καὶ κατὰ τὴν Ἀσίαν καὶ ὅσα τοῖς ἑῴοις ἐνίδρυτο μέρεσι, κατὰ τάχος ἐκάλει, καὶ παρῆν πανταχόθεν οὐκ ὀλίγον τι πλῆθος.

have been praesentals from Thrace and Asia Minor, who were supplemented perhaps by forces from Isauria.

Zeno initially appointed his fellow Isaurian Illus – an old associate of his who was holding the emperor's brother hostage – to command the army, but for reasons that are lost to a gap in our fragments of Malchos, he replaced Illus with Martinianus.[16] According to Malchos, the army deteriorated under Martinianus' command while Zeno coordinated a plan of attack using Theoderic the Amal. The emperor proposed a plan whereby Theoderic would bring his forces into Thrace, gathering Roman allies as he went. Near the pass across the Haemus range, he would rendezvous with the MMT, who would bring a force of 2,000 cavalry and 10,000 infantry. They would then proceed to Adrianople where they would find an additional 6,000 cavalry and 20,000 infantry. Zeno assured Theoderic that "there would be yet another force from Herakleia and the cities and towns that are close to Constantinople, if needed."[17] The phrase "another force" (ἄλλην δύναμιν) is identical to and correlative with that used to describe the main Roman battle force that Theoderic was meant to meet at Adrianople. This construction implies that the second army available from Herakleia and its surroundings would be roughly equivalent in strength to that found at Adrianople. Here at last we find in the sources evidence for the standard description of the praesental armies and the calculations inspired by the *Notitia*: two field armies of about 20,000 soldiers, not counting cavalry. If we follow the classic five-army model of the late antique eastern empire, Zeno planned to deploy about half of all the Roman field armies against Strabo: the two praesental armies and most of the army of Thrace.

Of course, we should not take Malchos' report at face value, or rather Zeno's promises, especially because the promised Roman forces never materialized. Instead, Theoderic the Amal marched alone past the Haemus range and Adrianople until he came upon Theoderic Strabo. Zeno had lured him, or both of them, into a trap. But the trap misfired and, after a skirmish, the two Goths joined forces in order to extort concessions from the emperor. But the failure of the Roman forces to join up with Theoderic should not be taken as evidence that these forces did not exist. Luring barbarian groups into mutually destructive conflicts was standard practice in Roman foreign policy. Moreover, Theoderic must have been convinced that the Romans could carry out whatever plan was

---

[16] Malchos, *History* fr. 18.1–2.

[17] Malchos, *History* fr. 18.2: ἀπὸ δὲ Ἡρακλείας καὶ τῶν πρὸς Βυζαντίῳ πόλεων καὶ φρουρίων ἄλλην ἔλεγον εἶναι δύναμιν, εἰ δεήσοι.

agreed upon, in other words that those forces really did exist, and, as a leading warlord in the Balkans, he was in a position to know. Also, as a teenager he had lived in Constantinople as a royal hostage for several years. In sum, he knew exactly what kinds of forces the eastern empire could muster and so Zeno's promises could not have been implausible. It is possible that Malchos has incorrectly reported the plan that was proposed by Zeno, but Malchos reports Zeno's massive mobilization in his own voice and the plan he outlines fits neatly into our picture of the strategic situation in Thrace during this period. We see, for instance, what are presumably praesental armies centered on Adrianople and Herakleia, the same cities that Attila had failed to capture in 447 due to determined resistance. Moreover, the number of soldiers in Zeno's plan closely matches the numbers that are cited for the praesental armies that were later sent to the east during the Persian war of 502–506.[18] Regardless of the sincerity of Zeno' plan, it appears to rest on valid information about the nature and disposition of Roman forces in 477.

Malchos reports that, following the agreement between Theoderic the Amal and Theoderic Strabo, the emperor announced his intention to take his massive army into the field himself. This rallied Roman spirits and is linked by Malchos to the successful defense of the Thracian Long Walls against an attack by Theoderic the Amal's bodyguard. This defense was perhaps led by praesental units stationed there (e.g., the *Matiarii* had been at Selymbria in 457). However, Zeno ultimately demurred, creating mutinous sentiments among the army, and, on the advice of Martinianus, the emperor sent the army to winter quarters. It is possible that the logistical challenges of supplying so large an army and the end of the campaigning season played a role in this decision.[19] Malchos is not specific about the location of these winter quarters, but he does not report units returning to the east, perhaps suggesting that most of the forces in Zeno's *grande armée* were praesentals.

After dismissing the army, Zeno concluded a peace with Theoderic Strabo in 478 that once again made the Goth an MMP. The office, which was stripped from Theoderic the Amal, also made Strabo the commander of two units of the *scholae*; reinforced his position as the predominant Gothic leader in the Balkans; and provided supplies for 13,000 of his followers.[20] Again, there is no reason to believe that Strabo

---

[18] A combined 40,000 soldiers for the praesental armies, plus 12,000 from the army of Oriens: pseudo-Joshua the Stylite, *Chronicle* 54. This war is discussed later in the chapter.

[19] Malchos, *History* fr. 18.3.   [20] Malchos, *History* fr. 18.4.

was in command of any Roman soldiers, just as there is no reason to believe that Zeno handed command of two units of imperial bodyguards to the self-appointed protégé of his old enemy Aspar. Rather, Strabo's Goths were likely being supported on the fiction that they were acting as praesentals (as "pro-praesentals" of a kind), a fiction that Strabo appears to have used in order to mask his support for Marcianus' attempted coup against Zeno in 479.[21]

Theoderic Strabo lost his praesental appointment shortly after Marcianus' coup and died two years later, in 481, in a freak accident after making an assault on the walls of Constantinople.[22] It is unclear where the praesental armies were during this attack, but Strabo's praesental command passed to the Isaurian Trocundes, the brother of Illus. Trocundes may have retained it until Zeno's final break with Illus in 484. Zeno also gave the senior praesental command, the one that had been briefly held by Armatus after Zeno's return to power in 476, to his recently freed brother Longinus, in 485.[23] It is unclear whether Longinus and Trocundes held honorary or real praesental commands, but there is no attestation of praesental units being used in the subsequent war between Zeno and Illus, and the campaign was led by Ioannes the Scythian, who was MMO at the time. Theoderic the Amal regained his praesental status in 483, but it is not clear for how long. Ioannes of Antioch reports that he was sent by Zeno to attack Illus in 484 but made it only as far as Nikomedeia before being recalled.[24] Theoderic the Amal presumably lost his appointment during his own revolt in 486–487, when he too approached the city of Constantinople, but he may have regained it prior to his departure for Italy given the close association between the office and his invasion in Jordanes.[25] Once again, our surviving sources make no mention of any mobilization of praesental units, even though Theoderic was as close to Constantinople in 487 as Attila had been in 447.[26] Perhaps Zeno opted to keep his praesentals in garrisons and to allow these Gothic attacks to crash uselessly against the Roman fortifications. Besides, much of the "warfare"

---

[21] Malchos, *History* fr. 22.

[22] Ioannes of Antioch, *History* fr. 234.5. Marcellinus Comes, *Chronicle* s.a. 481, reports that Strabo came to within four miles of the city.

[23] *PLRE* II, 1127–1128 (Trocundes); *PLRE* II, 689–690 (Longinus 6).

[24] Ioannes of Antioch, *History* fr. 237.5; see later in the chapter for Ioannes the Scythian. A slightly different version in Theophanes, *Chronographia* a.m. 5977, pp. 130–131.

[25] Jordanes, *Romana* 348; Jordanes, *Getica* 57.

[26] As close as Region: Ioannes of Antioch, *History* fr. 237.8; as close as Melantias: Marcellinus Comes, *Chronicle* s.a. 487. For these locations, see *TIB* 12: 615–618 and 526–527; Map 1.

among these warlords consisted of feints. At any rate, this is the last we hear of Zeno's armies before his death in 491.

The reign of Anastasius (491–518), who followed Zeno on the throne, is a high-water mark for information about the praesental armies. On January 1, 492, shortly after his accession and during his preparations for the opening campaign of his Isaurian war, Anastasius published a law addressed to the MMP Ioannes the Hunchback. The law deals largely with the processes and jurisdictions for bringing civil or criminal litigation against soldiers in the praesental armies. However, the law also clarifies the chain of command for praesental units that had been detached from the command of the MMP and stationed in the east. Apparently, this process was sufficiently advanced by 492 that a number of administrative complications had to be resolved.

> We perceived that it was necessary that the most dedicated soldiers from various praesental units who are known to be stationed throughout the districts of Oriens obey the orders of the *spectabiles duces* in order that, no matter what occurs, a suitable remedy . . . can be obtained as quickly as possible from the military garrison stationed in the closest locations.[27]

The law reveals that, far from being clustered tightly around Constantinople, praesental units in 492 could be found "throughout the districts of Oriens," subject to their local *dux*. The emperor confirms that both these units and their local *duces* were under the de facto command of the MMO, not the MMP (their de jure commander). The law also gives a clear sense of the powers devolved to these local commanders, who, in addition to taking command of praesental units in a crisis, are specifically allowed to direct the movements of nearby praesental units, including for the purpose of inspecting them. The law makes provision for a liaison between the courts of the MMP and the MMO, including the local *duces* in the east, so that legal cases involving praesental soldiers could be resolved efficiently and fairly. Moreover, the *duces* of the MMO are not to summon too many praesental soldiers for the purposes of inspection in a time of peace.[28] But, generally, praesental soldiers stationed in the east are directed to obey the *duces* of the MMO.[29]

The law gives us a unique glimpse into both the disposition of praesental units and their command structure. For all military intents and purposes, the units Anastasius describes in this law had ceased to be praesentals: they were operating in Oriens, were subject to the local *duces*, and fell under the

---

[27] *CJ* 12.35.18.pr.   [28] *CJ* 12.35.18.4.   [29] *CJ* 12.35.18.8.

command (*potestas*) of the MMO. Moreover, unless we assume that the emperor had reassigned these praesental units immediately following his accession, which is unlikely, they must then have been attached to the MMO during the reign of Zeno, if not earlier. Such a reading would help explain Malchos' description of the mustering of the armies Zeno intended to use against Strabo in 477. Malchos reports that Zeno summoned "as many units as were in the direction of the Pontos and throughout Asia and as many as had been assigned to the eastern divisions" (ὅσα τε πρὸς τῷ Πόντῳ καὶ κατὰ τὴν Ἀσίαν καὶ ὅσα τοῖς ἑῴοις ἐνίδρυτο μέρεσι).[30] It is possible that Malchos is distinguishing here between praesental units stationed at or near Constantinople, either in Thrace or Asia Minor, and praesental units that had been seconded to the MMO. Regardless of whether or not we can push these arrangements back to 477, by 492 there was an established (possibly long-established) system for detaching praesental units to supplement other commands, a practice that would expand dramatically under Justinian. While we cannot quantify these transfers, it is likely that this was a large-scale phenomenon. The alternative would be to assume that approximately 40,000 elite field army soldiers were kept on permanent station near Constantinople, a tremendous waste of resources in a period when the capital was not under threat.

Moreover, epigraphic evidence indicates that praesental forces were stationed in these very regions. Unfortunately, these inscriptions cannot be dated precisely, but they fall generally within this period. Two inscriptions attest to the posting of *Sagittarii Dominici* (under the MMP II in the *Notitia*) to Seleukeia on the Kalydnos in Isauria (modern Silifke), which hosted a sizable military base in this period. One of these burials identifies a soldier along with two women, an indication that the soldier's posting lasted long enough to merit relocating his entire household.[31] Inscriptions of the *Lanciarii* have been found in Lykaonia (two at Laodikeia "the Burned" and two at Ikonion) as well as in Galatia (in the Axylon district).[32] This distribution of positions seems designed to surround Isauria, which was a trouble spot for the empire during the reigns of Zeno (himself an Isaurian) and Anastasius, who waged an all-out war

---

[30] Malchos, *History* fr. 18.1.
[31] *CIG* 4: 9207 (soldier Leontinos, fifth or sixth century); *CIG* 4: 9230 (Ioannes with two women, Arkadia and Paula) = Le Bas and Waddington, *Voyage archéologique*, no. 1408 (i.e., *LBW*). For Seleukeia, see *TIB* 5: 402–403. The unit is *ND Or.* 6.56.
[32] Laodikeia: *MAMA* 1: 167 (Sanbatios, of the *Lanciarii iuniores*, by his mother Flavia Diogenia), 169 (the *augustalis* Flavios Euandrios for himself and his wife Maria); Ikonion: Cronin, "First Report," 353–354 (the *domesticus* Ioannes Aouros), and *CIG* 3: 4004 (the *actuarius* Flavios Paulos); Galatia: *MAMA* 1: 306 (the *ordinarius* Sanbatios for his son Konon). The units are *ND Or.* 5.42, 6.47.

against Isauria in the 490s. It is, however, impossible to draw conclusions about the location of units from the placement of epitaphs of individual soldiers, who may have been buried far from their units or after their discharge, especially when their epitaphs can be dated only within a broad range (e.g., fourth to sixth centuries), during which, we argue, these units were moved around.[33]

A few months after publishing his law of 492 on praesentals stationed in Oriens, Anastasius sent the praesental armies into battle in Isauria under the leadership of the MMP Ioannes the Hunchback and the MMO Ioannes the Scythian.[34] It is likely that praesental units served under both commanders in this brutal and fairly long war in the 490s by which Anastasius finally "pacified" Isauria. Ioannes of Antioch reports that the Isaurians had assembled a combined Isaurian and Roman army of 100,000 men, an impossible number. Unfortunately, a lacuna in the text interrupts his report on the imperial forces. However, we are told that Ioannes the Hunchback had arrived "after setting out from Selymbria," adding to the evidence for a praesental base in that city.[35] The two forces met at the battle of Kotyaion. The imperial forces prevailed, but the war continued for another six years, apparently with Ioannes the Hunchback, and presumably praesental units, active for the duration.[36]

Five years later, both praesental armies were once more deployed to an active front, this time in Mesopotamia. Hostilities with Persia broke out in 502, catching the Romans by surprise and leading to the capture of Theodosiopolis in Armenia and of Amida in Mesopotamia by the forces of the Persian shah Kavad. In 503, Anastasius sent large forces to reinforce the garrisons of the east, followed shortly by an army under the command of Patricius and Hypatius, who are both securely attested as MMPs (the latter was the emperor's nephew and a hapless leader in the field).[37] In spring 503, the praesental generals began a siege of Amida with a reported

---

[33] See, for example, the *Mattiarius* whose epitaph was found at Dyrrachion: Dana, "Notices épigraphiques," 166–167.

[34] Our main narrative is in Ioannes of Antioch, *History* fr. 239. Malalas, *Chronicle* 16.3 preserves a bare report as does Marcellinus Comes, *Chronicle* s.a. 492. For the careers of the two Ioanneses, see Appendix 3.

[35] Ioannes of Antioch, *History* fr. 239.5: καὶ αὐτὸς ἐκ Σιλυβρίας ὁρμώμενος.

[36] Theophanes, *Chronographia* a.m. 5986, p. 138, and a.m. 5988, pp. 139–140. Most sources do not mention Ioannes the Hunchback's participation, focusing instead on Ioannes the Scythian: see, among others, Malalas, *Chronicle* 15.13–14; pseudo-Joshua the Stylite, *Chronicle* 13–17. For the war in general, see Haarer, *Anastasius*, chap. 1.

[37] Prokopios, *Wars* 1.8.1–2; Malalas, *Chronicle* 16.9; pseudo-Joshua the Stylite, *Chronicle* 54; pseudo-Zachariah, *Chronicle* 7.4g; Theophanes, *Chronographia* a.m. 5997, pp. 145–147. Patricius and Hypatius are *PLRE* II, 840–842 and 577–581, respectively.

40,000 men, a number that closely corresponds to the notional strength of two praesental armies, while the MMO Areobindus led 12,000 men toward Nisibis.[38] Some of those praesental units, as we have seen, may already have been stationed in the east, while others would have seen recent action in Isauria, or would have been stationed around Isauria at the end of Anastasius' war there in order to ensure the region was quiet. Thus, they would not have had to march to the east all the way from Thrace or Bithynia but from central and eastern Asia Minor.

After some initial success, Areobindus faced a Persian counterattack and requested assistance from the praesentals. Patricius and Hypatius refused, and so Areobindos was forced back into Roman territory, prompting the MMPs to abandon their siege.[39] During subsequent maneuvers, the praesental generals suffered a major defeat, in which Patricius is said to have been the first man to flee and Roman casualties were heavy. Prokopios reports the near total destruction of the army, which is certainly an exaggeration, but significant losses might explain the dispatch of 2,000 soldiers under the *magister officiorum* Celer in winter 503/4 as well as the reluctance of Patricius' units to fight later in the war.[40] Celer's forces were perhaps drawn from the palatine *scholae*, which he, as *magister officiorum*, already commanded. Roman reverses in 503 also prompted the recall of Hypatius, the emperor's nephew, ostensibly due to his hostility to Areobindus.[41]

Patricius, who had retired to winter quarters at Melitene, remained in the theater and, early in 504, launched a surprise attack on Amida. A Persian army moved against him, and his soldiers were too scared to fight, so he retreated until he found his path blocked by a swollen river, forcing him to give battle. The Romans prevailed and returned to continue the siege of Amida.[42] It was during this period that Patricius' subordinate Pharesmanes killed the Persian commander in Amida after luring him into an ambush.[43] The size of Patricius' army during the siege appears to have been much smaller than that reported under his command in 503. When Kavad sent a force to relieve Amida, it reportedly had only 10,000 soldiers and was defeated en route by a cavalry force of 6,000 sent by Celer.[44] It is

[38] 40,000: pseudo-Joshua the Stylite, *Chronicle* 54. Areobindus: *PLRE* II, 143–144.
[39] Pseudo-Joshua the Stylite, *Chronicle* 55–56; Theophanes, *Chronographia* a.m. 5997.
[40] Pseudo-Joshua the Stylite, *Chronicle* 57; Prokopios, *Wars* 1.8.13–19. 2,000 men: Marcellinus Comes, *Chronicle* s.a. 503. Celer: *PLRE* II, 275–277.
[41] Pseudo-Joshua the Stylite, *Chronicle* 64; Malalas, *Chronicle* 16.9; Theophanes, *Chronographia* a.m. 5998, pp. 146–147.
[42] Pseudo-Joshua the Stylite, *Chronicle* 66. For the remainder of the war, see ibid. 75 and 87.
[43] Prokopios, *Wars* 1.9.5–15; pseudo-Zachariah, *Chronicle* 7.5a–b.
[44] Pseudo-Joshua the Stylite, *Chronicle* 69.

likely then that Patricius was commanding no more than 13,000 soldiers, the total of the Persian forces sent against him and present in Amida.[45] The reduced number of praesentals was likely the combined result of battle losses and a reorganization of the Roman command following the arrival of Celer.

After the recapture of Amida in 505, hostilities largely came to an end as the Romans and Persians negotiated a peace. It was now that Pharesmanes was made MMP, likely in recognition of his outstanding performance in the war (though others have argued that he was made MMO).[46] Operations continued over the next two years and Pharesmanes was present both for the defense of Dara during its construction and at the signing of the treaty ending hostilities.[47] It is not clear where the praesental units, who had been sent east in 503, returned to after the end of the war, or on what schedule. Given the implications of Anastasius' law of 492, it is possible that some or many of them remained in Oriens. Nor is it clear that their battle losses were made up. As we will see in Chapter 4, the history of the praesental armies was about to enter a different phase, which resulted in the dissolution of those armies as coherent institutions, though their individual units survived within other armies.

The period 450–506 was thus the high point of the praesental armies, the only one during which we can say that they existed and occasionally operated at their notional strength of 20,000 apiece. Those armies were probably assembled to defend the Balkans against Attila and against whatever successors his career of destruction and extortion produced, and they were subsequently used against the Goths who spilled out of his fragmenting empire. After 488, when Theoderic the Amal left for Italy, the praesental armies lost their primary *raison d'être*. In time, the high command came to believe that, after the departure of the Goths in that year, the field armies of Thrace and Illyricum sufficed to defend the Balkans. It is in this period specifically that we first have notices that those regional field armies were operating at what historians take to be their notional strength. In 499, for example, the army of Illyricum took the field with 15,000 men, a plausible figure.[48] In 505, it took the field with 10,000 men.[49]

[45] Pseudo-Zachariah, *Chronicle* 7.4e. Prokopios reports an even smaller garrison: *Wars* 1.8.33.
[46] Pseudo-Joshua the Stylite, *Chronicle* 88. For the argument that Pharesmanes was made MMP and not MMO, as claimed in the *PLRE* II, 873, see Appendix 3.
[47] Pseudo-Joshua the Stylite, *Chronicle* 90, 97.
[48] Marcellinus Comes, *Chronicle* s.a. 499.1 (under Aristus 2, for whom see *PLRE* II, 147); Jordanes, *Romana* 356.
[49] Marcellinus Comes, *Chronicle* s.a. 505 (under Sabinianus 5, for whom see *PLRE* II, 967); Jordanes, *Getica* 300–301; *Romana* 356.

As we have seen, many units of praesentals had already been shifted to Asia Minor by 492, probably to monitor the trouble spot that was Isauria. The law of Anastasius in 492 indicates that the gradual transfer of praesental units to the commands of Oriens was well advanced by then. The wars of both Zeno and Anastasius in Isauria, especially during the 490s, likely shifted more such units to Asia Minor, to surround the recently pacified provinces, and the outbreak of war with Persia in 502 called them to theaters further east. Justinian would significantly accelerate the process, such that we never again hear of praesental units active in the Balkans or in the defense of Constantinople. Anastasius himself, as we will see, did not have any at hand in the 510s when he faced the dangerous Balkan rebel Vitalianus.

Egyptian papyri have also been used to show that some units of the MMPs, or parts of those units, were stationed in Egypt.[50] For example, in the *Notitia*, the unit of the *Daci* is listed under the MMP II, but an anecdote in a theological text mentions one of the *Daci's* officers, a *primicerius*, stationed in Alexandria around 475 AD. Then, a papyrus dated to June 20, 531 involves the soldier Georgios "of the unit of the most brave *Daci*" in a transaction in the city of Arsinoe (adjectives such as "most brave" or "dedicated" were commonly used before the names of field-army units).[51] Such discoveries can and have been taken to mean that the *Daci* were transferred out of the command of the MMP II and redeployed in Egypt, but we do not have to push the evidence that far. The evidence signals only that a few soldiers from that unit were present in Egypt, where they might have been sent on all kinds of business, as we will see. And it is also not necessarily the case that field-army soldiers or units that were sent to Egypt fell out of the command of their MMs and were transferred to the authority of the local commanders in Egypt (in theory and in the *Notitia*, Egypt formed a separate military jurisdiction under one *comes* and two *duces*, and was not under the command of the big MMs).

What were soldiers of the field armies doing in Egypt? A papyrus of September 25, 488 attests some "most brave soldiers of the *Armigeri*" who arrived at the city of Oxyrhynchos with the governor Ioannes. These *Armigeri* (a name that just means "arms-bearers") could belong to a unit

---

[50] For divergent estimates of the size of the Roman military presence in Egypt in the fourth, fifth, and sixth centuries, see Mitthof, *Annona militaris*, and Zuckerman, *Du village à l'empire*, especially at 170–176.

[51] *Daci*: ND Or. 6.43; *primicerius*: John Rufus, *Plerophoriae* 27.1 (p. 68). Papyrus: *Studien zur Palaeographie und Papyruskunde* 20 (1921) no. 139 (p. 102); see Palme, "Verstärkung für die fortissimi Transtigritani."

under the MMP I (the *Equites armigeri seniores Gallicani*) or under the MMO (the *Equites armigeri seniores orientales*). There were also some units of *limitanei* whose names included the term *Armigeri* (specifically under the *duces* of Scythia and Moesia II), but these soldiers are unlikely to belong to those units.[52] We can imagine various scenarios that would lead field-army soldiers to accompany a governor without it entailing that their entire units had been transferred to Egypt, altering the *Notitia* structure on a basic level. Among other, more banal reasons (such as soldiers accompanying a governor), the emperors at this time were trying to foster, promote, or enforce ecclesiastical unity in the empire, and Egypt was a hotbed of resistance to the controversial Council of Chalcedon (451 AD). Soldiers were frequently dispatched to Egypt, especially to Alexandria, to remove or install bishops at the emperor's command. To give one striking example, the emperor Marcian (450–457) sent 2,000 "new recruits" to suppress popular opposition in Alexandria against the installation of the bishop Proterios after the Council of Chaldecon. It was prudent to entrust such missions to men from the central armies rather than to the (potentially compromised) local militias.[53]

Finally, despite its own complement of local units under a *comes* and two *duces*, Egypt often asked Constantinople for military assistance against marauders. For example, at some point between 425 and 450 the bishop Appion of Syene, in southernmost Egypt, petitioned Theodosius II to send more soldiers for the defense of the province, and to put them under the bishop's command. This request was granted in a famous papyrus that bears the emperor's signature, the only text in the hand of an emperor that survives from antiquity.[54]

We also have confirmed cases of field-army units stationed in Egypt, above and beyond individual soldiers or small detachments that may have been sent there for specific purposes. The *Transtigritani* are a curious case, listed last among the units of the MMO. The "transtigritanian" districts (i.e., those beyond the Tigris river) had been taken from Persia by Diocletian and Galerius in 298, though it is not clear what, if any, relationship the fifth-century unit mentioned in the *Notitia* had with that region. Interestingly, the *Transtigritani* are attested as present in

---

[52] MMP I: *ND Or.* 5.35; MMO: *ND Or.* 7.26; papyrus: *P. Oxy.* 16: 1888.
[53] Euagrios, *Ecclesiastical History* 2.5; for the history, context, and parameters of the ecclesiastical politics on this issue, see Blaudeau, *Alexandrie et Constantinople.*
[54] Feissel, "La requète d'Appion"; Millar, *A Greek Roman Empire*, 22–23, 63–64, and fig. 3. For an example of a conflict between the Romans and the Blemmyes and Noubades in the mid-fifth century, see Priskos, *History* fr. 27.

Egypt in papyri from 406, 449, 498, 508, and 531. Some of these documents pertain to the delivery of bulk goods to the unit, enough for some 1,100–1,200 men, which implies that the entire unit was actually stationed there.[55] It is typically assumed that the unit must have been removed from the command of the MMO in the brief window between the ostensible early date of the eastern *Notitia* (ca. 395–401) and the unit's first attestation in Egypt in 406, on the assumption that the MMO could not command units in Egypt.[56] But the whole notion of a formal "transfer" (and the narratives built up around it) is unnecessary and based on a "rule" about the late Roman army that modern historians have invented, namely that the generals' regional zones overlapped perfectly with the postings of all the soldiers under their command.

In reality, the late Roman administration operated in far more ad hoc ways, and nothing prevented the MMO from nominally commanding a unit that was stationed in Egypt. The law of Anastasius of 492, for example, reveals that the MMO and his *duces* were exercising de facto command over units that were de jure praesental but that were stationed in the east. We might imagine a different "rule" operating in Egypt with the *Transtigritani*, one based on status rather than geography (and therefore closer to late imperial Roman ways of thinking). At the time when the eastern *Notitia* was drafted in the 440s, a process that defined the regional commands of the various MMs, the *Transtigritani* happened to already be a pseudo-*comitatenses* unit – this was the lowest-ranked category of field-army units. Let us assume that it was already present in Egypt and needed to remain there for whatever operational-strategic reasons. As a unit of field-army rank had to be placed at least notionally under a general of MM rank, and not a "mere" *comes* or *dux* (i.e., the commanders of the local forces in Egypt),[57] the *Transtigritani* were placed under the nominal command of the nearest MM, the MMO, though at the bottom of his list. But whether the MMO exercised actual command over the unit is unknown.

We are less sure about a unit of the MMP I, the *Felices Theodosiani Isauri*, which is merely mentioned, with an unspecified link to Alexandria, in an extremely fragmentary papyrus from 592/3 AD. It is not clear whether the unit itself was in Egypt, or only some of its men, or whether it was being

---

[55] For this unit in the papyri, see Youtie, "P. Mich. Inv. 6223: Transtigritani"; Benaissa, "The Size of the Numerus Transtigritanorum"; and Palme, "Verstärkung für die fortissimi Transtigritani." For the *regiones transtigritanae*, see Marciak, *Sophene, Gordyene, and Adiabene*, 37–41.

[56] For example, Palme, *Dokumente zu Verwaltung und Militär*, 87–89.

[57] See Kaiser, "Egyptian Units," 246 and 248, for this assumption.

mentioned for some other reason. But it is likely that at least some of the unit's men were actually in Egypt at that time.[58] Some scholars have argued that the unit is first mentioned in Egypt in the 440s and that it may possibly have been present there throughout the period in between too. Specifically, the early reference occurs in the *Life of Sabas* written by the sixth-century monastic author Kyrillos of Skythopolis (Sabas was the founder of the famous monastery of Mar Saba outside Jerusalem). Yet what is mentioned in the text is only a "unit of Isaurians" that was stationed at Alexandria between the early 440s and the early 490s (and possibly before and after that too). This unit was joined by the saint's father, a native of "Cappadocia" and so possibly himself an Isaurian.[59]

One possibility is to see that "Isaurian" unit as the *Felices Theodosiani Isauri* and conclude that it was more or less permanently stationed in Egypt (or Alexandria specifically). As we saw earlier, this would not necessarily entail that the unit was removed from the authority of the MMP I (though it almost certainly was by the later sixth century, when the unit is last attested, for MMPs had ceased to be appointed by then, as we will see in Chapter 4). Alternatively, Sabas' father may have joined the unit *Prima Isaura Sagittaria*, which is under the MMO in the *Notitia*, a closer general, whose own *Transtigritani* were also stationed in Egypt.[60] There is a third possibility, which is that in the fifth and sixth centuries Isaurians appear to have been recruited outside the regular command structure, effectively as barbarian auxiliaries, though these "barbarians" were, notoriously, internal to the empire. A fourth-century list of provinces mentions the Isaurians among the foreign barbarians, along with the Saxons, Goths, and Persians.[61] Thus, the historian Prokopios refers to armies consisting of "Romans and Isaurians," as if the latter were a separate category of soldier, for all that they were native citizens of the empire.[62] The emperor Leo I issued a law in 468 against private individuals maintaining armed slaves, private armies, and Isaurians – a revealing use of their name.[63] But it is unlikely that a unit such as that of Sabas' father, stationed near Alexandria for at least fifty years during the fifth century, consisted of a bunch of irregulars who were recruited ad hoc. Be that as it may, the link between Sabas' father's unit and the *Felices Theodosiani Isauri* a century later is

---

[58] For a study of the papyrus, see Palme, "*Theodosiaci Isauri* in Alexandria." The unit is *ND Or.* 5.66.
[59] Kyrillos of Skythopolis, *Life of Sabas* pp. 87, 92, 109.
[60] *ND Or.* 7.56; for scholars who suggested this – Jones and Hoffmann – see Palme, "*Theodosiaci Isauri* in Alexandria," 168 n. 39.
[61] *Laterculus Veronensis* 13.44 (p. 252).
[62] For example, Prokopios, *Wars* 5.5.2, 5.29.44, 6.5.1, 7.6.2; possibly also 1.18.5–7.   [63] *CJ* 9.12.10.

tenuous, though not impossible. Even if this were the same unit, however, we do not know how its place in the overall command structure changed between the mid-fifth century and the end of the sixth.

Our knowledge of the placement of these units is extremely fragmentary and is hinted at rather than revealed by the papyri. A soldier here, a soldier there: these snippets rarely provide solid data on which we can base conclusions about overall military dispositions. Not only is it possible that the MMs commanded soldiers outside the regions named in their command – for example, that the MMO or MMP had soldiers in Egypt – individual units may have had detachments of soldiers stationed in very distant places. A possible case of such dispersal is the *Balistarii Theodosiaci* (operators of the ballista, the crossbow siege-engine), who are listed under the MMO in the *Notitia*. Some of these "dedicated *balistarioi*" are solidly attested by an inscription at Cherson in the Crimea in 487/8, repairing the walls of the city; then, a papyrus of 511, only a generation later, attests at least two soldiers of the "dedicated *Theodosiakoi*" in the region of Nabatean Nessana in the Negev desert. The only *Theodosiakoi* listed under the MMO were the *Balistarii Theodosiaci*.[64] To be sure, the Crimean and Nessana attestations are separated by almost a generation, and these soldiers may have been dispatched on short-term missions to any region in Oriens that needed their help, but it is also possible that they held long-term postings in these widely distant areas.

To conclude, the period 450–506 is the only period in late Roman history when the eastern empire possessed more or less the full complement of field armies that historians, based on the *Notitia*, usually ascribe to its entire history from 395 to the seventh century. It was only in this brief window that the eastern empire may have had up to 100,000 soldiers in its five field armies (i.e., not counting the *limitanei*). This was not the case before and, as we will see, the strategic disposition of the field armies changed dramatically during the sixth century. There was one crucial factor that made this possible. During the second half of the fifth century, the eastern emperors appear to have enjoyed significant cash revenues. At the end of his reign, Marcian (450–457) left a treasury of seven million solidi only ten years after the worst of Attila's extortions. Anastasius left a reported twenty-three million, even after he abolished the tax on urban

---

[64] Inscription: *CIG* 4: 8621; Vinogradov, "Von der antiken zur christlichen Koine," 257 no. 2. "Dedicated" means (among other things) that this was a unit name, and not generic *balistarii*. The unit is *ND Or.* 7.47. Papyrus: *P. Ness.* 3: 15, ed. Kraemer, *Excavations at Nessana*, vol. 3, 43. The soldiers in the papyrus are unlikely to have belonged to the *Equites Theodosiaci iuniores* under the MMT (= *ND Or.* 8.27).

businesses (*chrysargyron*) in 498.[65] Leo I's expedition to take back North Africa in 468 cost between seven and nine million solidi.[66] While the expedition itself was a disaster, these reports reveal the amounts of cash that the emperors had at hand. It was this that enabled them to maintain such large armies. A partial explanation for this bounty is the fact that this period was generally free of droughts, famine, and pestilence, while it was still benefitting from the gradual economic and demographic growth that historians now generally believe marked east Roman history before the Justinianic Plague.[67] It was also in the second half of the fifth century that the state economy of the eastern empire was increasingly monetized, transitioning away from the collection of taxes in kind. This provided the emperors with both the cash and the spending flexibility to maintain large armies and move them around the empire.[68]

In sum, the "classical" phase of the praesental armies was both much shorter and more transient than scholars imagine it. Originating in the 440s, the classic five-army system was already being reformed by the late 480s as praesental units were dispersed away from the region of the capital to provinces in the east. It is worth noting, moreover, that even in their classic mode, the field armies of the east Roman empire preserved much of the logic of the fourth century, according to which local units were supplemented by a large mobile reserve force. The difference is that local commands now included not only *limitanei*, but also field armies organized under the new regional commands in Illyricum, Thrace, and Oriens, while the praesental units functioned as a reserve force, first in the Balkans, then in Isauria, and finally in the east. The term praesental is thus misleading and we should be careful not to overstate the degree to which the arrangements of the *Notitia* reflect a totally new conception of Roman military strategy. Regardless of what role was imagined for them in the 440s, the praesental forces appear to have always acted as an old-school *comitatus*, going wherever their manpower was needed, only they no longer accompanied the emperor. They were not a stationary force designed to defend Constantinople and its approaches.

In recognizing this reality, we are forced to recast our understanding of the late Roman military almost completely. Where scholars have seen a largely stable five-army system in place by the late fourth century, representing a fundamentally new structure for the Roman military and

---

[65] Ioannes Lydos, *On the Magistracies* 3.43; Prokopios, *Secret History* 19.7.

[66] Kandidos, *History* fr. 2: seven million plus some extra; Ioannes Lydos, *On the Magistracies* 3.43: about nine million; compare Prokopios, *Wars* 3.6.1–2.

[67] Stathakopoulos, *Famine and Pestilence.*   [68] Monetization: see the Conclusion.

high command, the evidence instead points to a gradual process of evolution in which the mobile field armies assembled under the Tetrarchy morphed over the course of half a century (395–440) into regional commands, a transition that was facilitated by the political stability of the eastern empire after 400. As we will see, the reign of Justinian represents the upper limit of regional devolution of the Roman military command, one that would once again be reversed in the face of mounting military and economic pressure as well as rising political instability in the later sixth and seventh centuries.

CHAPTER 4

The Dispersal and Decline of the Eastern Field Armies (506–630)

The five-army system of the *Notitia dignitatum* was defined by the creation of multiple regional commands backed up by a central reserve force, the prae-sental armies. On its face, the particular distribution of this structure was imbalanced between the two major military frontiers of the eastern empire: Four armies were placed within striking distance of the Balkans, while a single army, that of Oriens, reinforced thousands of miles of *limitanei* stretching from the Caucasus to Arabia. This imbalance is yet another sign that the *Notitia* captures a distinct moment in the evolution of the armies of east Rome, rather than a general blueprint for a long-term military system. The *Notitia* system was sustainable only in the context of a quiescent Persia. It was designed in response to Attila, not the shahs.

It is not surprising, then, that our earliest evidence under Anastasius for the system's major modification coincided with threats from the east, first in Isauria and then on the Syrian border with Persia. The Persian war of 502–506, begun by the shah Kavad, initiated a new, escalatory period in Roman–Persian relations, which was stoked by the aggressive anti-Persian policies of Justin and Justinian in the 520s and then by the aggressive anti-Roman policies of Khusrow I after 540. As conflict with Persia intensified under Justinian, so, too, did the pressure on the Balkan-oriented *Notitia* system, and this pressure only increased after 533, when Justinian turned his attention to reconquering and occupying first North Africa and then Italy. The *Notitia* system was not designed for the realities of Justinian's empire, and so it is no surprise that it was partially dismantled and redeployed during this period, beginning with the praesental armies.

Let us pick up the story in the reign of Anastasius. The Isaurian and Persian wars were its largest conflicts, and probably resulted in more praesental units being stationed permanently in the east, in addition to those whose move to Oriens was already attested in the law of 492.[1]

---

[1] That is, *CJ* 12.35.18.

Meanwhile, fighting continued in the Balkans. Marcellinus Comes reports a series of Roman defeats: the death of an MM in Thrace in 493 (likely the MMT) "by the Scythian sword"; an MMI defeated by the Bulgars in 499; a Bulgar raid in Thrace in 502, during which "not a single Roman soldier resisted"; and an MMI killed fighting Mundo's Goths and Huns in 505.[2] Most of the attacks took place far from Constantinople, but the Romano-Gothic historian Jordanes, while reporting several of the same episodes, adds an undated battle at Adrianople under one Pompeius, possibly the nephew of the emperor Anastasius.[3] As we have seen, Adrianople was a staging point and likely garrison for praesental forces. These events indicate that praesental forces were needed in the Balkans, but they are not attested as active there, unless it was some of their units that were defeated at Adrianople.

These defeats in the Balkans, along with the dispersal of the praesental armies, may help explain the success of Vitalianus' rebellion in 514. This rebellion, which involved three marches on Constantinople, is lacking in clear evidence for a praesental response.[4] A former officer of barbarian descent, Vitalianus suborned some regular Roman units in the frontier provinces of Scythia and Moesia by fanning the grievances of the soldiers against their officers. He never claimed the throne for himself and posed as, or was, a champion of the Council of Chalcedon (AD 451) against the apparently anti-Chalcedonian policies of Anastasius. During his first march on Constantinople, he was persuaded by Patricius to withdraw after Anastasius granted various concessions. Patricius was perhaps still an MMP (as he had been during the Persian war of 503), but he is not named as such in connection with the rebellion, and his involvement in it was diplomatic anyway. The emperor appointed a new MMT, Cyrillus, whom Vitalianus promptly assassinated in his base at Odessus. Anastasius then sent out another army under his own nephew Hypatius along with Alathar, the new MMT, against Vitalianus. Our sources place Vitalianus' army at 50,000–60,000 men, while Hypatius is said to have led 80,000, of whom he lost around 60,000 in battle when he was defeated and captured.[5] These numbers are impossible and therefore useless – the total would

<hr/>

[2] Marcellinus Comes, *Chronicle* s.a. 493.2 (= Iulianus 15 in *PLRE* II, 639); 499.1; 502.1; 505 (= Sabinianus 5 in *PLRE* II, 967); Jordanes, *Getica* 300–301.

[3] Jordanes, *Romana* 356. The defeat is not attributed to any of the Pompeii in the *PLRE* II.

[4] The main sources for the rebellion are listed in the entry for Vitalianus 2, in *PLRE* II, 1175–1176. See now Laniado, "Jean d'Antioche."

[5] Ioannes of Antioch, *History* fr. 242.1, 242.6, 242.9; Marcellinus Comes, *Chronicle* s.a. 514; Jordanes, *Romana* 357; Theodoros Anagnostes, *Ecclesiastical History* 4.503. For Church politics under Anastasius, see Chatziantoniou, *Η θρησκευτική πολιτική*.

require the equivalent of six or seven full field armies, all drawn from Roman forces, while Hypatius' losses would by themselves represent three full field armies – but we note the absence of any explicit reference to an MMP or praesental units, many of whom, as we know, were already stationed in the east.

It is possible that Hypatius commanded praesental soldiers – projecting force into the Balkans had been the original purpose of these armies after all – but their contribution appears to have been minor. If this was the case, Hypatius' defeat only depleted their remaining numbers. It is also possible that praesental units were left to garrison the approaches to Constantinople in the event, as actually happened, of a Roman defeat. Perhaps this is why, despite beating Anastasius' armies in the field, Vitalianus was content to bargain rather than press his advantage toward Constantinople.

As part of further concessions, Vitalianus was made MMT, but he was later stripped of this position as his relations with Anastasius soured again. Vitalianus' final assault on Constantinople took a novel approach: the rebel sailed south from the Black Sea with a significant naval force. In the end, his strategy failed and he was defeated in 515. He remained independent but quiescent for the rest of Anastasius' reign. But it is noteworthy that his defeat before Constantinople in 515 came at the hands of Anastasius' praetorian prefect, Marinus, and the *comes* of the imperial bodyguard of the *excubitores*, Justin (the future emperor). No praesental generals or armies are explicitly attested in the final round of the conflict. In fact, the emperor scraped together an improvised local defense force that even included the celebrity charioteer Porphyrius and the fans of the hippodrome racing teams.[6] Even for the defense of Constantinople from a determined and dangerous enemy, the emperor was not using praesental forces. This is almost certainly not because they were too expensive (Anastasius died in 518 leaving a massive surplus of cash, twenty-three million solidi), but because their numbers had not been kept up, or they were not stationed near the capital, or both. Anastasius had a year (or more) during the revolt to call them up had they been available, but he did not.[7]

Even after this last attack failed, Anastasius allowed Vitalianus to continue operating unopposed in the Balkans. Roman emperors did not tolerate independent, much less openly hostile, warlords operating in

---

[6] *Greek Anthology* 16.350, 15.50 (also 16.347–348); see Cameron, *Porphyrius*, 126–130.

[7] The duration and chronology of the rebellion is uncertain, with some scholars preferring two and others three years. Based on Marcellinus Comes, *Chronicle*, we prefer the tighter chronology, but compare Geogakakis, "Το κίνημα του Βιταλιανού." Anastasius' surplus: Prokopios, *Secret History* 19.7.

their territories unless they were forced to, as was the case with the two Theoderics in the late fifth century. Anastasius had opened his reign by crushing precisely such a threat in Isauria. If Anastasius could have crushed Vitalianus' revolt, then we would expect him to do so. If he had at his disposal two praesental armies of the size described by the *Notitia*, he should have been able to. The fact that his regime made no attempt on Vitalianus after 514 strongly suggests that the praesental armies were no longer available to serve their original function, in part because they were playing an important role in the defense of the east. This was especially true in the aftermath of the recent massive war with Persia, which had drawn in the entirety of both praesental armies. Some praesental units were likely back in Thrace and available to Justinian in 532, during the Nika Insurrection, and he promptly called them up. But these did not play a major role, if any, during the rebellion of Vitalianus.

Vitalianus' revolt ended with Anastasius' death and the accession of Justin I in 519. Justin, like Vitalianus, was an ardent Chalcedonian and appointed the rebel as MMP. The emperor's nephew Justinian either became his colleague or was appointed soon after. There is no indication that either man was given direct command of praesental units, particularly Vitalianus, who was not fully trusted by the regime and was murdered in 520.[8] The position of MMP was already being treated as an honorary and prestigious court title, a new twist on the function it had served in negotiations with the two Theoderics and perhaps linked to a decline in the forces under its effective command after 492. The political significance of the office was eclipsing its military function and was possibly already independent of it.

In the 520s, the regime of Justin I chose to become involved in a series of escalating confrontations with Persia, which began in the Caucasus (Georgia and Armenia) and spread southward to northern Mesopotamia, the Syro-Palestinian desert frontier, and even to Arabia proper (Himyar). It is likely that Justinian was already pushing for war on this front, even during the reign of his uncle, for his personal retainers Belisarius and Sittas held command positions during the war in 526 or 527. The Persian shah Kavad also had reasons to escalate the conflict and so, during this decade, the two empires took fateful steps toward the state of near-permanent war that would mark their relations in the sixth and seventh centuries, in

---

[8] Compare Koehn, *Justinian*, 56–67; Koehn, "Justinian στρατηγός," who argues that Justinian's service as MMP involved an active military command on the basis of a tenth-century source, which is not only late but unclear on the point in question.

contrast to the relative peace that had prevailed since the late fourth century.[9]

When he took over the throne in 527, Justinian moved aggressively to militarize the eastern frontier. In the south, he created or significantly bolstered the position of a Saracen *phylarch*, basically a Saracen king (al-Harith) who was a client of the emperor and brought Saracen forces to fight alongside the imperial armies against the Persians and their Saracen allies. Scholars traditionally call the Roman Saracen allies Ghassanids (a tribal name) or Jafnids (a clan name) and the Persian Saracen allies Lakhmids (tribal) or Nasrids (clan), but these names are rarely or never used in contemporary sources.[10] During the conflict with Persia in 529–531, the armies of Oriens (under the MMO Belisarius) appear to have been operating at full strength and were reinforced by the forces brought by al-Harith. For example, during the campaign of 531, Belisarius commanded some 20,000 men.[11]

Justinian's most significant reform came in 528 when he created a new military command for eastern Anatolia and Armenia, that is, the northern sector of the arc of conflict with Persia. The holder of the command was called *magister militum per Armeniam et Pontum Polemoniacum et gentes* (MMA for short), and it was first given to Sittas, who would go on to marry the emperor's sister-in-law. In a law addressed to Sittas, the emperor indicates that the manpower for his new Armenian command would come in part from the praesental armies:

> We have placed under you certain units, not only the new ones We have just now formed, but also some taken from the soldiers at court (*praesentales*), from those serving in the Orient (*orientales*), and from others, without, however diminishing their number; for while We added many soldiers to them without burdening the state or increasing expenses, We removed some, but in such a way that after this reduction the soldiers should remain more numerous than they had been before Our happy times.[12]

The units transferred to the MMA from the MMO and MMP most likely included those that were already stationed in the new MMA's area of command, with the difference made up by newly conscripted soldiers and

[9] This arc of conflict is explained in Kaldellis, *New Roman Empire*; see also Greatrex and Lieu, *The Roman Eastern Frontier*, 82–96.

[10] Fisher, *Between Empires*; Hoyland, "Insider and Outsider Sources," 267–273.

[11] Prokopios, *Wars* 1.18.5.

[12] *CJ* 1.29.5 (trans. Blume and Frier, vol. 1, 347); Malalas, *Chronicle* 18.10. For the imperial involvement in the Armenian lands annexed by Justinian, see Adontz, *Armenia in the Period of Justinian*, outdated in many respects but still useful.

units transferred from other armies. Justinian claims that all of this resulted in a net gain of soldiers, but this claim is unbelievable on its face and is expressed in convoluted and elusive rhetoric.[13] Justinian had just come to the throne and it is impossible to believe that in a single year he had increased the total size of the Roman armed forces by some 15,000 men, the eventual – or immediate – size of the *per Armeniam* command. Justinian had created the Armenian command at the (initial) expense of Oriens and the praesentals and was rhetorically pledging that he would make up the losses to them through recruitment (but falsely implying that he had already done so). The losses to Oriens were (eventually) replaced, as Oriens continued to be a large and operational army. In fact, Oriens and Armenia went on to become the two main armies ("themes") of the Byzantine empire (under the Greek names Anatolikon and Armeniakon). By contrast, there is no proof that the losses to the praesentals were made good. It is likely, then, that Justinian was dissembling his intentions or at least taking for granted a future replenishing of the praesentals which likely did not occur, at least not to the pledged extent.

In fact, it seems that the soldiers of the new Armenian command were taken overwhelmingly from the praesental armies, and this is reflected in Sittas' career. He was appointed MMA when that command was first created but then, in 530, he was made MMP with authority over the MMA (who was Dorotheus in 530–533). Sittas then campaigned in the east against the Persians with an army that reached a maximum field strength of 15,000.[14] This army was separate from that of Oriens but it likely absorbed some of the praesental units that had formerly (under Anastasius) been transferred to Oriens along with additional praesental units that still remained under their own command, but were brought to the east by Sittas now.[15] Sittas' tenure was, then, effectively a period of transition during which a significant number of praesental units were converted into Armenian units. "Armenian" here refers not to ethnicity but to the territorial command only. In fact, Roman soldiers were brought in from elsewhere precisely in order to "make the Roman army less dependent militarily on local levies and the armed retinues of members of the indigenous Armenian aristocracy," who had proven unreliable and ineffective.[16]

---

[13] We are not as willing to trust Justinian as are Treadgold, *Byzantium and Its Army*, 15; Koehn, *Justinian*, 43; and others.

[14] Prokopios, *Wars* 1.15.3 and 1.15.11; Malalas, *Chronicle* 18.60; *PLRE* III, 1161 (Sittas 1), and 420–421 (Dorotheus).

[15] Compare Koehn, *Justinian*, 14–15 n. 16.

[16] Sarris, *Empires of Faith*, 143; sources: Prokopios, *Buildings* 3.1.27–29; Malalas, *Chronicle* 18.10. Theophanes, *Chronographia* a.m. 6032, p. 219: Justinian later added Bulgar soldiers to the army of the MMA.

Suggestive evidence for the state of the praesental armies following the creation of the MMA comes from the Nika Insurrection. This popular uprising against Justinian took place in January 532, shortly before the formal conclusion of peace with Persia. Over the course of several days, an ad hoc alliance between the Blue and Green circus factions, originally formed to protest the punishment of some of their members, escalated into a full-blown insurrection culminating in an attempt to replace Justinian with Anastasius' nephew, the former MMT and MMP, Hypatius. The Nika Insurrection was the nadir of Justinian's political fortunes and the closest he ever came to losing his throne. Large swathes of Constantinople were burned, Justinian considered fleeing the city, and the matter was ultimately resolved when a cadre of loyalist soldiers slaughtered the Greens and Blues in the hippodrome, arresting Hypatius and his brother Pompeius in the process.[17]

The Nika Insurrection was not the sort of crisis the praesental armies were designed to guard against, but it nevertheless appears that they factored into Justinian's reaction. Theophanes reports that Justinian planned to flee to Herakleia in Thrace, leaving 3,000 soldiers under the MMI Mundo to hold the palace, while the *Paschale Chronicle*, whose account of the insurrection is by far the most detailed in any of our sources, reports that Justinian summoned soldiers from Constantinople's western hinterland, namely Hebdomon, Region, Athyras, and Kalabria.[18] Both of these details implicate praesental units. Herakleia, as we have seen, was a major staging ground for praesental forces in the fifth century, and there is a good chance that the soldiers stationed just outside Constantinople were praesental units, especially those at the Hebdomon and Athyras, the latter of which is often referred to as a "fortress" (*phrourion*).[19] In fact, these locations may be precisely the "cities and towns" close to Constantinople from which Zeno promised Theoderic the Amal reinforcements in 477.[20] Admittedly, both Theophanes and the *Paschale Chronicle* are later sources, but this may enhance their reliability; both come from periods after the praesental armies had ceased to exist and so have no reason to invent these details.

---

[17] The main sources are Prokopios, *Wars* 1.24; Malalas, *Chronicle* 18.71; *Paschale Chronicle* s.a. 532; Pseudo-Zachariah, *Chronicle* 9.14; Theophanes, *Chronographia* a.m. 6024, pp. 181–186. For a modern reconstruction and timeline, see Greatrex, "Nika Riot."
[18] Herakleia: Theophanes, *Chronographia* a.m. 6024, pp. 184; Summoned soldiers: *Paschale Chronicle* s.a. 532, pp. 622.
[19] Priskos, *History* fr. 10.4; Palladius, *Dialogue on the Life of John Chrysostom* p. 23.
[20] Malchos, *History* fr. 18.2; See p. 52.

The units summoned by Justinian do not appear to have been large. All they did was engage in running street skirmishes with the protesters and eventually set fire to parts of the city to smoke them out. Ultimately, they failed, as the protesters gained control of the area around the palace and made the hippodrome their base. Our sources are uniform in reporting that the decisive role in ending the insurrection was played by palace units and the personal retinues of Belisarius and Mundo, both of whom happened to be in Constantinople when the violence broke out. Prokopios indicates that Belisarius, like many generals of that time, had a large armed retinue, while Mundo led "Herulian barbarians."[21] This general picture is confirmed by other sources, several of which have Belisarius leading a force of Goths, clearly distinguished here from Roman soldiers, early in the insurrection, and all of which give a prominent role to Mundo and palace units in the final confrontation in the hippodrome.[22]

We can draw several major conclusions from the Nika Insurrection. The first is that there were no praesental units stationed in Constantinople's Asian hinterland. Justinian planned to flee west to Herakleia and all of the praesental units he summoned came from the west. The second is that there were not substantial praesental forces available to the emperor. Whatever praesental forces Justinian pulled into the city from the surrounding hinterland were insufficient to suppress the insurrectionists and apparently small enough that they failed to be noticed by all but one of our sources. Moreover, there is no indication in any source that the availability of praesental forces factored into Justinian's planning, save as a potential refuge should he quit Constantinople. It is possible that, after being summoned early in the insurrection, these units adopted a posture of neutrality as they waited to see which way the wind would blow, as Prokopios indicates most soldiers did.[23] Hypatius' previous service as MMP may recommend this reconstruction, though it is unclear whether he would have been able to call upon any reserves of loyalty given his manifest military incompetence and the decades that had elapsed since his last command.

The final major conclusion we can draw is that there was no MMP active in Constantinople during the insurrection. We have remarkably good evidence for the officials around Justinian during the crisis, including the recent MMO Belisarius, the MMI Mundo, Constantiolus, Narses, and

[21] Prokopios, *Wars* 1.24.40–41.
[22] Belisarius leading Goths: Malalas, *Chronicle* 18.71, p. 475; *Paschal Chronicle* s.a. 532, p. 621. Palace units: Malalas, *Chronicle* 18.71, p. 476; pseudo-Zachariah, *Chronicle* 9.14b; *Paschal Chronicle* s.a. 532, p. 626; Theophanes, *Chronographia* a.m. 6024, p. 185.
[23] Prokopios, *Wars* 1.24.39.

Basilides, who was appointed acting *magister officiorum* to command the loyal *scholae* of the imperial bodyguard during the crisis.[24] Sittas was presumably still MMP, but he remained in the east supervising the Armenian sector of the Persian war. Given the potential importance of praesental soldiers in such a crisis and the sheer number of detailed sources we possess, the absence of a second MMP should be understood as definitive.

Taken together, the evidence of the Nika Insurrection paints a downsized picture of praesental forces in the process of dispersal. Some forces were still stationed west of Constantinople, but their numbers appear to have been small. At a moment when the emperor was in desperate need of military support, he relied not on an MMP, but on an out-of-favor former MMO (Belisarius), an MMI who just happened to be in the city (Mundo), and various palace officials. Likewise, he relied not on praesental soldiers, but on the personal retinues of his commanders and various units of palace guards. This was because significant portions of the praesental armies were in the east, serving under Sittas, the one MMP active during this period. The function of the praesental armies and their commanders were increasingly disconnected from the logic of the *Notitia* system.

In 532, with the conclusion of the peace between Rome and Persia, Sittas returned to Constantinople. In 535, he defeated some Bulgar raiders in Lower Moesia near the city of Iatros, which belonged to the diocese of Thrace and presumably fell under the authority of the MMT.[25] However, we are told nothing about the army he commanded and, as we saw when he was in Armenia, Sittas was empowered, either as MMP or as Justinian's favorite, to take command of other armies. Unfortunately, the MMT at this time is unknown. In 536, a law of Justinian regulating marriages was issued to a number of high officials, including no fewer than *three* MMPs: the emperor's cousin Germanus, an experienced general who would soon be sent to North Africa "with a few men" to suppress a mutiny; Sittas; and the otherwise unknown Maxentianus, listed in that order of precedence. These subscriptions hardly imply that there were now *three* praesental armies, a typical instance of the mistake of inferring armies from the mere appointment of MMPs.[26] It means only that Justinian had decided to honor three men with an office that was becoming a court rank, just as he and Vitalianus had been honored with it in 520. There is no proof that

---

[24] Constantiolus in *PLRE* III, 352–353; Basilides in *PLRE* III, 172–173.

[25] Additions to Marcellinus Comes, *Chronicle* s.a. 535.1.

[26] *Pace* the views laid out in Koehn, *Justinian*, 14–15. The law is Justinian, *Novel* 22, epilogue. The other two men are Germanus 4 in *PLRE* II, 505–507, and Maxentianus in *PLRE* III, 864. "Few men": Prokopios, *Wars* 4.16.1.

these men commanded praesental forces, though the forces Germanus took to Africa may have included praesentals, for all we know. In 538/9, Sittas was sent back to Armenia where, possibly still as MMP, he died fighting against local rebels while commanding the forces of the MMA. Those forces, we recall, consisted to some degree of former praesental units. We do not know whether the position of MMA was vacant or occupied at that time.[27] It may have been vacant, as the Eternal Peace with Persia (which lasted from 533 to 540) was still in effect.

In 533, Justinian sent Belisarius to conquer North Africa with an army of 10,000 infantry and 5,000 cavalry. We are not told where these units were drawn from specifically, but Belisarius was MMO throughout the entire campaign and he was accompanied by Dorotheus, the MMA. Therefore, it is reasonable to conclude that their forces were drawn from those two commands.[28] Prokopios confirms this picture, reporting that the soldiers who had fought Persia dreaded their transfer to the war in North Africa.[29] Justinian was counting on the peace with Persia to safeguard the east while he sent its armies to the west. This proved to be a costly mistake when the shah Khusrow I invaded in 540 and took the Romans by surprise. But let us keep our focus on North Africa for now. After its conquest, Justinian immediately established a new command for it under a *magister militum*, with subordinate *duces* for five provinces.[30] There is a technical debate over when the formal position of *magister militum Africae* was created, as opposed to an acting MM in charge of the new prefecture, but it need not detain us here.[31] Both an army and a general of sorts were established for the new prefecture of North Africa.

Presumably, in the long run the African army was recruited locally, but at first it consisted of the army of conquest, some of whose soldiers even married the widows or daughters of the Vandals whom they had defeated.[32] In 536, during the mutiny led by the Roman officer Stotzas, the rebels had about 8,000 Roman soldiers, which according to Prokopios amounted to two-thirds of the Roman army listed in the rolls for North Africa. This means that the army of occupation was about the same size as the army of conquest and likely consisted of the same men.[33] These were, then, not new recruits but units detached from Oriens and Armenia (and possibly other armies, too, such as the remaining praesentals, although we have no specific evidence to that effect). The standard size assumed in the scholarship for

---

[27] Prokopios, *Wars* 2.3.10–27.   [28] Prokopios, *Wars* 3.11.   [29] Prokopios, *Wars* 3.10.5.
[30] *CJ* 1.27.2; in general, see Pringle, *The Defence of Byzantine Africa*.
[31] Zuckerman, "Le haute hiérarchie militaire."   [32] Prokopios, *Wars* 4.14.8–10.
[33] Prokopios, *Wars* 4.15.2–4, 4.16.3.

the field army of Africa is 15,000 (not including the *limitanei*, who were also created by Justinian's edict on the army of Africa).[34]

In 535, Belisarius was sent to conquer Sicily with 4,000 soldiers from the regular Roman units and the *foederati* (barbarian auxiliaries) in addition to 3,000 Isaurians, 200 Huns, and 200 Moors.[35] After conquering Sicily, Belisarius invaded Italy, without having received any reinforcements. In 537, Prokopios reports that a unit called the *Regii* ('Ρῆγες), which is listed under the MMP II in the *Notitia*, fought at the Flaminian Gate during the siege of Rome.[36] This unit, therefore, must have been part of the 4,000 soldiers with whom Belisarius had crossed over from Sicily to Italy at the outset of the expedition, and they must have been drawn from the Roman armies, not the barbarian auxiliaries. Here is proof, then, that Justinian was cannibalizing the praesental armies to send expeditionary forces to the west, just as both he and Anastasius had previously done in the east.

Moreover, Justinian's difficulty in providing Belisarius with further reinforcements during the war in Italy makes it clear that this process of cannibalization was far advanced. The first reinforcements sent by Justinian to Italy – 1,600 cavalry drawn primarily from barbarian auxiliaries – arrived in the spring of 537, followed by 3,000 Isaurians, 1,800 cavalry (including 1,000 men from units of the regular army), and a unit of 300 cavalry.[37] These groups were not coordinated, arrived by different routes, and were for the most part not drawn from the regular army. It was not until 538 that a major and coherent relief force of 5,000 Romans and 2,000 Heruls arrived under the command of the eunuch chamberlain Narses.[38] Everything about these reinforcements suggests that Justinian was struggling to find military manpower for the Italian campaign despite the peace in the east and the relative quiescence of the Balkans, a fact that cannot be reconciled with large reserves of praesental units. As we have seen, the latter had been dispersed to Armenia and Oriens, and Justinian had subsequently drawn on Armenia and Oriens for the armies of conquest in North Africa and Italy. The emperor was not creating new armies, but shuffling existing ones around, and by the late 530s he was running out of units to move. Clearly, then, Justinian had not made good on his promise in his law of 528 to replenish the praesental armies.

This is not to say that the praesental armies had been completely broken up. In 541, we find a member of the *Equites Sexto Dalmatae*, a unit under the

[34] For example, Haldon, *Warfare*, 100; Treadgold, *Byzantium and Its Army*, 60–63, 74.
[35] Prokopios, *Wars* 5.5.2.   [36] Prokopios, *Wars* 5.23.3; the unit is *ND Or.* 6.49.
[37] In order: Prokopios, *Wars* 5.27.1–2, 6.5.1–2.   [38] Prokopios, *Wars* 6.13.16–18.

MMP II, attested in Constantinople in a loan contract that survives on a papyrus in the archive of Dioskoros of Aphrodite in Egypt. One scholar has suggested, on the basis of this papyrus, that his entire unit, the *Equites Sexto Dalmatae*, was based in Egypt by this time, as the soldier in question was already enmeshed in local affairs, even though his presence is strictly attested only in Constantinople, where the document was drawn up.[39] While this argument would support our view that the praesental armies were largely dispersed and away from Constantinople at this time, perhaps that is going too far, based on the sole evidence of this papyrus. A stronger argument can be made for the unit of the *Scythae*, listed under the MMP II in the *Notitia*: A dozen or so of its men are attested in two Oxyrhynchos papyri in 563 and 564, receiving deliveries of supplies, which implies an official posting.[40]

In addition, other documentary evidence makes it clear that by the middle of the sixth century some or many praesental units were taking up long-term, if not permanent, postings in the reconquered west. Specifically, some or all of the *Primi Theodosiani*, originally under the MMP I, were in Italy by 547, and the *Felices Theodosiani* and *Daci*, two units originally under the MMP II, were still in Italy around 600.[41] And we mentioned earlier the *Regii*, who were fighting at Rome in 537. Are any praesental units attested in the east after the mid-sixth century? A unit of the *Lanciarii iuniores* is attested epigraphically at some point in the sixth century at Ulmetum (modern Pantelimon in Romania, near the Danube delta). But in the *Notitia*, both the MMI and the MMP II commanded units with that name (which just means "Junior Lancers"). This could have been a unit of the Illyrian army that had been posted farther east. Moreover, even if this is the praesental unit, it, too, could have been transferred to the command of the MMT in the meantime.[42]

We likewise have evidence that Justinian continued Anastasius' deployment of praesental units to the east. In his *Edict* 13, issued in 538/9,

---

[39] *P. Cairo Masp.* 2: 67126, lines 65–66, ed. Maspero, *Papyrus grecs*, vol. 2. The unit is *ND Or.* 6.37. Posted to Egypt: Kaiser, "*Daci* und *Sextodalmati*." For the literary work and archive of Dioskoros, see Fournet, *Hellénisme dans l'Égypte*.

[40] The unit is *ND Or.* 6.44, and the papyri are *P. Oxy.* 16: 1920 and 16: 2046.

[41] *Primi Theodosiani* (at *ND Or.* 5.64): *CIL* 11: 1693, dated to May 14, 547 (= *ILS* 2806); *Felices Theodosiani* (at *ND Or.* 6.62): *CIL* 6: 32970 and the Italian papyrus cited by Rance, "The Battle of Taginae," 446 n. 83; *Daci* (at *ND Or.* 6.43): ibid and Schoolman, "Greeks and 'Greek' Writers." There are a range of other *potential* praesental or other field-army units attested in Italy in the late sixth and early seventh centuries: Brown, *Gentlemen and Officers*, 90–91, with the caveats of Rance, "The Battle of Taginae," 446 n. 83; and Pellegrini, "Una guarnigione bizantina."

[42] *Lanciarii iuniores*: *ND Or.* 6.47 (MMP II) and 9.38 (MMI); inscription: *L'Année épigraphique* 1922 (for year 1922) 18, no. 71: *pedatura militum lanciarium iuniorum*; Popescu, *Inscripțiile grecești și latine*, 224–226, no. 211.

Justinian specified that the Augustal prefect of Egypt would take the place of "the most brave *magistri* [στρατηγοί] of the praesentals and Oriens" and command units serving in Alexandria and both Egypts.[43] We also have papyrological confirmation of such deployments. The *Felices Theodosiani Isauri*, another unit under the MMP I in the *Notitia*, are attested in Egypt in 592/3, where they may have been stationed since the mid-fifth century.[44] Thus, legal documents, epigraphy, and papyrology confirm what we have inferred from the narrative sources: The praesental armies had been broken up and distributed across Justinian's expanding empire, from Egypt and Armenia to Italy.

The war in Italy dragged on in a desultory fashion throughout the 540s, as the Goths regained their footing under their energetic king Totila (also known as Baduila). The empire was now fighting in Italy against the Goths, in the east against the Persians, in the Balkans against Slavic raiders, and occasionally in North Africa against armies of Moors. It is likely due to the exigencies of Justinian's wars that the *PLRE* III, which covers the sixth century, contains many more MMs with unspecified regional commands than does *PLRE* II. We are dealing with a proliferation of ad hoc commands (i.e., commands that did not fit into the schema of the *ND*), which perhaps never had a territorial designation at all: They existed only in relation to the units that they commanded, which were sometimes assembled in relation to a specific crisis that these men were sent out to resolve. It is also possible that in these circumstances Justinian increased the empire's reliance on barbarian mercenaries, who could be paid on a campaign-by-campaign basis and were therefore cheaper than full-time, professional Roman soldiers, who were, in theory, career recruits.[45]

The largest ad hoc army assembled during Justinian's reign was in 551, under the eunuch Narses, who was finally given an army powerful enough to end the war in Italy against the Goths. A new command was created for Italy after its conquest by Narses, though it was not led by a *magister militum*. Narses himself held an ad hoc command there until the early 560s. His successors had to deal with the Lombard invasion of 568, which fragmented the Italian peninsula and led to the emergence of a different command structure under the so-called exarchs. (An exarch was also

---

[43] Justinian, *Edict* 13.2: ἐπέχοντα τὸν τόπον, ὅσον ἐπ᾽ αὐτοῖς τοῖς στρατιώταις τοῖς τε ἐν Ἀλεξανδρείᾳ τοῖς τε ἐφ᾽ ἑκατέρας Αἰγύπτου, καὶ τῶν ἐνδοξοτάτων καὶ ἀνδρειοτάτων στρατηγῶν τῶν πραισενταλίων τῶν τε τῆς Ἑῴας.

[44] *ND Or.* 5.66 and the papyrus studied in Palme, "*Theodosiaci Isauri* in Alexandria." For the identity of this unit and duration of its posting, see the discussion in Chapter 3.

[45] Teall, "The Barbarians"; Kaldellis, "Classicism, Barbarism, and Warfare."

appointed to command the North African forces.[46]) But the key issue for us is manpower. The Italian command at the high point of Narses' power is said to have had 18,000, a figure that possibly excluded garrison units and local defense forces.[47] Eventually, local recruitment must have kicked in to some degree, but the original core of these forces was formed by the army that Narses led there in 551–552. Prokopios does not give us an exact figure as to its size, but he does say that its core consisted of "a great many Roman soldiers from Byzantion," and that Narses "collected many [soldiers] from the lands of Thrace and Illyricum," and had many barbarian auxiliaries such as Lombards.[48] The clear implication is that Narses marched west, gathering units from the praesental, Thracian, and Illyrian armies as he went. We might wonder how it was that, after moments or periods when the praesental armies seem not to have existed in and around the capital, they still managed to yield active units in 552 for Narses to take. The answer is simple: More men must have been recruited to its remaining units in the meantime, possibly for the purposes of this campaign.

As far as we can tell, this was the end of the praesental armies stationed in or around the capital. They are not attested again after 551. This point must be stressed. There is no positive evidence for the existence of praesental armies for the next eighty years, despite the many wars the Romans fought during that period, which included major attacks on Constantinople. The assumption that these armies continued to exist is premised on reading the *Notitia* and its five-army system as normative in a way that our narrative demonstrates it had never been. When praesental units were dispersed to Armenia, Oriens, North Africa, and Italy, they were never replenished to a degree that warranted mention in any kind of source. The system that emerged in our sources in the 440s, in response to a new military reality on the Danube, gradually disappeared in response to the needs of Justinian's conquests. It is not a coincidence that MMPs largely cease to be appointed after the mid-sixth century. The last appointments known to have been made by Justinian were empty court titles: to the Armenian noble Artabanes who had foiled another major rebellion in North Africa, and then to the Herul Suartuas, who was appointed in 548/9 as a consolation prize for his failure to establish himself as a Roman client king over his people. In 551–552, as we saw, many of the soldiers nominally under his command marched to Italy with Narses. In 552, Suartuas was one of five commanders sent by Justinian to help the Lombards against the Gepids,

---

[46] Brown, *Gentlemen and Officers*; Shlosser, "The Exarchates."   [47] Agathias, *Histories* 2.4.10.
[48] Prokopios, *Wars* 8.26.10–13.

although the expedition was called off before reaching its destination. We are not told what soldiers Suartuas commanded then, and he is not heard of again.[49]

The nonexistence of the praesental armies after 551 is indicated by their absence from defensive operations when they would surely have been mobilized, had they existed. In particular, in 559 a large army of Huns and Slavs invaded the Balkans and reached almost to the walls of Constantinople. We are told that they killed many during their advance and captured two high officials, including a *magister militum* – the infamous Sergius, son of Bacchus, whom Prokopios reports had ruined Africa – but the account is vague and it is not clear if the invaders faced organized Roman resistance.[50] The Hunnic and Slavic approach caused panic in the capital and Belisarius was pulled out of retirement. He had to assemble a ragtag force of veterans and some farmers in order to mount a show of resistance.[51] This is not the first time praesental units failed to appear in the field when we might have expected them, but the details of this late Hun attack cannot be reconciled with the presence of *any* praesental forces in the vicinity of Constantinople. The testimony of Agathias, a contemporary and our most detailed source for this event, reflects this.

Agathias interrupts his narrative of the invasion of 559 with a digression on the decline of the Roman army under Justinian, in which he gives precise figures for the army in 559 and at an unspecified earlier date. These numbers have attracted significant scholarly attention, and we will return to them later, but what has gone largely unnoticed is the other half of his explanation. Agathias blames the disaster of 559 on both the decline in Roman military strength and the manner of its deployment. His critique is specific. The success of the Hunnic and Slavic assault of 559, that is, the failure of the defensive systems of which the praesentals were once the lynchpin, is a result of the dispersal of units to Italy, North Africa, the Caucasus, and Egypt.[52] These are precisely the regions for which we have the strongest independent evidence of praesental deployment under Justinian. The correspondence is unlikely to be a coincidence: Agathias knew where the armies were and where they had come from.

Moreover, Theophanes' narrative suggests that the function of the praesental armies had been taken over by units of palace guards. In 559, he reports that units of *scholarii*, *scholae*, and *protectores* manned the

---

[49] Prokopios, *Wars* 8.25.11–13.   [50] Malalas, *Chronicle* 18.129. Sergius 4 in *PLRE* III, 1124–1128.

[51] Agathias, *Histories* 5.11–25; Theophanes, *Chronographia* a.m. 6051, pp. 233–234; Menandros, *History* fr. 2.

[52] Agathias, *Histories* 5.13.8.

Theodosian walls against the Huns and Slavs.[53] In 562, Justinian redeployed guard units from "Nikomedeia, Kios, Prousa, Kyzikos, Kotyaion, and Dorylaion" to Herakleia and surrounding cities.[54] That is, he redeployed units from the eastern approaches to Constantinople to the west, to precisely the same city that had served as a praesental base of operations in the fifth century. Here, then, is our clearest evidence for the classic distribution scholars have imagined for the praesental armies – bracketing Constantinople to east and west – being explicitly held by units of what had once been palace guards. Though we cannot be certain, it is tempting to understand these palace units as filling the gap left behind by the dispersal of the praesental armies, at least in part.

Significantly, the praesentals never appear in action in accounts of fighting in the Balkans during the whole of Justinian's reign. All raids by the Huns or Slavs were answered by the field armies of Thrace and Illyricum, the empire's barbarian mercenaries, and the local defense units of the border provinces. Justinian had apparently decided that those forces, backed by the extensive fortifications that he built across the Balkans, were sufficient for the defense of the peninsula. He may have been correct in this calculation, and a recent study finds that his approach to this theater of war was successful, even if it also entailed great risks.[55] Justinian entangled the empire in costly foreign wars that diverted its military resources to overseas fronts, while his gradual dispersal of the praesentals made the Balkans more vulnerable to future enemies, especially to those who could mount more determined attacks than the Slavs and Huns. The Avars would prove to be just such an enemy. Justinian reaped the short-term benefits of his risky expansionist policies, but he left the debt on that risk to be paid by his successors and his subjects.

The Avars arrived on the scene late in Justinian's reign but for some years they were consolidating their control over territories north of the Danube. They did not become a major problem for the Romans until the 570s.[56] The Avars could deploy about 20,000 soldiers, the equivalent of a Roman field army at full strength, and they had many thousands of Slavic auxiliaries.[57] To the best of our knowledge, the Roman response relied entirely on the field armies of Illyricum and Thrace and various local defense units. Our main narrative source for the reign of Maurikios (582–602), the history of Theophylaktos, focuses on Maurikios' generals,

[53] Theophanes, *Chronographia* a.m. 6051, p. 233.
[54] Theophanes, *Chronographia* a.m. 6054, p. 236. There is debate over whether the units in question here are *scholarii* or *scholae*, but this does not affect our argument.
[55] Sarantis, *Justinian's Balkan Wars*.   [56] Pohl, *The Avars*.
[57] 20,000: a Turkish envoy in Menandros, *History* fr. 10.1.83.

including Ioannes Mystakon ("the Moustache"), the emperor's brother-in-law Philippikos, Priskos, Komentiolos, and, in the 590s, the emperor's brother Petros. Maurikios would rotate these men in and out of the top positions, reflecting his alternating favor and disfavor for their successes and failures. Theophylaktos, who was writing in the 620s and possibly the 630s, reflected a later tradition that favored Priskos and disparaged the others,[58] but there is no reason to believe that his focus on this cast of characters led him to somehow omit from his narrative the presence in this war of two major field armies (the praesentals) and their commanders. They simply were not there. Moreover, when credible numbers are given in the sources for the size of the Thracian and Illyrian field armies, they rarely exceed 10,000 men.[59] This means that even these armies were operating at reduced strength, in fact at about half their full capacity as laid out in the *Notitia* of the previous century. The reliance on two armies of about 10,000 men unsupported by a praesental reserve explains why the Romans found the Avars to be a match.

The last attested MMP was Maurikios' general Komentiolos, appointed to the position in 585 after he defeated some Slavs in Thrace. By this point the title MMP was a veritable archaism and does not imply the continued existence of a designated praesental force, save perhaps for some skeletal, ceremonial, or bodyguard units. The title and remit had been revived, but whatever forces Komentiolos commanded were praesental by virtue of their commander's office, not the other way around. Komentiolos went on to prosecute the war against the Avars in the following year, but it is not clear whether he did so as MMP or MMT. The army of 10,000 that he led in about 587 was certainly that of Thrace, and he could have commanded it in either capacity, that is, as either MMT or MMP.[60] We saw earlier how Sittas led the armies of the MMA while he was MMP on assignment to the east.

Thus, the late Roman field armies of the east never reached the maximum size that most historians give them. In theory, and before Justinian, around 100,000 men served in those armies (for Illyricum, Thrace, Praesentals I and II, and Oriens), with each army having at most 20,000 men. Historians believe that Justinian added another 15,000 for Armenia, 15,000 for North Africa, and 18,000 for Italy (which are approximate numbers, factoring in some slight reductions in the old field armies).

---

[58] Whitby, *The Emperor Maurice*.
[59] For example, Theophylaktos, *History* 3.7.10, 3.10.7 (Persian), 5.11.4, 7.7.1–2 (numbers depleted by war), 8.3.11; see Whitby, "Recruitment," 100–101.
[60] Theophylaktos, *History* 1.7.4, 2.10.8–9; *PLRE* III, 322 (Comentiolus 1).

The new total in 565 would, then, have been about 150,000 (for field armies only, not the *limitanei*). This nicely matches the figure given by the historian Agathias, writing around 580, who says that the army of Justinian in 559 numbered only 150,000 men, down from 645,000 "in former times."[61] Agathias intends for the contrast to show how low the empire had sunk, though he does not specify when the empire had 645,000 soldiers. To produce the "low" figure of 150,000 for Justinian, Agathias is supposed to have omitted the frontier soldiers (*limitanei*) and to have cited the full paper strength of the army of past times. To match the figure that Agathias cites for "former" times, one scholar, A. H. M. Jones, managed to produce a paper-strength total of around 600,000 for all units listed in the *Notitia dignitatum*, combining West and East, though he admitted that this was both speculative and (even if it is a correct reading of that source) only a nominal figure.[62] Other scholars do not believe that the Roman empire ever had that many soldiers, and some estimates are much lower, sometimes less than half that figure, even for the peak of Roman military recruitment.[63]

On the other hand, it is possible that Agathias did intend for the figure of 150,000 to represent *all* the soldiers employed by Justinian toward the end of his reign, both the field armies and the *limitanei*. This is impossible to verify because we do not know the numbers of the remaining *limitanei*. Prokopios, writing in the early 550s, accuses Justinian of basically demobilizing the *limitanei* and not treating them as soldiers anymore. But we have seen that Justinian did garrison his North African provinces with *limitanei*, and some scholars have argued that Prokopios is referring to a small-scale demobilization restricted to Palestine, Prokopios' home province.[64]

Of course, it remains possible that the figure of 150,000 in Agathias reflects the total paper strength of all the field armies "in the books," therefore including the praesentals. But that paper strength, we now realize, was even further removed from reality than previously suspected, and here we are primarily interested in the reality. The creation of the armies for Armenia, North Africa, and Italy came at the direct expense of other armies, especially the praesentals who ceased to exist as an effective fighting force. So up to 40,000 men must be deducted from the operational total to reflect

---

[61] Agathias, *Histories* 5.13.7–8.
[62] Jones, *Later Roman Empire*, 684; compare Treadgold, *Byzantium and Its Armies*, 48, 60–63; Haldon, *Warfare*, 100; Decker, *Byzantine Art of War*, 17.
[63] Bang, "The Roman Empire II."
[64] Prokopios, *Secret History* 24.12–14. Coin finds indicate the reform was limited to Palestine: Casey, "Justinian, the *limitanei*"; Sivan, *Palestine*, 88–89.

praesental soldiers who were reassigned but never replaced. (In fact, we suspect that significant numbers of praesental units had either been posted to the east or were not being replenished already by the 510s, which is why Anastasius could not use them against the rebel Vitalianus.) Moreover, by the 580s (and possibly earlier still) the field armies of Illyricum and Thrace were operating at close to half their capacity, at around 10,000 men apiece. Similarly, it would also be surprising if, by that time, the exarch of North Africa could bring more than 5,000 men to the field. Italy too was in shambles after the Lombard invasion of 568. We do not have reliable figures for the forces that its local commanders and exarch could muster, but they would not have exceeded 10,000, and even that force was dispersed across the Italian peninsula and pinned down.

The only armies that seem to have been kept up to something resembling their regular strength were Armenia and Oriens. They more or less held their own against the Persian imperial army in the second half of the sixth century, and the warfare between the two empires along the eastern frontier, their most populous and wealthy territories, was nearly constant. In 591, Maurikios decided to intervene in a Persian civil war on the side of the deposed heir Khusrow II. He mustered a large invasion force that marched into Mesopotamia and defeated the pretender Bahram at the battle of the Blarathon river, near lake Urmia. Theophylaktos says that the Roman side had 60,000 men at the battle – note that this was roughly the size of Julian's invasion force in 363 – and Bahram had 40,000. These numbers seem high, but nothing less than control of the Persian empire hung in the balance, and both sides would have mustered their full strength. In fact, we can make sense of these figures. An eastern source (in Syriac) says that each Roman field army in this campaign (i.e., Armenia and Oriens) had 20,000 men, which matches their nominal strengths, and they were joined by 10,000 Persian allies who fought for Khusrow II.[65] Perhaps the Romans and Khusrow had 50,000 rather than 60,000, and there might be some rounding up in the figures to yield more impressive totals, but it is close enough to what Theophylaktos reports to confirm his account.

Let us, then, attempt an operational tally for the years around 590. Armenia (15,000 or 20,000), Oriens (20,000), Thrace (10,000), Illyricum (10,000), Italy (10,000), and North Africa (5,000) give us a total of 70,000

---

[65] Theophylaktos, *History* 5.9.4; *Chronicle to 1234* 7–8 (trans. Palmer, pp. 116–117). Pseudo-Sebeos, *History* 11 (77) mentions 15,000 for the Armenian field army (mistaking it for a national Armenian army); at 11 (70) he mentions 8,000 allied Persians.

or 75,000 soldiers for the empire's field armies. The actual total for the eastern empire since the death of Theodosius I would never have been higher than 100,000, and that high point was reached around AD 500. So the empire had lost significant operational capacity, of the order of 30 percent, during the sixth century. Into the tally of 590, we have folded an army of (allegedly) 15,000 barbarian federates, recruited by the emperor Tiberios II Konstantinos in about 581 and called Tiberianoi, into the armies of Oriens and Armenia, because that is where he sent them. They are never mentioned again as a separate unit.[66]

Why did the numbers go down? The first answer is that the praesentals had been dispersed to Oriens and then from there to Armenia, North Africa, and Italy. Then, in the latter half of the sixth century all the field armies of the empire seem to have suffered a general diminution in their recruitment figures, including Illyricum and Thrace, though this affected the commands of Armenia and Oriens to a lesser degree. Why did this happen?

We cannot give a full answer to that question here. It would require a global analysis of the circumstances of the Roman empire in a challenging period of its history.[67] Yet an outline can be hazarded. The impression given by the sources, as well as by the actions and reactions of the court, is that the emperors lacked the money with which to pay new soldiers, not the manpower from which to recruit them. Whereas Anastasius left a surplus, after 540 Justinian and his successors were regularly short on cash and frequently unable to pay their soldiers on time, which often led to desertions and mutinies. If they could not pay their current, actual soldiers, they could not easily recruit new ones. So the size of the armies decreased largely because the emperors were unable or unwilling to pay for the recruitment and subsequent salaries of the soldiers necessary to bring them to strength. The emperor Maurikios in particular was notorious for his penny-pinching when it came to the army, even though he was a former general himself. His monetary policy suggests that the regime was desperately short on cash.[68] He periodically tried to reduce military pay and benefits while squeezing more dangerous service out of soldiers in ways that would also save him money (such as asking them to winter north of the Danube and forage). This led to a number of major mutinies, including one that finally destroyed his regime and brought the centurion Phokas

[66] Theophanes, *Chronographia* a.m. 6074, pp. 251–252; Euagrios, *Ecclesiastical History* 5.14 (gives the figure 150,000); for the recruitment drive, see also Theophylaktos, *History* 3.12.4. Archaeological evidence points to their deployment under the MMO: Fourlas, "Eternal Rest."

[67] See Kaldellis, *New Roman Empire*.

[68] Gândilă, "Heavy Money," on the numismatic policies of Maurikios in the Balkans.

(602–610) to the throne. Maurikios' austerity politics led to his death, and this, in turn, precipitated a major war with Persia when the shah Khusrow II cynically sought to avenge his so-called father Maurikios by conquering Maurikios' empire. This war destroyed the old imperial order of Rome and Persia and enabled the Arabs to conquer the Near East in the 630s.

Why, then, were the emperors short on cash after 540? One answer is the plague. A fierce debate is currently raging between maximalists and moderates about the extent of the death that it caused (there are no minimalists in this debate). We are moderates, which means that we find a mortality of around 10 percent to be more likely than 50 percent (both numbers are guesses). Even with 10 percent, state revenue would have been dramatically impacted. At the same time, Justinian had embroiled the Roman state in difficult wars and protracted quagmires on many fronts: in Italy against the Goths and then the Lombards; in North Africa against the Moors (although they were an occasional threat only); in the Caucasus, Mesopotamia, and Syria against the Persians; and in the Balkans against Hunnic, Bulgar, and Slavic raiders. The problems in the Balkans became vastly worse when the Avars appeared. The short, local wars of the fifth century had given way to a series of forever-wars against increasingly powerful enemies along virtually every Roman border.

Active wars cost more money than just maintaining field armies to be idle, which meant that Justinian and his successors had to pay more for the same number of soldiers at war than, say, Anastasius had to pay for them to be at rest in 500. Also, during the course of these wars the empire's cities and agricultural lands were damaged and sometimes even destroyed, which resulted in a further loss of revenue, whether permanent or temporary, as the emperors granted tax breaks or remissions so that the devastated regions could recover. Enemy attackers (on all fronts) also carried off thousands of prisoners to sell as slaves beyond the frontier or to use for their agricultural labor and crafts, especially on Mesopotamian estates owned by the Persian elites. These losses also resulted in a further decrease in taxpayers and therefore revenue.[69] Roman policy from the mid-sixth century onwards was thus constrained by a vicious cycle of military insecurity and economic retrenchment, in which foreign wars were exacerbated by shocks both natural (such as the plague) and systemic (such as mutinies).

Just before he died, Justinian managed to tie up most of the loose ends on the military side of things by making a series of peace treaties with his neighbors on all fronts. He did this with Persia and with a number of

---

[69] Sarantis, "The Socio-Economic Impact of Raiding."

Germanic tribes to the north of the Danube. In Italy as well his general Narses defeated the Goths and brought the peninsula under control. It has therefore been argued recently that the late-sixth-century decline of the eastern empire was not Justinian's fault, but due to the bad decisions, failures, and incompetence of his heirs, who did not manage the international scene as adeptly as he did.[70] The plausibility of this defense of Justinian, however, depends on the scale against which we examine the issue and the facts on which we base our conclusions. For example, those studies take the continued existence of the praesental armies for granted and do not realize how deeply Justinian's conquests had eroded the *Notitia* framework, which was not, it should be noted, a framework for reconquest and occupation. He did not add new armies but moved the existing ones around. That process had already begun under Zeno and Anastasius, but they still kept the armies within the borders of the eastern empire presupposed by the *Notitia* (i.e., in Isauria and the east). Justinian, by contrast, sent them abroad.

As a result, Justinian obliged his heirs to defend increasingly far-flung territories while facing escalating crises along their traditional borders. This pressure was especially acute after 540, which saw renewed Persian aggression in Mesopotamia and Armenia, and the onset of the plague. Moreover, the treaties of peace that he concluded in the final years of his life were fragile and proved to be temporary. They were short-term patches on mounting structural problems in the empire's overall geostrategic position. It is, therefore, not a convincing defense to say that Justinian could not have foreseen that the Lombards would invade Italy in 568, or that the Avars would invade in the 570s, or that Constantinople, at a time when it began to face severe budget deficits, would find itself at war with two major enemies simultaneously (the Avars and the Persians). Justinian internalized the benefits of conquest (e.g., glory and political legitimacy) and externalized the risk that they created to his successors. His choices limited the options of those who ruled after him, so he was, to a great degree, responsible for the eastern empire's negative long-term outcomes.

The history of Theophylaktos ends in 602. After that, the Roman state gradually fell apart on all sides. The Avars and Slavs eventually conquered or overran most of the Balkan provinces, though we do not know how exactly this played out. It is likely that by 620 the Roman state was deriving no revenue from most of the Balkans. The field army of Illyricum effectively disappeared so that not even its name lived on in later, Byzantine times. If any of its units survived, it would have been by seeking refuge in Thrace or

---

[70] Heather, *Rome Resurgent*, ch. 11; Sarantis, *Justinian's Balkan Wars*; Koehn, *Justinian*.

garrisoning the surviving cities of the Greek coastline, which were the only two Balkan regions that remained under imperial control.[71] In 608–610, a vicious civil war was fought between the regime of Phokas in the capital and some rebels in North Africa, who put up Herakleios as their counter-emperor, and this further degraded the empire's armies, specifically the army of North Africa, which marched into Egypt, and that of Oriens, which was sent by Phokas to meet the rebels there.[72] Herakleios seized the throne in 610, but over the course of the following decade the Persians overran Syria, Palestine, and Egypt, defeating all the Roman armies that tried to stop them. This time they did not come as raiders but as conquerors. It took a long time for Herakleios to muster the forces with which to respond. In late 624 and during winter 624–625, he invaded the Caucasian territories of the Persian empire, causing extensive damage and repeatedly defeating and brilliantly outmaneuvering the two Persian armies that were sent against him. Herakleios' movements were rapid, complex, and deep in enemy territory, so it is unlikely that he had more than 20,000 soldiers with him, drawn probably from the field armies of Armenia and Oriens.[73]

In response, in 626 the Avars, who had allied at a distance with Persia, besieged Constantinople with a force reported at some 80,000 men, though this number seems high, and with support from the Persians, who had marched to the opposite shore of the Bosporos. To meet this challenge to the very existence of the empire, Herakleios, who was based in eastern Asia Minor, divided his forces. He sent a partial-strength field army of 12,000, whose identity is not specified, to defend Constantinople in his absence in 626, which they did successfully.[74] It is not clear whether this army then stayed on in the capital or returned to Herakleios. The emperor dealt the Persian empire a knock-out blow in 627–628, when he invaded

---

[71] Pillon, "*L'Illyricum* byzantin," 66–74.   [72] John of Nikiou, *Chronicle* 107.1–109.17.

[73] *Paschal Chronicle* s.a. 624; pseudo-Sebeos, *History* 38 (124–125), with additions from Thomas Artsruni, *History of the House of the Artsrunik'* 2.3 (trans. Thomson p. 159); Theophanes, *Chronographia* a.m. 6113, pp. 302–303; and a.m. 6114–6116, pp. 307–314; Georgios of Pisidia, *Heracliad* 2.160–230; Movses Dasxuranci, *History of the Caucasian Albanians* 2.10 (trans. Dowsett pp. 78–81); for a modern reconstruction, see Howard-Johnston, "Heraclius' Persian Campaigns," with the corrections by Zuckerman, "Heraclius in 625." Pseudo-Sebeos, cited earlier in this note, impossibly gives Herakleios an army of 120,000, of whom 20,000 were elite. The latter figure is plausible.

[74] For Herakleios' division of his armies, see Theophanes, *Chronographia* a.m. 6117, p. 315; see *Paschal Chronicle* s.a. 626 (p. 718) for the 12,000 men he sent to Constantinople. Our sources for the siege include the *Paschal Chronicle* s.a. 626; Theodoros Synkellos, *On the Attack by the Atheist Barbarians and Persians on This God-Protected City*; Georgios of Pisidia, *Avar War*; Nikephoros, *Short History* 12–13.

Mesopotamia, defeated the Persian armies sent against him, ravaged the agricultural estates of the Persian nobility, and weakened the regime of the shah Khusrow II, who was deposed and killed in a coup hatched by his own disaffected aristocracy. However, much of this success was likely due not to the Roman armies of Herakleios but to the Turkish allies whom the emperor had been cultivating for years and who now finally showed up for this showdown with the Persian empire, their common enemy. In his dispatches to Constantinople, Herakleios essentially took credit for the victory but, if we read between the lines and take seriously the testimony of the eastern sources, a scenario emerges in which the Roman armies were only accompanying a much larger force supplied by their Turkish allies, the latter possibly as large as 40,000.[75]

In his postwar negotiations with the Persians, Herakleios restored the status quo that prevailed before 602. But then, in the 630s, the Arabs rapidly conquered Palestine, Syria, Egypt, and Roman Armenia, as well as, on the Persian side, Mesopotamia. The Roman empire's remaining field armies were pulled back into Asia Minor. In a process that has been extensively studied and is now fairly well understood, the army of Oriens became Anatolikon (in south-central Asia Minor), that of Armenia became Armeniakon (in north-central Asia Minor), and that of Thrace became Thrakesion (in western Asia Minor).[76] As the praesental units had long since departed from the scene, it is not likely that the elite force of Opsikion, which appears after the mid-seventh century, originated in the praesental forces, even though Latin *obsequium* does mean something similar to *in praesenti*, that is, "following the emperor."[77] The connection lacks institutional and historical continuity, given the early demise of the praesentals. Nor, if there were institutional continuity between the two, would there have been a reason to change the army's name to something synonymous in Latinate Greek, especially since the Greek transliteration

---

[75] Campaign of 627–628: Herakleios' dispatches in Theophanes, *Chronographia* a.m. 6117–6118, pp. 316–327; *Paschal Chronicle* s.a. 628; also Nikephoros, *Short History* 12–15; Movses Dasxuranci, *History of the Caucasian Albanians* 2.11 (from one source), 2.12–14 (from a more reliable source) (trans. Dowsett pp. 85–95); pseudo-Sebeos, *History* 38–39 (126–127). The *Chronicle to 1234* 37 (trans. Palmer, p. 137), along with its related eastern chronicles and Nikephoros, reveal that the Turks accompanied Herakleios (they are wrongly called "Khazars" in some sources); also Michael the Syrian, *Chronicle* 11.3.

[76] Haldon, *The Empire That Would Not Die*, 266–269, citing previous scholarship.

[77] Haldon has tentatively postulated a connection between the praesentals and Opsikion, but is lately more cautious about it: compare *Byzantine Praetorians*, 173–178, with "More Questions." Either way, these are (and are correctly represented as) highly conjectural reconstructions.

praisenton (πραισέντον) had been in use since at least the fifth century.[78] Opsikion (both the name and the thing) was likely a new creation.

The praesental armies lasted as integral units for less than a century. They were assembled in their "classical" form around 440 and began to be stationed in the east by the later fifth century. In the sixth century, they were dispersed to the new field armies created by Justinian in his newly occupied provinces. Their units were not disbanded but incorporated into other armies and are attested in Italy and Egypt as late as about 600. A set of plans drawn up in Constantinople for an attack on Arab-held Crete in 949 lists two units, the *Theodosiakoi* and *Viktores*, as part of the contributions made by the Thrakesian thematic army, the descendant of the field army of Thrace. This is the last known attestation of the subunits of the late Roman field armies. The *Notitia dignitatum* lists *Victores* for the first Praesental, and *Theodosiaci* for the second Praesental, Oriens, and Thrace.[79] These units were probably shuffled from army to army many times in their long history, and the configuration reflected in the *Notitia* was only a relatively brief moment within the long arc of Roman military history.

---

[78] For example, Justinian, *Novel* 22, epilogue; Malalas, *Chronicle* 14.46, 15.3, 15.5, 15.7, and passim; *ACO* vol. 3, pp. 101.30, 102.12; *Paschal Chronicle* s.a. 478 (p. 601) and passim; Theophylaktos, *History* 1.7.4.

[79] Konstantinos VII, *Book of Ceremonies* 2.45 (ed. Dagron and Flusin, vol. 3, 315). See also *ND Or.* 5.22, 5.63, 6.33, 7.57, 8.27; and Haldon, *Byzantine Praetorians*, 238–239.

Conclusions

This book has argued that the "canonical" five-army system of the eastern empire that is reflected in the *Notitia* emerged only after the 440s, and that we should neither project its titles and structures of command onto the armies of the previous period nor assume that it lasted until the seventh century. Before the battle of Adrianople (AD 378), it is unlikely that the eastern empire (under Valens) had much more than the equivalent of two Roman field armies of 20,000 each. For the generation after that battle, it may have had even fewer soldiers than that, with the difference made up through the recruitment of barbarian auxiliaries, both those who agreed to the peace of AD 382 and others who immigrated later. These barbarian armies, led by the likes of Alaric, Tribigild, and Gaïnas, proved repeatedly to be unreliable and dangerous. After the pogrom and ensuing war of AD 400, the east began to build up its own defense forces, a process that went into overdrive in response to Attila the Hun and other challenges, in the 440s.

The classic phase of five armies also did not last as long as historians have commonly believed. The two praesental armies were already in an advanced state of dispersal, especially to Oriens, by the end of the fifth century. Justinian finished that process off in creating his new armies for Armenia, North Africa, and Italy. The empire now had six field armies but not many more soldiers than it used to have with five, because Justinian's many wars overstretched his resources and he often left his soldiers unpaid and units undermanned. This process of decay accelerated after 540, when the plague and constant war on many fronts weakened and impoverished the empire. Despite having more armies, by the end of the sixth century the eastern empire was operating with fewer soldiers than it had a century earlier, possibly up to 30 percent fewer. By the 620s, when Herakleios had to face both the Avars in the Balkans and the Persians in the east – enemies more powerful than any the eastern empire had ever previously faced, though on a par, perhaps, with Attila – he was likely doing so with the equivalent of only two field armies. The Balkans were essentially sacrificed to this merciless calculus. By contrast, Anastasius could defend the empire against Persia alone in the early 500s with three such armies at full strength.

As we said at the outset, many facets of current scholarship will need to be revised in light of our arguments. The most immediate effects will be in *Notitia* studies, a field that has been trapped for decades in a cul-de-sac created by the nature of the text itself and the misdating of at least half of its contents. It is not yet clear what scholars armed with a new date might discover. At the very least, virtually every theory of its composition will need to be revised in major ways.

Political narratives, too, will need to be revised. The military was one of the most important institutions in the Roman world, and our revision of its history has implications for everything from political legitimacy to the personal security of Roman citizens. In particular, breaking the current orthodoxy about the *Notitia* system grants greater agency to emperors and their courts, neither of which were as constrained by earlier structures as scholars have previously imagined. Imperial administrations during this period made more and more meaningful choices about military policy than we realized. Both these decisions and their consequences must be reassessed accordingly.

Roman identity is also implicated in our argument, especially its political function. We have thrown new light on the arrangements Rome made with the various barbarian generals who populate the history of the fifth century, men such as Gaïnas, Aspar, and the Theoderics, whose ethnic identities continue to be controversial. We have laid out our view in the relevant chapters, but even scholars who disagree with our conclusions must now reconcile their views with a new narrative of the fifth century. The east Roman empire swung rapidly from a state of relative demilitarization facilitated by reliance on barbarian manpower to the *Notitia* system, which allowed it to suppress and purge groups perceived as non-Roman, especially Goths and Isaurians. The Roman army had once been a major driver of Romanization, but in the fifth century it was used to enforce the boundaries of Roman identity. Both this shift and its motives require explanation.

Perhaps the most significant questions our reconstruction raises concern the imperial budget and the broader economy. Our reconstruction implies that Constantinople was spending considerably more money on its armies after the 440s than it was in the later fourth and early fifth centuries. The decision to do so made sense: in 441, it was trying to save the western empire by sending a massive expedition against the Vandals in North

Africa; it faced a simultaneous war with Persia in the east; and it suffered a massive invasion by Attila along the Danube in the same year. The relative demilitarization of the early reign of Theodosius II was henceforth untenable. But where did Constantinople find the money to pay for so many more soldiers, starting in the 440s, and what had it been doing with those resources before that?

We can only gesture toward a possible answer to these important questions here, as anything more would take us too far into a different technical domain of research on the later empire. First, it is now universally understood that the fifth century was a period of general economic growth for the eastern empire, and this must have translated into greater revenues for the state. Emperors between 450 and 518 were able not only to pay for these larger forces but also occasionally to leave significant surpluses to their successors. The court at Constantinople was also run by competent civilian officials, the praetorian prefects, who had more power at this time than they had in the fourth century or in the collapsing fifth-century west. These officials created an efficient apparatus for generating revenue and were able to crack down on exemptions that had been granted to the aristocracy. An author writing at the court around 440 called the prefect the "second power in the state after the emperor."[1]

In sum, the eastern empire was wealthier than before, and it was precisely when these revenue-streams began to dry up after 540 that the armies began to contract, as one would expect. There was a second factor at play here. It is likely that the state economy of the eastern empire became increasingly more monetized during the fifth century.[2] Taxes and other revenues that, in the fourth century, had been collected in kind or in the form of services, were commuted to cash payments during the course of the fifth, giving the state precisely the kind of fiscal flexibility that it needed in order to pay for mobile armies, as opposed to the relatively stationary *limitanei*, who could more easily be supplied in kind by their provinces. We have no way to estimate the scale of this shift toward monetization, but on any level it would have helped Constantinople to hire more professional soldiers. Thus, comparing the cost of the armies between the later fourth century and the later fifth would, from a budgetary point of view, be like comparing apples to oranges, or, more literally, apples to gold coins.

---

[1] Sokrates, *Ecclesiastical History* 2.16.2; compare Ioannes Lydos, *On the Magistracies* 2.20; see Jones, *Later Roman Empire*, 207.

[2] Jones, *Later Roman Empire*, 207–208, 397, 443, 449, 460–461, 630; Banaji, *Agrarian Change* (some aspects of this book are controversial, especially that regarding capitalist economics in late antiquity, but monetization is not really among them).

Even so, the difference between two and five field armies is significant, and we might ask what Constantinople was doing with the extra revenue during the first decades of the fifth century, whatever form that revenue took. This is a real question, though it is impossible to answer as we lack the empire's budget sheets. Some obvious items come to mind, such as the expansion of Constantinople and the construction of the Theodosian walls, in addition to the defensive walls that were newly built around many cities throughout the Balkans and Asia Minor in the aftermath of Alaric and Tribigild's depredations.[3] It is also possible that the court had been under-taxing its aristocracy. The contemporary historian Priskos reports that massive levies on the aristocracy were needed in order to gather the tribute that Attila demanded in 448. Priskos' account is cast in a tragic mode, with senators reduced to poverty or taking their own lives in desperation, and so it should not be taken at face value. But he does note that the court and aristocracy had previously been spending their money on vanities and luxuries rather than on the army. If there was any truth to this report, priorities changed after the 440s.[4]

The *Notitia* system also has macroeconomic implications. State expenditures played a major role in structuring economic activity in the Roman world. The expansion of the armies after the 440s, especially when paired with increased monetization, likely represented a quantitative and qualitative shift in the state's role in the economy. The field armies were mobile vectors of money and demand; wherever they went, economic activity followed. The gradual dispersal of these armies, especially their redeployment outside the core territories of the east Roman empire, to Africa and Italy, must have had significant economic consequences for the empire.

Another distinct set of questions focus on the praesental armies. Upon reflection, they appear to be the most idiosyncratic component of the *Notitia* system; indeed, the origins of this book project lie in a sense of unease that modern scholarship on the praesental armies did not add up, in particular that it did not account for the relative silence on those armies in the sources. The other field armies in the system make geographical and strategic sense, but what was the point of having a further 40,000 men stationed around Constantinople? Why were those two armies attested in use only in the period between the 470s and 506, when scholarship assumes that they were present for the whole range of the years 395–630? Why was the position of MMP treated more like a ceremonial honor and often

---

[3] Jacobs, "The Creation of the Late Antique City" (not linked there to the Gothic marauders).
[4] Priskos, *History* fr. 9.3.

bestowed upon barbarian warlords whom the palace was courting, but without also giving them command over the armies themselves, making it difficult for us to determine whether those armies even existed at that time?

Our research has shown that the praesental armies were likely maintained as a reserve force during a period, namely the 440s–480s, when Constantinople was preoccupied with its Balkan challenges. When its needs shifted to the east, that is, to Isauria in the 490s and the eastern frontier after that, the praesental armies were accordingly dispersed to those regions, and then the same thing happened again when Justinian created new armies for Armenia (528), North Africa (534), and Italy (552). The position of MMP began to be treated as a court honor already in the 470s or 480s and given to barbarians (such as the two Theoderics) whom the palace needed to pay without losing face.

Even generals of Roman origin did more than just command armies, or less than that, depending on how we view it. They were also high court functionaries who performed a wide range of important tasks for the court, such as attending ceremonies in the capital; going on embassies (as the first MMPs did in 450 and 451, to Attila); supervising a host of legal, financial, and bureaucratic issues of military administration; organizing and even presiding over some of the Church Councils; and negotiating with urban protesters. More than for the other "masters of soldiers," the attestation of MMPs does not necessarily imply the existence of praesental armies or, in periods when those armies did demonstrably exist, active command over them. In the second half of the fifth century, that office was traded back-and-forth between barbarian generals (the two Theoderics), while also being held by high-ranking members of the imperial family. This trend may have begun as early as the reign of Leo (457–474), who gave the office to his two sons-in-law Zeno and Marcianus. The usurper Basiliscus (475–476) gave the office to his nephew Armatus. This mix of dynastic and military appointees continued under Anastasius (491–518), who appointed his nephew Hypatius (along with Patricius and Ioannes the Hunchback). Justin I (518–527) appointed his nephew and future emperor Justinian and the ex-rebel Vitalianus, both for political and not primarily military reasons.

Justinian went on to appoint his cousin Germanus and brother-in-law Sittas to the post, along with the otherwise unknown Maxentianus. The first two were active generals, the third almost certainly not. Toward the middle of his reign, the office of MMP declined further in value. It was now being offered as a sop to foreign generals whom the regime was cultivating, such as the Armenian Artabanes and the Herul Suartuas. Artabanes sought to marry Justinian's niece Preiecta at the same time that he was appointed MMP, but was prevented by Theodora.[5] We must remember that by this time there hardly were any praesental units left. Narses probably took the last of them with him to Italy in 551. In all likelihood, many of the last MMPs spent most of their time in office at the court decked out in splendid uniforms. They were essentially MMP-*vacantes*.

Thus, the trajectory of the office of MMP was noticeably divorced from the history of the praesental armies themselves. Of the twenty-odd men we know to have been praesental generals, only nine are clearly attested leading any kind of army while in office: Theoderic Strabo, Armatus, Theoderic the Amal, Ioannes the Hunchback, Hypatius, Patricius, Pharesmanes, Sittas, and Komentiolos. But of these nine, the two Theoderics are never attested leading Roman soldiers, whether praesental or other. Instead, they and their followers appear to have been deputized as proxy-Roman armies under the high court title of MMP. In addition, just because a praesental general engaged in military action does not mean that he was leading distinctly constituted praesental armies. This is a concern especially in the cases of Sittas, who is said to have been leading the newly created armies of the MMA in Armenia (though he possibly brought some praesental units with him to the east), and of Komentiolos, the last man attested in that office who was almost certainly commanding the army of Thrace. That brings us down to five MMPs who commanded praesental armies, all between 475 and 506. As it happens, this is also the brief period during which, we have proposed, the *Notitia* system actually reflected the reality of the eastern military command.

Conversely, praesental units were not always led by the MMPs. In 478, Zeno appointed Illus, who was *magister officiorum*, to take command of a large army he was assembling against the Goths, which almost certainly did include praesental units.[6] In the long Isaurian war of 492–498, it is again likely that praesental units served under both the MMP Ioannes the Hunchback and the MMO Ioannes the Scythian.[7] In the Persian conflict of the early 500s, Anastasius appointed the *magister officiorum* Celer to take overall command of the war after the initial failures of his two MMPs Hypatius and Patricius, which means that Celer was effectively commanding praesental units.[8] By this point, of course, many of those units had been transferred to the east and had come under the command of the MMO and his *duces*, as ratified by Anastasius' law of 492. The "classical" phase of the praesental armies was thus much shorter than scholars imagine it, ranging

---

[5] Prokopios, *Wars* 3.31.10–11.   [6] Malchos, *History* fr. 18.1.   [7] See Chapter 3.
[8] *PLRE* II, 275–276 (Celer).

from the 440s to the late 490s. Even in that brief period, there were likely years when MMPs were not appointed even though the praesental armies existed, just as some MMPs were appointed after the armies had ceased to exist.

The historical oddity of the praesental armies can be understood better if we situate their brief history against the background of Roman military strategy in the *longue durée*. The history of the Roman army from Augustus to Herakleios is generally divided into three phases, based on how Rome organized and strategically distributed its forces. In the first phase, Augustus converted the civil war legions into increasingly stationary armies of frontier defense, a process that was completed by the reign of Tiberius. Though campaigns of conquest and terror against barbarians continued, the legions were primarily a defensive force dispersed across the frontiers of the empire, and the emperors, who were mostly based at Rome during this phase, did not keep a large strike force at their side. Campaigning armies were assembled by supplementing regional forces with units drawn from across the empire and the strike-force armies were concentrated under their command.[9]

In the second phase, which began in the third century, the rise of more formidable enemies on all of Rome's major borders forced the adoption, under Diocletian and Constantine, of a system of defense-in-depth. *Limitanei* and a denser network of forts guarded the borders against minor threats, but true striking power was invested in the emperor's mobile *comitatus*, which he brought to bear wherever needed, against both foreign invaders and domestic rivals. In this phase, emperors were always on the move along the frontiers.[10]

The second phase is traditionally understood to have ended during the reigns of Valens and Theodosius, when the earlier system was destroyed at Adrianople and Theodosius reorganized the army along the lines of the *Notitia* system. This inaugurated the third phase. Yet this transition is broadly under-theorized in terms of military strategy due to a combination of poor sources and the tendency to use the *Notitia* to look backward rather than forward, and westward rather than eastward.[11] Nevertheless, the broad

[9] Keppie, *The Making of the Roman Army*, 161–168; Gilliver, "The Augustan Reform"; Goldsworthy, *Pax Romana*, 309–326.

[10] Jones, *Later Roman Empire*, 607–611; Southern and Dixon, *Late Roman Army*, 4–38; Treadgold, *Byzantium and its Army*, 8–14. Scholars have begun to argue for greater continuity in this development, but nevertheless accept the broader trends: Strobel, "Strategy and Army Structure."

[11] Under-theorized: Jones, *Later Roman Empire*, 654–657; Southern and Dixon, *Late Roman Army*, 55–60; Treadgold, *Byzantium and Its Army*, 14–21. Two works with a noteworthy backward focus in their use of the *Notitia* are Southern and Dixon, *Late Roman Army*, and Hoffmann, *Das spätrömische Bewegungsheer*.

outlines of this third phase, premised on the operation of the *Notitia* system, may be sketched. The *comitatus* was unfolded and reorganized into a set of regional field armies that were backed by a central reserve of praesental units that was also tasked with defending Constantinople. In this phase, the emperor reverted to residing at "Rome," only it was New Rome this time. Essentially, the third phase trended back in the direction of frontier defense that marked the first, while preserving regional striking power. This is the *Notitia* system, which is thought to have operated until it collapsed, along with much of the east Roman empire itself, in the seventh century.

This three-phase narrative is useful because it captures an essential dynamic that characterizes the history of Rome's armies, namely the trade-off between firm frontier defense and mobile striking capacity. The *Notitia* system seems to strike middle ground between the significantly different choices of the first and second phases.

The narrative given above, however, is problematic on a number of grounds. It is built on an erroneous privileging of the evidence of the *Notitia* itself – whose arrangements it misdates – over the evidence of all of our other sources for the period; and it also assumes a relatively static approach to issues of frontier defense that lasted roughly from the reign of Theodosius I to the seventh century. In this book, we have argued instead that the *Notitia* captures only a short-lived configuration of the east Roman military that was designed to meet a specific set of challenges that arose in the 440s and that had changed considerably by the end of the fifth century. How does this realization change our grand narrative of Roman military history?

Far from operating within a relatively fixed institutional shape, as previous reconstructions based on the *Notitia* have assumed, the armies of east Rome were in a continuous state of evolution between the fourth and the seventh centuries as the empire's strategic circumstances changed. The mobile *comitatus* of the fourth century grew out the reforms of Diocletian, whose army was created by the simultaneous need for effective striking power against (on the one hand) Sasanian Persia and the increasingly powerful Germanic confederations and (on the other hand) the proliferation of domestic rivals that defined the crisis of the third century. The strategic disposition of the army was therefore dictated by considerations of both foreign and domestic security. However, by the reign of Constantius II political stability had been largely restored, allowing for the creation of a number of quasi-formalized regional commands, specifically for Gaul, Illyricum, and Oriens. Nevertheless, imperial insecurity was still such that emperors continued to keep their armies at their side. Thus Constantius II, Julian, Jovian, and the brothers Valentinian and Valens spent their reigns accompanied by a large, centralized striking force. This was not always strategically sound. The eastern frontier was exposed to Persian attack when Constantius traveled to the west in the 350s to suppress a domestic rival (Magnentius), and Valens' presence in Antioch in the 370s left the defense of the Balkans in the hands of *limitanei* who were not equipped to deal with the scale of the Gothic influx after 376. But emperors still tended to prioritize their personal command of Rome's military power over an occasional breach of the frontiers. The need to prevent (through sheer intimidation) or suppress (through force) domestic challenges was paramount.

Following the battle of Adrianople, the political calculus of the eastern empire shifted. Theodosius inherited a shattered eastern *comitatus* that could threaten neither the Goths nor his own rule. In other words, the disaster of 378 paradoxically reduced the political threat posed by the central army enough to allow Theodosius to spend much of his reign in Constantinople, erecting monuments and dictating his religious preferences, rather than leading the wars in the Balkans, which was mostly done, in the years 380–382, by western forces. It is noteworthy that he accompanied his armies only on their marches to the west to suppress domestic rivals, in 388 (Magnus Maximus) and 394 (Eugenius). It made sense for Theodosius to accompany his armies on those two expeditions (although not, we suspect, to actually lead them) because the distances involved and the potentially destabilizing political apparatus of the western empire made imperial action from such a great distance riskier. Under Theodosius I, domestic challenges remained more important than barbarian threats. But the two halves of the empire followed divergent trajectories after Theodosius' death in 395, with each one investing in a different aspect of his rule. In the west, the court and imperial policy was dominated by a series of powerful generals, starting with Stilicho, who had to suppress many barbarian invasions and domestic usurpers. The east, by contrast, remained relatively demilitarized and was governed for decades by a series of civilian officials, such as the praetorian prefect Rufinus, the eunuch Eutropius, the praetorian prefect Anthemius, and the senatorial class generally.

It is important that, for two generations after 378, we can rarely hear of the eastern *comitatus* in our sources. Having lost much of its striking power in 378, the eastern empire had de facto reverted to a policy of frontier defense, as the victory of Promotus over the Greuthungi in 386 indicates. When a *comitatus* was required, as it was for Theodosius' civil wars in 388 and 394, it was assembled with difficulty, left the Balkans relatively exposed (hence the troubles with the Goths that Theodosius faced in Macedonia in 391), and relied heavily on hired barbarian manpower. The army could still cause problems for the court during this period, but, because it was now so reliant on barbarian auxiliaries, the threat that it posed was fundamentally different. Warlords such as Alaric, Tribigild, and Gaïnas could ravage provinces but they could never become emperors. Facing the hostility of Constantinople, they even failed to establish themselves as the eastern equivalents of Stilicho. The civilian authorities in the capital remained in control, in part because they did not have to worry about the ambitions of a large *Roman* strike force in their backyard. Civilian control was enabled by under-militarization.

East Rome's under-militarization had come to an end by the 440s, when the invasion of the Huns, coupled with the existential threats faced by the western empire and the potential for war with Persia, forced the government in Constantinople to redevelop its striking power against formidable, organized, and highly mobile enemies. It was in this context that it devised and implemented the *Notitia* system, with its clear concentration of military power in the Balkans and its devolution of large armies to regional commanders, albeit with the praesental forces presumably held in reserve. The *Notitia* system thus marks a step away from both the centralization of the *comitatus* (marking the period from Diocletian to Adrianople) and its marginalization (after Adrianople) and toward a model of frontier defense like that which had prevailed under the Principate, with large armies entrusted to generals in Illyricum, Thrace, and Oriens. This system required the level of political stability and civilian control over the military that was available to Theodosius II as it had not been to his grandfather. But once the system was in place, the political power of these new armies required that the emperors again be military men (Marcian, Leo I, Zeno) backed by military factions, and not dynastic non-entities such as Arcadius and Theodosius II.

The program of remilitarization that began under Theodosius II was both a product and a producer of political stability. In the aftermath of Adrianople, the court at Constantinople had struggled to contain the ambitions of powerful barbarian generals, especially of Alaric and Gaïnas, who had one foot inside the Roman system and another outside of it. A similar dynamic played out in the second half of the fifth century. After the empire had rearmed itself (thus offering new opportunities to ambitious warlords), it was forced to cope with the fallout from the disintegration of Attila's empire, namely more barbarian migration. Thus, the politics of the second half of the fifth century was defined by the ascendancy of new barbarian warlords such as Aspar, Zeno, Illus, Theoderic Strabo, and Theoderic the Amal. The increasingly Roman field armies of the *Notitia* system gave Constantinople the means to curtail such ambitions. Leo I murdered Aspar and then used Roman armies to check the forces of Aspar's barbarian clients. When Theoderic Strabo sought to succeed Aspar as the most powerful military man at court, he was rebuffed and contained. His contemporary Theoderic the Amal repeatedly attacked imperial positions, even Constantinople itself, but he, too, was eventually repelled and checked. The field-army system proved its worth and so there was no repetition of the troubles of the years 376–400 and no east Roman parallel to the western disasters of 410, 455, and 476. In 488, Theoderic the Amal was induced to seek his fortune in Italy, as had Alaric before him. By 491, the major threats had been overcome and the court was able to once again install a civilian emperor, Anastasius (491–518). Numerous factors contributed to the parting of ways between eastern and western Rome during the fifth century, but the ability of the civilian administration in Constantinople to contain the ambitions of barbarian warlords, even through military violence, deserves a high position among them.

The *Notitia* armies thus functioned as intended, though this was not a simple or linear process. The east Romans were aided in resisting the fifth-century Goths by the Isaurians, the empire's only remaining internal barbarians. But Constantinople had had enough of the Isaurians' own infighting and high-handed treatment of the senatorial elite. That elite, along with the Roman field armies and populace of Constantinople, authorized (or required) Anastasius to suppress and finally pacify the Isaurians in a long, all-out war in their homeland (in the 490s). When Anastasius came to the throne in 491, he inherited a quiescent Balkan front (at least until Vitalianus' rebellion in the 510s), which allowed him to reorient the *Notitia* system toward the east, first to crush the Isaurians in Asia Minor and then to defend the empire against Persian aggression in Oriens (in 504–506). His reign also inaugurated a century of unprecedented political stability, during which the army was a solid supporter of the reigning emperor, both militarily and politically. While eastern pressure led to the dismantling of the Balkan-oriented *Notitia* system and the shift of its forces in an ever-eastward direction, it was political stability that facilitated a new, increasingly decentralized military disposition: The praesental armies were gradually broken up and dispersed to the east. Eventually they were absorbed into the new regional armies created by Justinian in Armenia, North Africa, and Italy.

As discussed in Chapter 4, Justinian leveraged his financial resources, political stability, and what remained of the praesental units to launch his wars of reconquest. At his death, he left the empire over-leveraged and it would fall to his successors to pay that debt. Imperial resources gradually contracted during the second half of the sixth century due to a combination of constant war on many fronts and the plague. By 582, a man with some (albeit not much) military experience, Maurikios, was once again on the throne. Initially his regime was secure and, when it came time for a push into Persia in 591, he could entrust the campaign to the generals of Oriens and Armenia. Maurikios' regime, however, fell to a military rebellion prompted by austerity measures, the first successful military usurpation in the history of the east Roman empire (if we discount the unfinished war against Constantius II begun by Julian). What followed Maurikios' overthrow was a period of rapid political and military collapse that left the Romans in desperate need of striking power in a context of low political stability. After the Avar and Persian invasions of the early seventh century, the Romans no longer had functional borders. So it was that Herakleios, the second successful military rebel in a row, essentially revived the *comitatus* in order to launch an invasion of Persia. The emperor as field commander was back. Following Herakleios, the emperors of the middle Byzantine period would frequently take the field in person, marking a new phase of Roman military planning and response.

In conclusion, it is worth looking at the middle Byzantine period for just a few moments, for it displays a striking iteration of the same underlying dynamic that we have seen play out in ancient and late antique Roman history. In the mid-seventh century, after the Arab conquest of Egypt, Palestine, and Syria, and the Roman withdrawal from most of the Balkans in the face of Avar, Slavic, and Bulgar aggression, what remained of the field armies were pulled back into Asia Minor and became local-defense forces, known after about 800 as the "themes" (*themata*).[12] As we have seen, units of the old field armies still survived under their own names embedded in the tenth-century thematic armies. Yet in time, the emperors felt the need to supplement these local-defense forces with a mobile, central striking force, the *tagmata*, which began to be built up in the mid-eighth century by Konstantinos V (741–775).[13] And thus the cycle began anew, following well-worn Roman precedent. In the ninth and tenth centuries, wars were fought primarily with these *tagmata* – the new *comitatus* – supplemented by the pick of the thematic armies, the descendants of the

---

[12] Haldon, *The Empire That Would Not Die.*   [13] Haldon, *Byzantine Praetorians.*

old field armies. By the eleventh century, after a series of spectacular conquests, the professional striking forces began to be posted increasingly in the provinces to guard the (now more distant) frontiers, leading to a relative demilitarization of the local-defense forces, who commuted their service obligations to cash payments.[14] Thus, in the *longue durée*, from Augustus to the era of the crusades, Roman strategic dispositions cycled through centuries-long patterns that oscillated between a focus on frontier defense and an investment in mobile striking power. The remarkable continuity of this pattern was due to the survival of the one and only "polity of the Romans" that had to chart its way through increasingly troubled waters. Its oscillations, by contrast, were due to the changing balance of foreign threats, which affected the Romans collectively, and the potential for domestic military subversion of the emperor and his regime. In the period of transition examined in this book, Constantinople cycled through most of the options that were available to the emperors of the Romans in the long arc of their history. Flexibility and pragmatism rather than "Byzantine" formalism characterized the east Roman armies during late antiquity, and beyond.

[14] Kaldellis, *Streams of Gold, Rivers of Blood.*

The Roman High Command at Adrianople (378)

Scholars have seen in the battle of Adrianople the beginnings of the five-army system described by the eastern *Notitia* and have argued for a proliferation of *magistri militum* heading into the battle. However, this inflated number of *magistri* is probably the result of misinterpretations resulting from (a) Ammianus' imprecise literary language and (b) the retroactive influence of the *Notitia*. Specifically, scholars have identified up to seven *magistri* serving in the eastern army in 378: Iulius, Victor, Arinthaeus, Profuturus, Traianus, Saturninus, and Sebastianus. Demandt claims all seven as *magistri militum*, but he views Saturninus and Traianus as supernumeraries and is evasive as to whether or not Arinthaeus fought at Adrianople. In any case, he explicitly links this proliferation of generals to the *Notitia* system, which he believes was introduced under Theodosius I.[1] The *PLRE* I claims that only three *magistri* were active at Adrianople (Victor, Iulius, and Sebastianus), but lists six men who held that rank during the year 378 (it does not claim Profuturus was ever a *magister*) and assigns two of them as *in praesenti*, one to Oriens, and no fewer than three to Thrace.[2] Lenski claims five, arguing that Profuturus and Arinthaeus were dead before the battle, and he explicitly links this number to the imminent development of the five-army *Notitia* system under Theodosius I.[3]

Of these men, the evidence for Iulius and Victor is unimpeachable, and it is likely that they were in fact the only *magistri militum* in the east Roman empire in 378. In other words, we do not accept that the Roman high command at Adrianople reflected the multiple-*magister* system that we see in the *Notitia*, at least not to the same degree other historians have. We do see an evolution in that direction, but it was much more gradual and likely did not develop significantly in the crisis years 376–378.

---

[1] Demandt, "Magister," 703–709, 789–790.   [2] *PLRE* I, 1113–1114 (fasti).
[3] Lenski, *Failure of Empire*, 362–363.

To begin with **Arinthaeus**, he had almost certainly died before the outbreak of the Gothic crisis, though most scholars have missed this. At issue are three pieces of evidence: the narrative of Ammianus, an undated letter of condolence from Basil of Caesarea to Arinthaeus' widow that confirms the general's death, and a story in the *Ecclesiastical History* of Theodoretos. In Ammianus' narrative, Arinthaeus disappears after 370 but we can independently confirm him as *magister peditum* in his consular year of 372.[4] Even so, Arinthaeus' absence from Ammianus narrative of 376–378 suggests that he was dead before 376.[5] Basil's letter, meanwhile, makes no mention of Adrianople, an event that was already seen by contemporaries as a universal calamity for the Roman state, suggesting a *terminus ante quem* of August 9, 378. Moreover, the bishop presents the general's death as a quiet and private loss. Now, Basil died on January 1, 379, a few months after the battle, so any letter that he would have written after the battle would necessarily have been in its immediate aftermath.[6] Scholars argue that Arinthaeus continued to serve through 378 based solely on a tendentious and apocryphal story in Theodoretos in which Traianus, having been defeated by the Goths in an initial encounter before Adrianople, is berated by Valens but responds by shifting blame for the defeat onto the emperor's heresy, an accusation that is endorsed by Victor and Arinthaeus.[7] This story is an unambiguous piece of religious propaganda and should be dismissed as chronologically garbled fiction.

Theodoretos' story has also been used to establish the rank of **Traianus**, for Theodoretos specifically calls him a στρατηγός, often (but not always) the Greek equivalent of *magister militum*, and equates his rank to that of Victor and Arinthaeus.[8] However, Theodoretos is extremely loose with his terminology and uses the term στρατηγός for a range of ranks.[9] Combined with the fictional nature of the broader story, we cannot use this attestation to signify anything beyond the fact that Traianus was a high-ranking military commander. Leaving Theodoretos aside, Ammianus reports that Traianus served in Armenia in 373 "in command of military affairs" (*curans rem militarem*), a vague phrase that is widely taken to indicate that he was *comes rei militaris*.[10]

---

[4] See the papyri cited in *PLRE* I, 103 (Arinthaeus).
[5] Woods, "Dating Basil of Caesarea's Correspondence." Woods' specific date for Arinthaeus' death (373), based on the promotion of Traianus, is possible but not certain.
[6] Basil of Caesarea, *Letter* 269; universal calamity: Lenski, *"Initio mali Romano imperio."*
[7] Theodoretos, *Ecclesiastical History* 4.30.
[8] Theodoretos, *Ecclesiastical History* 4.30: στρατηγὼ γὰρ ἤστην καὶ τούτω.
[9] For example, Theodoretos, *Ecclesiastical History* 4.29. Terentius was a *dux*: *PLRE* I, 881–881 (Terentius 2).
[10] Ammianus, *Res gestae* 30.1.18; *comes rei militaris*: *PLRE* I, 921–922 (Traianus 2); see Lenski, *Failure of Empire*, 330, 336, 339, 363.

He next appears co-commanding, alongside Profuturus, the east Roman forces at the battle of Ad Salices before Adrianople: "[Valens] sent Profuturus and Traianus ahead, both *rectores*" (*Profuturum praemisit et Traianum, ambo rectores*).[11] Although Ammianus sometimes uses *rector* to mean *magister*, he also uses it for other offices too, including provincial governors and the captains of smaller units.[12] Moreover, Ammianus' language implies a strict equivalence between Traianus' rank and that of Profuturus.

Unlike Traianus, **Profuturus** is a relatively obscure figure who appears only in relation to this command, and his obscurity argues against *rector* meaning *magister* here.[13] The nature of the military force that Traianus and Profuturus were leading also argues against a high command. Ammianus is specific that they were pulling their soldiers from the forces in Armenia, but is vague about numbers.[14] Ammianus is likewise imprecise about the units brought from the west by Richomer, which included some under-strength cohorts as well as Pannonian and transalpine auxilia, and he does not reveal the number of Goths that they faced. Thus we have a poor understanding of the size of the armies that fought at Ad Salices, but it was likely not a large engagement. No other historian records this battle, and the Gothic army there was an ad hoc assembly of groups pillaging the region. Despite this, Ammianus reports that the Goths significantly outnumbered the Romans, whose forces were better suited to a campaign of harassment and containment.[15] It is therefore unlikely that the east Roman forces at Ad Salices were large enough to merit one, much less two, *magistri militum*.

The details surrounding the battle of Ad Salices argue strongly against either Traianus or Profuturus being a *magister* at the time of the battle. Yet scholars are not inventing Traianus' rank out of whole cloth. When describing the army that Valens led to Adrianople, Ammianus specifically calls attention to the presence of experienced soldiers:

> [Valens] had joined to these forces a great number of veterans, among whom both other *honoratiores* and Traianus, who had a little before [*paulo ante*] been *magister armorum*, had been reappointed.[16]

> quippe etiam veteranos isdem iunxerat plurimos, inter quos et honoratiores alii et Traianus recinctus est, paulo ante magister armorum.

[11] Ammianus, *Res gestae* 31.7.1.
[12] *Magister*: Ammianus, *Res gestae* 26.1.6 and 26.4.1; unit commanders: 31.10.9 and 31.13.18.
[13] Lenski speculates that Profuturus was killed at Ad Salices to explain his subsequent absence as a top-tier general from the narrative: *Failure of Empire*, 330, 363. He may simply not have been important enough to warrant mention.
[14] Ammianus, *Res gestae* 31.7.2.   [15] Ammianus, *Res gestae* 31.7.3 and 9.
[16] Ammianus, *Res gestae* 31.12.1.

This passage is generally understood to mean that Traianus was a *magister* at Ad Salices (*paulo ante*), but such a reading ignores the broader context in which his magisterial command is mentioned. The focus in the passage is on the veterans recruited into Valens' army ahead of Adrianople. It is in relation to these (*inter quos*) that we meet Traianus and the other *honoriatiores*, that is, a number of high-ranking officers, all of whom should be understood to have been reappointed (*recingo*). This is the clear force of the *et . . . et* construction, while the *recinctus est* is singular by attraction to Traianus. Traianus is separated from the rest of the officers only because he had once held a much higher, magisterial command. The best reading of this passage, then, is that Traianus and the other *honoratiores* were reappointed as officers in command of the veterans, which does not suggest that Traianus had been a *magister* at Ad Salices and neither claims nor suggests that he was one at Adrianople. Indeed, the force of the *paulo ante* specifically argues against his holding that rank in 378 (see the discussion of Sebastianus below for the likely dating of Traianus' magisterial command).

The second piece of evidence that scholars use to claim Traianus as a *magister militum* at Adrianople is Ammianus' report that Sebastianus, a commander sent by Gratian from the west at Valens' request, took command of the "infantry army" (*pedester exercitus*) "that Traianus had previously commanded" (*quem regebat antea Traianus*). Once again Ammianus' terminology is vague but the simplest interpretation of the phrase *pedester exercitus* is a military force composed primarily of infantry, which matches the available evidence for the forces Sebastianus commanded.[17] We do not need to infer that Traianus and Sebastianus were *magistri peditum* simply from the fact that they commanded this infantry unit, in part because, as mentioned above, the forces involved were too small to merit such a high-ranking command. The force that Traianus

---

[17] For the use of *exercitus* for forces not associated with the *comitatus*, see Ammianus, *Res gestae* 19.11.17 and 20.6.9. As far as we can tell, Ammianus uses *exercitus* only for actual armies as opposed to branches of the Roman military, which is signified by the term *militia*. Thus, there is no reason to assume that *pedester exercitus* is equivalent to *pedester militia*, a phrase that Ammianus often uses to signify the command of a *magister*. Moreover, the phrase *pedester exercitus* occurs only twice in the extant text of Ammianus, the other time to describe a force led by one Severus: 29.4.3. Although Severus was certainly a *magister peditum* at the time of this campaign, the context makes clear that the *pedester exercitus* that he was leading does not refer to his office or even to the entire army on campaign, but rather to the advance force that he led across the Rhine, which he feared was too small. Thus *pedester exercitus* by itself cannot be taken to imply the office of *magister peditum*, and the same logic applies to the phrase *equester exercitus*, discussed later in the text in the context of Saturninus' office. See also the parallel phrases for units smaller than an *exercitus*: 14.2.12 (*equestres cohortes*); 25.1.7 (*equester numerus*); 15.4.10, 16.11.6, 16.12.7, 17.6.1, and 18.6.16 (*equester turma*); 18.9.4, 23.3.4 and 24.4.9 (*equestres turmae*); 21.6.6 (*turmarum equestrium numerus*); 16.12.21 (*equestres copiae*); and 16.12.7 and 24.4.9 (*pedestres copiae*).

had previously commanded and that Sebastianus took over can only be the Armenian legions that he led at Ad Salices, and Ammianus' narrative of the battle describes a primarily infantry engagement with cavalry playing a minor role in chasing down retreating units.[18]

Sebastianus' subsequent actions do not imply that he held a magisterial appointment either. Operating in Thrace ahead of the emperor and presumably of the main Roman battle force in early 378, Sebastianus launched an opportunistic attack on a group of Goths retreating from the approaching imperial armies. Under his command were "three hundred soldiers selected from each *numerus*" (*cum trecentenis militibus per singulos numeros lectis*).[19] According to Eunapios and Zosimos, the total force was 2,000 men, which suggests that Sebastianus was operating with a total of no more than seven *numeri*, hardly a field army.[20] Similarly, it is difficult to reconcile Sebastianus as a *magister* with his reception by the people of Adrianople during this action. The city initially refused to admit him fearing that he had been captured and was being used to trick them into admitting Goths inside. How can we reconcile this event with the presence of a large field army under the command of a formal *magister militum*, unless we assume that a campaigning army of Rome's most elite soldiers was indistinguishable in appearance and number from a band of marauding Goths? Finally, neither Eunapios nor Zosimos, our only other sources for Sebastianus' command, call him a *magister*. In Eunapios, he is given a generic command (ἡγεμονία), while Zosimos says he was a general (στρατηγός) and "entrusted with command of the whole war" (τὴν ἡγεμονίαν τοῦ παντὸς πιστεύει πολέμου).[21] Although στρατηγός can mean *magister* in Greek sources, it does not have to mean that.[22] Moreover, ἡγεμονία is a vague term and Zosimos' claim that Sebastianus was the commander-in-chief of the Roman war effort is irreconcilable with Ammianus' detailed narrative.[23] The simplest reading of Zosimos is that Sebastianus had been placed in command of the specific action that he is shown in Zosimos' narrative as leading, not the entire war against the Goths. On balance, then, there is insufficient evidence to make Sebastianus

---

[18] Armenian legions: Ammianus, *Res gestae* 31.7.3; Infantry battle: Ammianus, *Res gestae*, 31.7.10–15.
[19] Ammianus, *Res gestae* 31.9.2.
[20] Eunapios, *History* fr. 4.4; Zosimos, *New History* 4.23.2. Zosimos is likely using Eunapios of Sardeis as a source for this information.
[21] Zosimos, *New History* 4.23.1.   [22] See the discussion of Hormisdas and Arinthaeus at p. 5 n. 17.
[23] Sebastianus also appears in Eunapios, *History* fr. 44.3 (known from the *Souda*). However, the entry is vague and exaggerated, perhaps reflecting Sebastianus' own self-promotion: Ammianus, *Res gestae* 31.12.1.

a *magister*, which further erodes the case for Traianus' magisterial commands in 377–378, in particular his supposed stint as *magister peditum* that is associated with the battle of Ad Salices.[24]

In short, there is nothing in our sources for 377–378 to suggest that either Traianus or Sebastianus was a *magister* during those campaigns. So when was Traianus *magister armorum*? The likeliest answer is that he was appointed to that rank while serving in Armenia. Traianus disappears from Ammianus' narrative between 373 and 376/7, but his disappearance does not mean that he was militarily inactive. Both Victor, *magister equitum* throughout this period, and Arinthaeus, the *magister peditum* who likely died in this interval, are likewise absent from the narrative during roughly the same period despite the ongoing conflict with Persia. It appears likely that Traianus, who was in charge of the Armenian theater in 373, was either then or was later promoted to be a *magister equitum et peditum*, possibly as a regional command analogous to that held in Oriens by Lupicinus and Iulius. This reconstruction is recommended by the logistics of the Persian front, which stretched from the Caucusus to Arabia and was geographically divided into distinct theaters of operation. We know that Valens managed the southern stretch of the border from Antioch, which is where the news of the Gothic uprising reached him, so there was an obvious need for a largely independent military force in Armenia.

There is one more possibility for which we have good evidence: Traianus may have held an honorary rank as *magister equitum et peditum*, not an actual command with that rank. Laws preserved in the *Theodosian Code* explicitly attest to honorary appointments as *magister equitum* in the west by 372 and as *magister equitum et peditum* in the east by 384.[25] In both cases, the mention of honorary *magistri* is incidental and delimiting. That is, neither law treats the existence of honorary *magistri* as an innovation, but rather as a potential source of confusion with genuine *magistri*, so it is likely that such honorary ranks were awarded in both halves of the empire from the 370s, if not earlier. Thus it is possible, but less likely, that the rank Ammianus refers to here is an honorary one.

It must be admitted that both of these reconstructions are hypothetical. No source tells us that Traianus was ever *magister equitum et peditum*

[24] Den Boeft et al., *Philological and Historical Commentary . . . XXXI, ad* 12.2. Incidentally, this also helps to clarify the meaning of the title *magister armorum* that Ammianus uses, which scholars have linked to both the offices of *magister equitum* and *magister peditum*. However, Traianus is the only supposed *magister peditum* whom Ammianus calls by the title.
[25] West: *CTh* 6.22.4; East: *CTh* 8.5.44.

in Armenia nor do we have any evidence that his office was honorary. Moreover, we are dubious that Ammianus would have bothered to report an honorary military rank. However, both options are recommended by their grounding in observed precedent during the period in question. The alternative is to postulate a rapid and unprecedented multiplication of magisterial commands in the two years between the Gothic crossing and Adrianople, a multiplication that is inherently suspect because it has been drawn by scholars in the shape of the *Notitia* system.[26] Put differently, scholars who argue for the proliferation of magisterial commands prior to Adrianople postulate this proliferation in order to smooth the way for the introduction of the *Notitia* system, which they place under Theodosius I, at least half a century too early. However, absent the *Notitia*, the evidence for this proliferation of commands consists only of a handful of ambiguous phrases in Ammianus. Our proposed reconstructions, hypothetical though they may be, ultimately rest on firmer ground than does the prevailing, *Notitia*-inflected consensus.

The final supposed *magister* for the period 376–378 is **Saturninus**, who, in the words of Ammianus, was "given temporary command of an army of cavalry" (*equestris exercitus ad tempus cura commissa*).[27] We should not necessarily see this as a roundabout reference to a specific office. Rather, we should take Ammianus' report literally: Saturninus, whatever his rank, was given command of a large force of cavalry. And this makes sense in context. Saturninus was dispatched by Valens while the emperor was still at Antioch after he had received further reports on the deteriorating state of affairs in the Balkans, but before news of the battle of Ad Salices had reached him. Under the circumstances, it makes perfect sense that Valens would dispatch a fast-moving force of cavalry to reinforce the Armenian legions he had already sent to the area. There is nothing here that requires us (or Valens) to make Saturninus a *magister equitum*, and he is better understood as a *comes rei militaris*, a rank he is explicitly attested with, holding an extraordinary (and temporary) command.[28] Saturninus' turn to be a *magister* would come in the early 380s.

Thus, of the seven *magistri* proposed by various scholars to have been active in the years 376–378, we find that only two survive close scrutiny: Iulius and Victor. It is worth noting in this connection that we know of no *magister peditum* active during this period. However, this was not

[26] Demandt, "Magister," 789–790; Lenski, *Failure of Empire*, 363. The *PLRE* I is less explicit about the connection, but, in its fasti, it assigns the *magistri* of the period to regional commands modeled on the *Notitia*: *PLRE* I, 1114–1115.
[27] Ammianus, *Res gestae* 31.8.3. [28] *Comes*: Basil of Caesarea, *Letter* 132.

unprecedented. Julian had likewise operated without a *magister peditum* during his Persian expedition, having instead a *magister equitum in prae-senti*, Nevitta, and another *magister equitum* in a regional command in Illyricum, Iovinus. That is precisely the arrangement we propose for Valens in 376–378. Scholars have been misled by their assumptions about the full emergence of the *Notitia* system under Theodosius I, and they have taken advantage of the occasional vagueness of Ammianus' terminology, in order to anachronistically impose a preliminary version of that system on the Roman high command in 378.

Magistri militum *under Theodosius I (379–395)*

As mentioned, our sources for military affairs under Theodosius I are poor. We rely primarily on the narrative of Zosimos, whose terminology, as we will see, is often imprecise. To Zosimos, who himself relied heavily on the contemporary fifth-century history of Eunapios of Sardeis, we add the testimony of the ecclesiastical historians (Sokrates, Sozomenos, and Theodoretos), whose interest in military affairs is inconsistent but sometimes technically precise; court panegyrics and invectives, which tend to be vague and allusive; and public speeches (including sermons) and letter collections, which survive in abundance from this period but often avoid mentioning specific offices. By far our most reliable source for military offices is the *Theodosian Code*, which preserves a large number of laws from Theodosius' reign, along with the names and titles of their addressees, many of whom were senior military officers.

Of the fourteen men identified by Demandt or the *PLRE* as definite or potential eastern *magistri* under Theodosius, only six are explicitly so named in the *Theodosian Code*: Hellebicus, Timasius, Richomer, Abundantius, Addaeus, and Stilicho.[1] The magisterial rank of these men is beyond doubt, however, the nature of their commands is not always clear. Despite the lack of evidence in either official or narrative sources that the *Notitia* system was being implemented at this time, both Demandt and the *PLRE* argue that key elements of that system, in particular formalized regional commands in Illyricum, Thrace, and Oriens, came into effect under Theodosius (Demandt claims this only for Illyricum and Oriens).[2] Neither reconstruction, however, assumes the

---

[1] Demandt, "Magister," 710–726 and 790; *PLRE* I, 1114. We have excluded Iulius and Victor from this count because neither is clearly attested in office under Theodosius. We also will not discuss Gildo in detail; see p. 16 n. 69.

[2] Demandt, "Magister," 719–722. Demandt is generally beholden to the *Notitia* system despite acknowledging that magisterial commands were irregular during the late fourth century and that the *Notitia* cannot have been implemented before the death of Theodosius I: ibid. 736–739.

existence of formalized praesental commands during this period. Instead, Demandt sees the continued operation of *magistri equitum / peditum in praesenti* despite the introduction of the new title of MVM, whereas the *PLRE* classifies generals as *magistri equitum et peditum in praesenti*.[3] They do so based simply on which generals they believe were in proximity to the emperor, not because that title is officially attested. In what follows, we survey the evidence for the various generals thought to be operating in this period and demonstrate that nothing like the *Notitia* system can be detected in the eastern empire during the reign of Theodosius, with one major exception, as noted in Chapter 1, the first element of that system to appear in its gradual evolution toward the *Notitia* form. We begin with that exception, the *magister militum per Orientem* (MMO), whose office is first formally and securely attested by 393 with Addaeus (see p. 16), though previous occupants have been proposed.

Ammianus and Zosimos both report that **Iulius**, the functional though not titular MMO under Valens, continued in command of Oriens in the immediate aftermath of Adrianople, when he coordinated the slaughter of Gothic recruits in the region.[4] This is his last attested action in office, and it is not clear when he left office or under what circumstances. The *PLRE* claims **Sapores** as the next MMO on the basis of the general's role in reinstalling Nicaean bishops in the east prior to the accession of Theodosius, as well as his appearance in Libanios' corpus (he is mentioned in an oration dated to 381 and is the addressee of an undated letter).[5] However, all of this evidence is circumstantial. To begin with, Sapores' role in restoring the bishops comes from Theodoretos, whose terminology is demonstrably loose.[6] Thus we cannot necessarily read στρατηγός, the rank that Theodoretos gives Sapores, as implying a magisterial command. Likewise, the testimony of Libanios works against Sapores' appointment as MMO. While defending himself against the accusation that he was overbearing (βαρύς), Libanios reports that "Saporeses, and Iuliuses, and Victors came to visit me while I was sick and unable to flee."[7] All three of these figures were military men, but Libanios does not say or imply that they were all of the exact same rank, which is how the letter has been read. In fact, it is possible that their order here is as a tricolon crescendo of rank.

[3] Demandt, "Magister," 723–724.
[4] Ammianus, *Res gestae* 31.16.8; Zosimos, *New History* 4.26.2–9.
[5] *PLRE* I, 803 (Sapores); Theodoretos, *Ecclesiastical History* 5.2–3; Libanios, *Oration* 2.9 and *Letter* 957.
[6] Theodoretos, *Ecclesiastical History* 3.14.
[7] Libanios, *Oration* 2.9: Σαπῶραι δὲ καὶ Ἰούλιοι καὶ Βίκτωρες ἀρρωστοῦντος οὐκ ἔχοντος φυγεῖν ἧκον.

This reading fits both the rhetorical nature of the speech and our independent information: Victor was Valens' *magister peditum* for the entirety of that emperor's reign, while Iulius was a *magister militum* with an ad hoc (not formalized) regional command in Oriens and presumably ranked below Victor. The order therefore suggests that Sapores was of lower rank than Iulius. Finally, Libanios' letter to Sapores describes him as "commanding soldiers" (στρατιωτῶν ἡγούμενος), an imprecise phrase that does not require him to have held the highest command. The letter also makes it clear that Sapores had until recently been out of favor with Theodosius, making a high command less likely.[8] There is thus no compelling reason to make the otherwise unattested Sapores a *magister*, far less one with a regional command over Oriens.

The same is true of **Richomer**, the western *comes domesticorum* who fought at Adrianople in 378. The *PLRE*, but not Demandt, assigns him a brief command over Oriens prior to 383 on the basis of Libanios' report of his presence in Antioch prior to his consulship in 384.[9] Richomer subsequently served as a *magister* under Valentinian II during the civil war of 388.[10] As mentioned, he is assigned a formal command over Oriens under Theodosius I in the *PLRE* based solely on his presence in Antioch, but this is a weak argument. It is not clear that Richomer was ever formally a part of the east Roman military, and Antioch was one of the three largest cities in the eastern empire, as well as a major administrative, military, and economic center. Richomer might have visited the city for any number of reasons.

After Richomer, Demandt and the *PLRE* agree in naming **Hellebicus** as MVM of Oriens.[11] As mentioned in Chapter 1, Hellebicus is, in 383, the first general in the eastern empire attested with the title of MVM, but the single law addressed to him does not specify that he served in Oriens. All other references to his military command are equally imprecise, though a letter from Gregory of Nazianzos makes it clear that his appointment was not honorary, as he commanded soldiers and was embarking on a war.[12] Once again, the case for his assignment to Oriens is circumstantial and relies on letters from Libanios as well as his role in investigating the Riot of the Statues in Antioch in 387. However, none of Libanios' letters to Hellebicus contain any clear indication that he served as *magister* in Oriens.[13] Our major sources for the riot, on the other hand, confirm that Hellebicus was sent to Antioch

[8] Libanios, *Letter 957*.   [9] *PLRE* I, 765–766 (Richomeres); Libanios, *Oration* 1.219.
[10] Philostorgios, *Ecclesiastical History* 10.8.
[11] Demandt, "Magister," 711; *PLRE* I, 277–278 (Ellebichus).
[12] Gregory of Nazianzos, *Letter* 225.4; military command: Libanios, *Oration* 22.15–16, 22, 28.
[13] Libanios, *Letters* 2, 868, 884, 898, and 925.

to investigate.[14] That is, in 387 he was not already stationed in the city nor, it seems, the region, and he was recalled to Constantinople after his investigation.[15] There is thus no good reason to assume that he held a regional command over (or even in) Oriens in the later 380s.[16]

After Hellebicus, Demandt and the *PLRE* once more diverge. Demandt claims that one **Moderatus** was *magister* over Oriens in 392 on the basis of two letters of Libanios.[17] However, the letters are undated and the *PLRE* is right to understand Moderatus as a low-ranking officer, perhaps a *tribunus*, as he is mentioned in command of a λόχος, a term generally used to refer to a smaller unit.[18] The *PLRE*, meanwhile, suggests that **Eutherius** occupied the post of MMO between 388 and 393, although it flags this as doubtful in both his entry and the fasti. Eutherius is attested solely by an inscription in the Crimean Chersonese that is heavily reconstructed and does not mention his office.[19] This is insufficient evidence to support the proposed assignment.

It is in 393 that we find our first explicit attestation of the office of MMO, which is held by the general **Addaeus**, and the office appears regularly in the *Theodosian Code* from this point forward.[20] Addaeus was in office through the death of Theodosius and organized the defense of Oriens against a Hunnic incursion in 396.[21] We lose track of him in the sources after that, but he may have been replaced in office by 398.[22]

Thus the only securely attested *magistri* holding a command in Oriens in this period are Iulius, who was appointed by Valens and held an ad hoc regional command, like others in the fourth century, and Addaeus, who appears in office at the end of Theodosius' reign in what appears to be a formally constituted regional command. It is noteworthy that both Demandt and the *PLRE* assume that a magisterial command analogous to the MMO was continually in place in Oriens between the tenures of Iulius and Addaeus. This explains their willingness to rely on demonstrably insufficient evidence to fill out the otherwise empty roster for the office. There is, however,

---

[14] Military officer: Libanios, *Oration* 22.15–16; arriving from elsewhere: ibid. 22.12; John Chrysostom, *Homilies on the Statues to the People of Antioch* 17.1.

[15] Libanios, *Oration* 22.41.

[16] Demandt identifies him as the unnamed *comes orientis militarium partium* from whom Ambrose received the report of the destruction of a synagogue in Kallinikos (Callinicum) in 388, but this is just a guess: "Magister," 711.

[17] Demandt, "Magister," 711.   [18] *PLRE* I, 605 (Moderatus); λόχος: Libanios, *Letter* 1057.

[19] Eutherius: *PLRE* I, 315 (Eutherius 3).

[20] Addaeus: *CTh* 16.8.9; continued appearance: ibid. 7.8.8 (400 or 405), 12.1.175 (412), and 7.4.36 (424).

[21] Office: *CTh* 6.24.6; Huns: pseudo-Joshua the Stylite, *Chronicle* 9; Greatrex and Greatrex, "The Hunnic Invasion."

[22] *CTh* 7.7.3. The content of this law, which deals with grazing rights in Apameia, strongly suggests that Simplicius was MMO in 398: *PLRE* II, 1013–1014 (Simplicius 2).

no reason to expect a designated *magister* for Oriens during this period. The position occupied by Iulius appears to have been ad hoc, which explains both the inconsistent nomenclature Ammianus uses for it and the lack of a regional title in the inscription that attests Iulius' rank and office (*Iuli | v(iri) c(larissimi) com(itis) magistri equitum et peditum*).[23] Although there had been a series of generals assigned to a regional command in Oriens under Valens, his reign coincided with a period of elevated tensions with Persia, when the emperor himself took command of operations there. These tensions were likely eased by whatever arrangements Victor made in 376, which allowed Valens to withdraw the field army and march to Adrianople, and they were fully resolved by Theodosius' partition of Armenia in 387, which inaugurated the most peaceful period in the history of Roman–Persian relations. It is therefore entirely possible that the appointment of *magistri* for Oriens, an ad hoc arrangement during the fourth century, ceased between Iulius' departure and Addaeus' appointment. The notion that a formally constituted magisterial command both existed there and was continually filled during this period is yet another shadow cast over the fourth century by the proposed early date for the *Notitia*.

The MMO is the first formally attested regional command in the east Roman empire. It is also the only regional command for which we have evidence during the reign of Theodosius. Nevertheless, both Demandt and the *PLRE*, in thrall to the *Notitia*, argue that a parallel command operated in Illyricum, and the *PLRE* adds yet another in Thrace. However, there is no reason to believe that formally constituted regional commands existed in either place during the reign of Theodosius.

Like the MMO, there were ad hoc forerunners of the *magister militum per Illyricum* (MMI) in the fourth century. In Chapter 1, we saw how the emperor Julian made **Iovinus** his *magister* in Illyricum in 361. We also know of one **Equitius** who was placed in charge of the Illyrian army (*Illyricianus exercitus*) in 364 and then promoted to the rank of *magister* in 365.[24] Equitius' initial appointment was explicitly not at the top level as *magister* (he was a *comes rei militaris*), and his subsequent promotion was a direct result of the rebellion of Procopius. In other words, Valentinian promoted Equitius in response to an unforeseen emergency and not as part of a formalized command structure. In fact, the promotion may have been intended to ensure Equitius' loyalty, as he had been rumored as a candidate for emperor prior to Valentinian's own election.[25] There is therefore no

---

[23] *CIL* 3: 88.
[24] *Illyricianus exercitus*: Ammianus, *Res gestae* 26.5.3; *magister*: ibid. 26.5.11; *CTh* 7.1.8; *CIL* 3: 5670a.
[25] Ammianus, *Res gestae* 26.1.4.

reason to see any continuity between Equitius and the subsequent office of MMI, which is not attested until the *Notitia* (which we place in the 440s). Instead, we should understand Equitius as evidence that Illyricum had traditionally been managed by generals holding sub-magisterial commands, and we may speculate that his forces, even after his promotion to the rank of *magister*, were primarily composed of *limitanei*.

There is therefore no evidence for a formally constituted magisterial command in Illyricum prior to the reign of Theodosius. There is, on the other hand, good reason to doubt that a coherent regional command *could* have appeared in Illyricum during that reign. At the death of Valens, the region was under the nominal control of Valentinian II (375–392), but Gratian ceded the territory, or at least the southeastern portion of it, to Theodosius in 379 to facilitate his war against the Goths. When Theodosius was defeated and withdrew from combat in 380, Gratian stepped into the gap and sent two of his own commanders, Bauto and Arbogast, to prosecute the war, effectively bringing it back into the western orbit.[26] Even after the Gothic settlement of 382, the region continued to be troubled and contemporaries lamented the destruction and dislocation that afflicted it.[27] This history argues strongly against a formalized and unitary east Roman military command in the region during this period.

Demandt and the *PLRE* claim **Maiorianus** as the first MMI under Theodosius on the basis of a panegyrical poem composed in the fifth century by Sidonius Apollinaris for his grandson, the emperor Maiorianus (457–461).[28] According to Sidonius,

> It is said that the grandfather of this man [the emperor Maiorianus] ruled alone as king over Illyricum and the region of the Ister [Danube] in Pannonia where Mars' Acincus stands strong. For Theodosius, when he assumed the title of Augustus in Sirmium and was about to leave for the eastern regions of the kingdom, made Maiorianus *magister per utramque militiam*.[29]

This is our only source for the elder Maiorianus and it presents several problems. To begin with, the praise of ancestors was an established requirement of panegyric, and these often incorporated fictitious genealogies. Thus emperor Constantine was said to be related to Claudius Gothicus, Theodosius I to

---

[26] Zosimos, *New History* 4.31–32; see Errington, "Theodosius and the Goths"; Heather, *Goths and Romans*, 157–188.

[27] Ambrose, *Commentary on the Gospel of Luke* 10.10 (380s); Jerome, *Letter* 60.16.

[28] Demandt, "Magister," 716; *PLRE* I, 537 (Maiorianus).

[29] Sidonius Apollinaris, *Carmina* 5.107–112: *Fertur, Pannoniae qua Martia pollet Acincus,* | *Illyricum rexisse solum cum tractibus Histri* | *huius avus; nam Theodosius, quo tempore Sirmi* | *Augustum sumpsit nomen, per utramque magistrum* | *militiam ad partes regni venturus Eoas* | *Maiorianum habuit.*

Trajan, and Anastasius to Pompey the Great.[30] In this context, the claim that the elder Maiorianus "ruled as a king" (*regno*) – a clear exaggeration – is best understood as an attempt to embellish the grandson's modest genealogy. The dubiousness of the story is compounded by the fact that Sidonius does not report the story in his own voice, but instead attributes it to rumor (*fertur*). That is, even the panegyrist distances himself from the claim. Moreover, the scene described is difficult to reconcile with our knowledge of Theodosius' reign. The phrase "eastern regions" (*partes Eoae*) implies the eastern frontier of the empire, but Theodosius never traveled east of Constantinople as emperor. The division of the kingdom implied by Sidonius would in fact have been little more than a division of the Balkans. Sidonius is exaggerating the emperor's distance in order to amplify the independence of Maiorianus' office. Taken together, the independence and authority that Sidonius assigns to the elder Maiorianus more accurately reflects the office of MVM as it operated in the fifth-century west, where its holders functioned as de facto heads of state for a series of weak emperors, rather than in the fourth-century east. In light of all these problems, we cannot securely make Maiorianus the *magister* for Illyricum, much less use his office to demonstrate the creation of the office of MMI or an analogous command. Not even Sidonius explicitly attests the office of MMI for the elder Maiorianus. At most he was a standard kind of MVM.

After Maiorianus, Demandt and the *PLRE* both name **Butheric** as the *magister* of Illyricum.[31] Butheric is famous for causing the massacre in Thessalonike for which Theodosius made a show of penance before Ambrose of Milan, but we know little about him. Sozomenos, who gives us our most complete account of the story, says that he was "at that time commanding soldiers among the Illyrians" (ἡγούμενος τότε τῶν παρ' Ἰλλυριοῖς στρατιωτῶν), meaning "in Illyricum," but this statement is vague and does not require Butheric to be the only or the supreme commander in the region. Moreover, this command is not reported by our other sources for the incident. Theodoretos does not mention Butheric at all, while Rufinus calls him "a man from among the soldiers" (*quidam ex militaribus vir*).[32] We therefore cannot confidently assign to Butheric the rank of *magister*, much less make him MMI simply because he held some sort of command in Thessalonike, which was located in the prefecture of Illyricum.

---

[30] Kaldellis, "The Politics of Classical Genealogies."
[31] Demandt, "Magister" 717; *PLRE* I, 166 (Butherichus). Demandt also claims Vitalianus as *magister*, but he was appointed by Gratian and so is not of interest to us here: "Magister," 602–603; compare *PLRE* I, 969–970 (Vitalianus 3).
[32] Sozomenos, *Ecclesiastical History* 7.25.3; Rufinus, *Ecclesiastical History* 11.18; Theodoretos, *Ecclesiastical History* 5.17.

The evidence is similarly thin for **Abundantius**, the final MMI claimed by Demandt and the *PLRE* for the reign of Theodosius. His rank is clear from the *Theodosian Code*, in which he appears as an MVM in 392 and 393, but no mention is made of his posting and the content of the laws themselves is unrevealing.[33] Because he is not listed among the generals who accompanied Theodosius to the west and because the Illyrian command was supposedly "open" following the death of Butheric, Demandt assigns him to that post.[34] The *PLRE*, meanwhile, suggests that post for him in the fasti, but makes no mention of Illyricum in his entry.[35] Once again, absent the expectation that the *Notita* system was already in effect, there is no reason to assign Abundantius to any regional command or to assume the office of MMI even existed.

Unlike Demandt, the *PLRE* also assigns designated *magistri* to Thrace (i.e., MMTs), specifically three men: Modares, Saturninus, and Stilicho. Our evidence for **Modares** comes from a passage of Zosimos and two letters of Gregory of Nazianzos. According to Zosimos, he was "promoted to a military command" and won a victory over a group of Goths early in Theodosius' reign, while Gregory of Nazianzos claims that he "settled the foreign war with his right hand and his intelligence, while bravely presiding over us."[36] He is addressed as στρατηλάτης in several manuscripts of this letter. Taken together, this is enough evidence for both Demand and the *PLRE* to make him a *magister militum*. While this is possible, it is not definitive. A "military command" is a vague phrase, and Zosimos does not give a clear sense of the size of Modares' forces. Zosimos does report the spoils of the battle – 4,000 wagons and as many women and children as those wagons could carry – but this seems exaggerated and makes the entire account difficult to credit.[37] So, too, does its reliance on broad stereotypes, namely the drunkenness of the Goths that facilitated the Roman ambush. Gregory's letter is similarly non-specific about Modares' rank and we may suspect that he is overstating Modares' achievements because his praise is directly linked to a request for help at the Council of Constantinople (381). Given the ambiguity of the evidence and the lack of other attestations of Modares, it is unlikely that he held a magisterial command. Even if he were a *magister*, the sources provide no grounds for assigning him the specific office of MMT.[38]

---

[33] 392: *CTh* 12.1.128; 393: ibid. 7.4.18. [34] Demandt, "Magister," 717.
[35] *PLRE* I, 4–5 (Abundantius) and 1114 (fasti).
[36] Zosimos, *New History* 4.25.2: στρατιωτικῆς προβεβλημένος ἀρχῆς; Gregory of Nazianzos, *Letter* 136: τὸν ἔξωθεν πόλεμον τῇ σεαυτοῦ δεξιᾷ καὶ συνέσει καταλύεις γενναίως ὑπὲρ ἡμῶν ἱστάμενος.
[37] Zosimos, *New History* 4.25.3.
[38] Demandt makes him *magister peditum in praesenti*: "Magister," 713–714.

Unlike Modares, we can be relatively confident that **Saturninus** was a *magister*. A senior commander at Adrianople, though not yet a *magister*, he was responsible for organizing the peace with the Goths in 382 and was made consul in 383, on which occasion he received a panegyric from Themistios.[39] Although no source calls him a *magister*, he is frequently referred to as στρατηγός, while Themistios claims that he had reached the highest levels of military command.[40] Moreover, it seems unlikely that a non-*magister* would be entrusted with the high-level negotiations that Themistios reports or be given the consulship as a reward. Although we can be confident of Saturninus' rank, we know virtually nothing of his specific post, if any, and Demandt and the *PLRE* once again offer different conjectures. The *PLRE* claims him as an MM in Thrace based on the description of his embassy by Themistios.[41] However, Themistios implies that Saturninus was not leading soldiers during this embassy, and we have no evidence that he played a military, rather than a diplomatic, role in Theodosius' Gothic campaigns, which were in any case largely resolved through western military intervention. There is thus no strong reason to associate him with a specific regional command.[42] Demandt, meanwhile, makes Saturninus the holder of a supernumerary magisterial command.[43] This is certainly possible, and we know that by this point *magistri militum vacantes* were present at court (i.e., men who were appointed to the office but had no specific duties), but it is ultimately speculative.[44] Regardless of his specific posting, Saturninus remained important at court: he oversaw the trial of Timasius in 396 and was one of the men whose dismissal was demanded by Gaïnas in 400.[45]

The final proposed MMT, **Stilicho**, was one of the most influential generals of the period and had a long and well-documented career as a *magister militum* in the west. We are interested here only in his rank and assignment prior to his departure for the west in 394. The *Theodosian Code* makes it clear that Stilicho was MVM by 393, and the *PLRE* attempts to link this to reports in various works of Claudian that Stilicho campaigned against the Goths in Thrace.[46] It is on these grounds alone that the *PLRE* suggests

---

[39] *Consular History of Constantinople*, s.a. 382 and 383; Themistios, *Oration* 16.208a–210a. For the nature of his command at Adrianople, see Appendix 1.

[40] Themistios, *Oration* 16.206a.   [41] *PLRE* I, 807–808 (Flavius Saturninus 10) and 1114 (fasti).

[42] Themistios, *Oration* 16.208d.   [43] Demandt, "Magister," 717–718.

[44] For *vacantes* generals, see Chapter 2.

[45] Trial: Zosimos, *New History* 5.9.3–5; demand: ibid. 5.18.7–9; Sozomenos, *Ecclesiastical History* 8.4; Sokrates, *Ecclesiastical History* 6.6.

[46] 393: *CTh* 7.4.18. Thrace: Claudian, *On the Consulship of Stilicho* 1.94–115; *Against Rufinus* 1.308–322; *Praise of Serena* 207–209.

that Stilicho served as MMT.[47] Demandt, meanwhile, makes Stilicho the *magister peditum in praesenti* based on his later co-command of the army that Theodosius took west against Eugenius in 394 and the fact that he does not believe the office of MMT existed at this time.[48] However, almost any commander serving in the early reign of Theodosius would have had experience fighting the Goths in Thrace, and the claim that Stilicho avenged Promotus need not imply anything about his specific post. All we can say for certain is that Stilicho was a *magister* who served under Theodosius in Thrace. There is no reason to make him an MMT.

It is worth reflecting on how different the careers of Modares, Saturninus, and Stilicho are in the reconstructions of Demandt and the *PLRE*. The evidence is slender, although Saturninus and Stilicho are better documented than Modares. Yet both reconstructions confidently assign these generals to specific commands that they are never attested as holding in the sources. In the process, these scholars reinforce the (erroneous) impression that we can detect the operation of an underlying command structure in our accounts for the period, namely the *Notitia* system. The tendentiousness of that conclusion is thrown into sharp relief by the radically different reconstructions that result from a single difference in their assumptions, namely whether or not the office of MMT had been established by the reign of Theodosius. Put differently, the proposed careers of these three generals illustrate how circular the arguments are about the high command under Theodosius. Scholars find generals in the offices they think existed, regardless of whether or not the sources support those attributions.

It is clear from the survey above that there is no reliable evidence that the posts of MMI and MMT existed during the reign of Theodosius. Even the position of MMO, which we know for a fact did exist by the end of this period, appears late in Theodosius' reign and there is no good evidence that a proto-MMO was regularly in place after the departure of Iulius (ca. 379?). The evidence therefore suggests that the MMO did not evolve directly from the ad hoc posts held by Lupicinus and Iulius under Valens, despite their obvious role as precedents. This is important because it indicates that the military arrangements found in the *Notitia* were not necessarily a formalization of a directly preexisting practice. In other words, even though we have clear ad hoc precedents for both the MMO and MMI in the late fourth century (and for

---

[47] *PLRE* I, 853–858 (Stilicho). The *PLRE* appears to be confused here. The entry suggests that Stilicho replaced Promotus as MMT, but neither Promotus' entry nor the fasti claim for him the office of MMT: *PLRE* I, 750–751 (Promotus) and 1114 (fasti).

[48] Demandt, "Magister," 715–716. Command: Zosimos, *New History* 4.57.2; Ioannes of Antioch, *History* fr. 212.2.

the MMT in 412), it is not necessary to assume that these assignments anticipated or were directly formalized into the arrangements found in the *Notitia*. Temporal gaps in regional commands were possible, and the institution of regional magisterial commands was not necessarily motivated by the same considerations that drove the ad hoc appointment of men such as Iulius (Oriens) and Equitius (Illyricum).

Who, then, were Theodosius' *magistri*? Victor continued in that post in the aftermath of Adrianople and possibly through to the accession of Theodosius, though we have no direct evidence for this. He is last attested in office bringing Gratian news of the defeat at Adrianople, and when we meet him for the final time in 381/2, in a letter of Gregory of Nazianzos, it is implied that he has retired.[49]

After Victor there is a significant gap in explicitly attested *magistri equitum* and *magistri peditum* until 386, when **Timasius** is addressed in a law as *magister equitum*.[50] Two years later, in 388, Zosimos reports that Timasius was placed in charge of the infantry for Theodosius' campaign against Magnus Maximus, which would make him the *magister peditum*. Shortly after this campaign, in 388 or 389, Ambrose reports an interaction with Timasius to his sister and refers to him as *magister equitum et peditum*.[51] Timasius continued to serve as a general for Theodosius until he was appointed, along with Stilicho, "to command the Roman armies" that Theodosius led west against the usurper Eugenius in 394.[52] Many generals are attested for this campaign, but our sources emphasize the Romanness of the forces commanded by Timasius and Stilicho, which suggests that the field army in the emperor's presence continued to have the traditional two commanders through to the defeat of Eugenius.[53] In light of the evidence, it is likely that Timasius was a *magister militum* and *in praesenti* throughout the period from 386 to 394, though we have to stress that there is no explicit evidence that he commanded anything like a distinct and formally constituted praesental army of the type described by the *Notitia*. Instead, he appears to have been playing the same

---

[49] News to Gratian: Zosimos, *New History* 4.24.3; retired: Gregory of Nazianzos, *Letter* 134: Νικῶν γὰρ τοῖς ὅπλοις τοὺς πολεμίους, ἕως ἐξῆν, καὶ νῦν πάντας νικᾷς χρηστότητι. Both Demandt and the *PLRE* claim that he is addressed as στρατηλάτης in another letter of Gregory, but this title is given in only one manuscript and cannot be relied on: Demandt, "Magister," 712; *PLRE* I, 957–959 (Victor 4); Gregory of Nazianzos, *Letter* 133; see Gallay, *Saint-Grégoire de Nazianze: Lettres*, v. 2, 22.

[50] *CTh* 4.17.5.

[51] Zosimos, *New History* 4.45.2; Ambrose, *Letter* 1.27* (= *Letter* 41.27, ed. *PL*). The latter is dated based on its contents, which deal with the destruction of the synagogue in Kallinikos (Callinicum) in 388.

[52] Continued service: Zosimos, *New History* 4.49.1; 394: ibid. 4.57.2: τῶν μὲν Ῥωμαϊκῶν στρατοπέδων ἔταξεν ἡγεῖσθαι Τιμάσιον καὶ ἐπὶ τούτῳ Στελίχωνα; Ioannes of Antioch, *History* fr. 212.2.

[53] Other officers: Zosimos, *New History* 4.57.2–3; Eunapios, *History* fr. 60.

role for Theodosius as Victor and Arinthaeus had for Valens, albeit with a slightly different title. We cannot securely date Timasius' retirement from office, but a *terminus ante quem* is provided by his exile in 396.[54]

Timasius was paired in office first with **Promotus**, who commanded the cavalry against Magnus Maximus in 388, and then with Stilicho, who was his co-commander against Eugenius in 394. In 386, Promotus was "commander of the infantry in Thrace" (ὁ στρατηγὸς τῶν κατὰ Θρᾴκην πεζῶν) according to Zosimos, a confused title that combines elements of the nomenclature for the MMT and the *magister peditum*, but should likely be identified with neither office.[55] Zosimos names Promotus' office in the context of a battle against the Greuthungi under the leadership of Odotheos, which he reports twice, first in a summary notice and then in a fully developed set piece. Promotus' office is mentioned in the first account of the battle, in which Zosimos reports that "[Timasius] opposed the enemy with infantry and river boats" and annihilated the invaders as they attempted to cross the Danube.[56] The second, more detailed account confirms the image of a largely naval engagement.[57] Every element of these accounts strongly suggests that, at this time, Promotus was a *dux* or *comes rei militaris* responsible for *limitanei* and river patrol craft, and not a *magister* leading field-army units. Moreover, at the end of the more extended account, Zosimos reports that Promotus called Theodosius' attention to his victory and preserved some Greuthungi alive for use against Maximus, but nevertheless "continued in the defense of Thrace (to which he had been assigned)."[58] The implication appears to be that Promotus was angling for a promotion and hoped to use his recent victory to bolster his credentials. The gambit apparently worked, and Promotus went west as *magister equitum* in 388.[59] Upon his return, Promotus was awarded the consulship for 389 alongside Timasius and subsequently served in Thrace with a broader, albeit still ad hoc, command.[60] It was in this capacity that he was killed in battle in 391.[61]

After Promotus, Timasius was next paired with **Stilicho**, who is attested as MVM by a law of 393.[62] As discussed, the *PLRE* tentatively suggests that

[54] Zosimos, *New History* 5.8.3–9; Eunapios, *History* fr. 65.3.
[55] Zosimos, *New History* 4.35.1. Based on its placement in Zosimos' narrative, this event should date to 381/2, but Claudian links it to Honorius' first consulship and this matches the evidence of the *Consular History of Constantinople*: Claudian, *On the Fourth Consulship of Honorius* 619–633; *Consular History of Constantinople*, s.a. 386; *PLRE* I, 750–751 (Promotus).
[56] Zosimos, *New History* 4.35.1: ἀπαντήσας πεζῇ τε καὶ ποταμίαις ναυσί.
[57] Zosimos, *New History* 4.38–39. [58] Zosimos, *New History* 4.39.4–5.
[59] Zosimos, *New History* 4.45.2. [60] Zosimos, *New History* 4.50.1.
[61] Zosimos, *New History* 4.51.2–3; Claudian, *On the Consulship of Stilicho* 1.94–96 and 102–103; *Against Rufinus* 1.316–317.
[62] *CTh* 7.4.18.

he was assigned to Thrace, and he certainly served in the region, but our evidence does not permit a more granular chronology. It is just as likely that his service in Thrace earned him his post as *magister* as it is that he was appointed *magister* and then sent to Thrace. In any case, by the time he is attested in office in 393, it is likely that he was already involved in preparations for the expedition against Eugenius the following year.[63]

To this survey of Theodosius' *magistri* we must also add two more: Abundantius and Richomer. **Abundantius'** rank is attested as MVM by the *Theodosian Code* in 392, and he also received a law addressed to "Abundantius, Stilicho, and the other counts and *magistri utriusque militiae*" along with the consulship in 393.[64] His consulship and equal billing with Stilicho suggest a high office, but there is no indication that he went west with Theodosius in 394. He is similarly never attested as leading an army between his first appearance as *magister* in 392 and his exile in 396, though Zosimos claims that he served as a general under Gratian.[65]

Richomer is a peculiar case. After Adrianople, where he held the rank of western *comes domesticorum*, he appears to have served as a *magister* at the court of the western emperor Valentinian II. He was consul in 384 and then served as a commander in the army that Theodosius led west to defeat Magnus Maximus and reestablish Valentinian II in 388.[66] Despite this link to the east, he continued to serve in the west, where we find his office attested as MVM by a law of 391.[67] The following year, Richomer was in the east during Eugenius' usurpation, which was undertaken with the backing of Arbogast, who had been Richomer's pro-Theodosian colleague in the earlier civil war against Maximus. Zosimos reports that Richomer was Theodosius' initial choice to command the cavalry in the war against Eugenius but he died before the expedition departed in 394.[68] It is unclear to what extent Richomer was formally integrated into the command structure of the eastern empire, but, if Zosimos is to be believed, it appears that his (western) status as *magister* was recognized by Theodosius, who was going to appoint him as his *magister equitum*. Richomer was a unique figure in the later fourth century, a western officer whose most important recorded campaigns took place under eastern emperors, and his career neatly encapsulates the shifting balance of power between the eastern and western empires during this period. Whereas Richomer began his recorded

---

[63] *PLRE* I, 853–858 (Stilicho).   [64] *CTh* 12.1.128 and 7.4.18.   [65] Zosimos, *New History* 5.10.4–5.
[66] Philostorgios, *Ecclesiastical History* 10.8.   [67] Zosimos, *New History* 5.53.1; rank: *CTh* 7.1.13.
[68] Zosimos, *New History* 4.55.2–3.

career by bringing aid to the beleaguered east, he ended up relying on eastern support to maintain the political stability of the west.

In the end, we find seven men for whom there is just enough evidence to assign magisterial commands in the eastern empire during the reign of Theodosius: Saturninus, Hellebicus, Timasius, Promotus, Stilicho, Abundantius, and Addaeus. Of these, the offices of four are clearly attested: Addaeus, who was MMO, and Timasius, Promotus, and Stilicho, who were MVMs serving in the emperor's presence during Theodosius' civil wars. It is noteworthy that all but one of these, Saturninus, is attested in the *Theodosian Code*, which speaks to the value of that document's testimony on high military officials. To the list of MVMs we can likely add Saturninus, whose consulship and role in the Gothic peace of 382 argue for a high appointment, and Abundantius, whose consulship and address alongside Stilicho in the *Theodosian Code* suggest the same office. Hellebicus appears to have spent much of his career in the environs of Constantinople, but we have no information about his military service. As for the regional *magistri* that Demandt and the *PLRE* have seen operating in this period, not a single assignment can meet the burden of evidence without the support of the *Notitia*, with the sole exception of Addaeus, the MMO, whose office is attested by the *Theodosian Code*. In the light of the evidence, then, it is clear that the Roman high command continued to operate under Theodosius within the same general structure as it had under Valens.

A Revised Fasti of the Eastern Praesental Generals (MMPs)

The late Roman armies themselves are sometimes difficult to see directly because our narrative sources often focus on the generals themselves rather than their armies. For this reason, constructing a reliable list of the men who held the post of *magister militum praesentalis* (MMP) is an essential first step in assessing the function of this office and its associated armies. It is also the most difficult of the various generals' offices to pin down, because the MMI, MMT, and MMO are often identifiable by their geographical location, whereas modern prosopographies want to assign the position of MMP to any general who happened to be present in the capital. This has resulted in serious distortions of the record and, by extension, a skewed history of the (often putative) armies themselves.[1]

Most modern discussions of praesental generals rely on two reconstructions, Alexander Demandt's entry in Pauly-Wissowa's *Real-Encyclopädie* on the office of *magister militum* and, more prominently in Anglophone scholarship, on the *PLRE*, or *Prosopography of the Later Roman Empire*. Both of these reference works often identify MMPs on thin or circumstantial evidence. Moreover, both reconstructions make four assumptions about the office that are not justified by the evidence of the sources: 1. that the office existed and was functioning by 395 (following the nearly universal early dating of the *Notitia dignitarum*); 2. that the office was continually filled from 395 until at least the later sixth century, or beyond; 3. that generals physically present in Constantinople are likely to have been praesental generals regardless of whether or not this specific office is attested for them; and 4. that "generically" attested generals (i.e., MMs or MVMs) must in reality have held one of the specific regional commands

---

[1] For a discussion of *vacantes* generals, see Chapter 2.

(MMI, MMT, MMP I and II, or MMO), even if that is not specifically attested for them. We separately address the third and fourth assumptions in Chapter 2. Despite these questionable assumptions, the reconstructions of Demandt and the *PLRE* have been widely accepted, reproduced by scholars, and used to construct the military history of the empire.

In an effort to construct a more reliable list of holders of the office of MMP, the present discussion will, in chronological order, scrutinize the offices of all men who have been proposed as holding it.

According to both Demandt and the *PLRE*, **Timasius**, a general under Theodosius I, was the first MMP.[2] Yet this identification immediately creates problems, especially for the *PLRE*. Timasius appears as an MMP in the fasti of *PLRE* II while his entry appears in *PLRE* I and makes no mention of the office of MMP, in part because he is never attested with that title. In the sources, he appears with the typical fourth-century titles of *magister equitum* or *magister equitum et peditum*.[3] Demandt's account contains a similar inconsistency. Although he lists Timasius as an MMP (under Arcadius in the chart at the end of his entry) and explicitly identifies him as a praesental (under Theodosius) in his analysis, he nevertheless understands Timasius to have held a unit-specific command that is irreconcilable with the office of MMP as described in the *Notitia*.[4] It is thus unclear why we should consider Timasius a praesental, rather than descriptively *in praesenti*, or what the implications of Demandt's identification are.

The next cluster of proposed MMPs comes early in the reign of Arcadius during the revolt of Gaïnas in 399–400, a notoriously complicated episode.[5] In question are the offices of three commanders: Gaïnas, Leo, and Fravitta. The *PLRE* claims that Gaïnas and Fravitta both served as MMP during these events, while Demandt adds Leo to that list. We will take the evidence for **Gaïnas** and **Leo** first. The fasti of *PLRE* II identify Gaïnas as an MMP, but in the actual entry for the general, found in *PLRE* I,[6] this identification is marked as uncertain and not argued for in the text. Demandt, meanwhile, argues that Gaïnas was made MMP along with Leo at the beginning of

---

[2] *PLRE* II, 1290 (fasti). For a reconstruction of Timasius' career and offices, see Chapter 1 and Appendix 2.

[3] *PLRE* I, 914–915 (Timasius); *magister peditum* for the campaign against Maximus in 388: Zosimos, *New History* 4.55.2: [Theodosius] τοῖς δὲ στρατιώταις, ἱππεῦσι μὲν Πρόμωτον, πεζοῖς δὲ Τιμάσιον ἐπέστησεν; as *magister equitum et peditum*: Ambrose, *Letter* 41.27; unspecified command in the campaign against Eugenius in 394: Zosimos, *New History* 4.57.2: τῶν μὲν Ῥωμαϊκῶν στρατοπέδων ἔταξεν ἡγεῖσθαι Τιμάσιον καὶ ἐπὶ τούτῳ Στελίχωνα.

[4] Chart: Demandt, "Magister," 789–790; praesental: ibid. 714–715; unit-specific command: ibid. 713 and 723–724.

[5] For this episode, see also the discussion in Chapter 2.   [6] *PLRE* I, 379–380 (Gaïnas).

Tribigild's rebellion (before they set out to suppress him) on the grounds that the object of their campaign was an internal foe and thus the posts of MMT and MMO were inappropriate (this is a "rule" about these commands that Demandt seems to have invented).[7]

There are overwhelming objections against identifying either Gaïnas or Leo as an MMP. To begin with, neither of them is given that title in the sources. It is also fairly clear from the sources laid out in the *PLRE* I that Gaïnas was not an MM of any kind when he was sent to suppress Tribigild's rebellion. He was awarded that title, in its MVM form, later, when he marched on the capital after having joined forces with Tribigild. The sources are explicit on this point: The office that Gaïnas extorted from the court is unusually well-attested and there is no indication that it included a praesental title.[8] Nevertheless, some modern historians give him that title and make it central to their interpretation of his career, because they believe (with no basis in the sources) that it gave Gaïnas command of the (in reality nonexistent) praesental armies.[9] This point also needs to be specified: no source for these events attests the existence at this time of "praesental" armies as known from the *Notitia* (e.g., formally constituted armies near Constantinople that were not under the emperor's immediate command). Others who have scrutinized the events closely have correctly denied that praesental titles and praesental armies were part of this story at any point.[10] Our analysis of events in Chapter 2 rules out the possibility that either man was commanding praesental armies. Gaïnas' forces are consistently described as containing mostly barbarian auxiliaries. Leo, meanwhile, is not given a title in the sources, even though he, in 399, was at least commanding Roman soldiers. Zosimos says that he acted from the start as Gaïnas' subordinate (ὑποστρατηγέω), which argues against him being an MMP.[11]

If neither Gaïnas nor Leo was leading a praesental army, there is, in turn, no reason to assign that same command to **Fravitta**, who opposed Gaïnas' crossing to Asia after the rebel was driven out of

[7] Demandt, "Magister," 732.58–736.41.
[8] Sokrates, *Ecclesiastical History* 6.6.1: στρατηλάτης Ῥωμαίων ἱππικῆς τε καὶ πεζικῆς ἀναδείκνυται; Sozomenos, *Ecclesiastical History* 8.4.5: πεζῶν καὶ ἱππέων τὴν ἡγεμονίαν ἐκ βασιλέως ἔχων; Theodoretos, *Ecclesiastical History* 5.32: πολλοὺς μὲν καὶ τῶν ὁμοφύλων ὑπηκόους ἔχων, ἄγων δὲ μετὰ τούτων καὶ τῶν Ῥωμαίων τήν τε ἱππικὴν καὶ τὴν πεζὴν στρατιάν; Ioannes of Antioch, *History* fr. 216.1: ὁ τῶν ἑῴων στρατοπέδων ἔξαρχος βάρβαρος ὢν τὸ γένος καὶ ὑπὸ Ῥωμαίων κατ' ὀλίγου ἐπὶ τὴν στρατηγίδα προελθών; as a generic "general": Zosimos, *New History* 5.13.1, 5.14.1; Philostorgios, *Ecclesiastical History* 11.8.
[9] For example, Cameron and Long, *Barbarians and Politics*, 20, 204–209.
[10] For example, Liebeschuetz, *Barbarians and Bishops*, 101–102.
[11] Zosimos, *New History* 5.16.5. Demandt claims that this reflects Gaïnas' status as senior MMP. Leo's Roman soldiers: Zosimos, *New History* 5.17.1. For Leo in general, see *PLRE* II, 661–662 (Leo 2).

Constantinople.[12] Unfortunately, we are not informed what forces Fravitta used for this operation. The *PLRE* is once again inconsistent: The fasti have no doubt about Fravitta being an MMP, while his entry marks his praesental command as suspect. Demandt argues that Fravitta, who was MMO at the time, was appointed as MMP during the crisis, citing a fragment of Eunapios that calls him "the general of the Romans" (ὁ στρατηγὸς Ῥωμαίων).[13] Our other sources are consistent in calling him simply a "general," not even giving him the more specific title of MVM that they use for Gaïnas.[14] The arguments that we used against Gaïnas being an MMP weigh against Fravitta as well, and we may add an additional argument: the fight around Constantinople was a sea battle and no naval units are attested in either praesental command by the *Notitia*.

After Fravitta, the *PLRE* and Demandt diverge. Demandt argues for Arbazacius, while the *PLRE* prefers Simplicius. Demandt argues for **Arbazacius** on the grounds that he is attested as a στρατηγός and there are no other options but for him to be an MMP, but he offers no specifics on the date of his tenure. The *PLRE* simply makes him a *comes*.[15] Demandt's argument again assumes that the post of MMP existed and was continuously filled, although he elsewhere argues that the court eunuch Eutropius left those offices vacant between Timasius and Gaïnas. The case for **Simplicius** in 405, which is found only in the *PLRE*, is similarly thin.[16] Both the fasti and the text of the *PLRE* express doubt about the assignment and cite as evidence only his appointment of a *dux Libyarum*, arguing that "he was presumably *magister militum* and by now will have been *praesentalis*." No further explanation is given. There is no reason to assign a praesental command to either man.

More promising candidates than any discussed so far are **Varanes** and **Arsacius**, who helped to diffuse a grain riot in Constantinople in 409/10.[17] The key source here is the seventh-century *Chronicon Paschale*, which reports that "the two generals, the consul Varanes and Arsacius" (οἱ δύο στρατηλάται, Οὐαρανᾶς ὁ ὕπατος καὶ Ἀρσάκιος), assisted Synesis, the *comes largitionum*, in confronting the populace and promising to carry out

---

[12] *PLRE* I, 372–373 (Fravitta).   [13] Demandt, "Magister," 736.4–23; Eunapios, *History* fr. 69.2.

[14] Zosimos, *New History* 5.20.1 (στρατηγόν); Sokrates, *Ecclesiastical History* 6.6.39; Philostorgios, *Ecclesiastical History* 11.8; Ioannes of Antioch, *History* fr. 216.3. Likewise implied by Sozomenos, *Ecclesiastical History* 8.4.19: στρατιὰ κατὰ γῆν τε καὶ θάλασσαν παρὰ βασιλέως ἀπεσταλμένη, ἧς ἡγεῖτο Φραβίτας.

[15] Demandt, "Magister," 736.42–737.2. Στρατηγός in Zosimos, *New History* 5.25.2. *PLRE* II, 128 (Arbazacius).

[16] *PLRE* II, 1013–1014 (Simplicius 2).   [17] *PLRE* II, 1149–1150 (Varanes 1) and 152 (Arsacius 3).

their wishes.[18] The phrase οἱ δύο στρατηλάται implies the expectation for a linked pair of generals, which, along with their presence in Constantinople, has suggested to many scholars the offices of MMP I and MMP II (it should be noted that there is no mention of any soldiers under their command). This is perhaps a big conclusion to base on a single article ("the") in an entry that has clearly been edited and redacted between its original source and the seventh-century *Paschal Chronicle*, and misplaced chronologically to boot.[19] It is possible that, in the transmission of the original notice, the later system of paired MMP commands was projected onto this event. But there is a simpler explanation for why Varanes and Arsacius appear as "the two generals," an explanation that is truer to the practices of those years than the office of MMP.

Specifically, the practice of appointing paired sets of *magistri equitum* and *peditum* ("masters of cavalry" and "of infantry") was standard in the late fourth century and continued into the fifth. For example, in 388, in the war against Maximus, Theodosius I appointed Promotus to be his *magister equitum* and Timasius to be his *magister peditum*.[20] In 408, after the murder of Stilicho, Varanes himself – the very same man who appears a year later in Constantinople – was made *magister peditum* and Turpilio was made *magister equitum* in the western empire.[21] Soon afterward in a political disturbance, Turpilio was replaced as *magister equitum* and many other officers were replaced too, but Varanes is not named among them in Zosimos' detailed account.[22] Varanes must have left for the east where he appears in 409 as one of the "two" generals. His western command may have just carried over to Constantinople, which means that Arsacius, his colleague in facing down the populace, was *magister equitum* to Varanes' *magister peditum*. While still speculative, this is a far likelier explanation for their "paired" command than that they held offices that are not otherwise attested for another thirty years.

There is an even simpler explanation that is also better than projecting the later realities of the *Notitia* onto the early fifth century: It is possible that Varanes and Arscacius were just the two active MMs or MVMs at the

---

[18] *Paschal Chronicle* s.a. 412 (p. 571.8–11). The *Paschal Chronicle* erroneously dates the event to 412. The correct date is in Marcellinus Comes, *Chronicle* s.a. 409.

[19] For the fifth-century sources of the *Paschal Chronicle*, see Whitby and Whitby, *Chronicon Paschale*, xv–xxii; Treadgold, *The Early Byzantine Historians*, 345.

[20] Zosimos, *New History* 4.45.2: ἱππεῦσι μὲν Πρόμωτον, πεζοῖς δὲ Τιμάσιον ἐπέστησεν. See our narrative in Chapter 1.

[21] Zosimos, *New History* 5.36.3: Τουρπιλλίωνα μὲν τοῖς ἱππεῦσιν, Οὐαράνην δὲ τοῖς πεζοῖς ἐπιστήσας; *PLRE* II, 1133 (Turpilio).

[22] Zosimos, *New History* 5.47.2–5.48.1.

court of the emperor Theodosius II at that moment. They were "the two generals" who happened to be at the court when a crisis occurred, just as Belisarius and Mundo happened to be present for the Nika Insurrection in 532. At any rate, our argument does not depend on any specific version of the offices held by these two men, only on the likelihood that they were not paired MMPs, which is not the office that our sole source explicitly gives them anyway.

Demandt and the *PLRE* both argue for the joint praesental command of **Florentius** and **Sapricius** in 415.[23] Demandt makes the argument on the basis of *CTh* 1.8.1, which is addressed to Florentius with a copy sent to Sapricius. Because both men hold the rank of MM and are, according to Demandt, in Constantinople, he views them as praesentals, which we regard as an insufficient argument.[24] The *PLRE* cites the same evidence for both men and argues that they were "probably" MMPs, though their appointments are not flagged as suspect in the fasti. These two men are attested nowhere else. Moreover, the fact that the law was issued at Constantinople is immaterial: It simply indicates the location of the emperor and not of the addressees. In short, these men were generic MMs, two among many at the court, and there is no positive reason to think that they were MMPs.

The career of **Plinta** (early fifth century), a relative of Ardabur and Aspar, illustrates how scholars have used mere location to assign the office of MMP.[25] Both the *PLRE* and Demandt identify Plinta as MMP, even though no source gives him that title. Our most specific source calls him "commander of the cavalry and infantry armies" (ἵππου τε καὶ πεζῆς στρατιᾶς ἡγεμών), a standard Greek translation of the title *magister equitum et peditum*.[26] Elsewhere he is just called a *magister militum*, that is, "general."[27] The *Notitia* titles had evidently not kicked in yet. But Demandt makes Plinta an MMP on the basis of his influence at court as reported by Sozomenos. The *PLRE*, meanwhile, offers no argument for

---

[23] *PLRE* II, 477 (Florentius 2) and 977 (Sapricius).

[24] Demandt, "Magister," 745.58–68. Demandt cites Jones, *Later Roman Empire*, 181, who in turn cites the same law. For the argument against all generals in Constantinople being praesentals, see Chapter 2.

[25] *PLRE* II, 892–893 (Plinta).

[26] Sozomenos, *Ecclesiastical History* 7.17.14. For other Greek renditions of the MVM title, associated with a variety of commands, see, for example, Olympiodoros, *History* fr. 14 and 43.1; *ACO* 3, p. 101.29–30; Ioannes of Antioch, *History* fr. 237.6; Theophylaktos, *History* 6.5.13.

[27] Sokrates, *Ecclesiastical History* 5.23: στρατηλάτης; *ACO* 1.4, p. 88.20: *magister militiae*; Priskos, *History* fr. 2: Πλίνθας μὲν τοῦ Σκυθικοῦ, Διονύσιος δὲ τοῦ Θρᾳκίου γένους, ἀμφότεροι δὲ στρατοπέδων ἡγούμενοι καὶ ἄρξαντες τὴν ὕπατον παρὰ Ῥωμαίοις ἀρχήν; ibid. fr. 15.4: Πλίνθου τοῦ παρὰ Ῥωμαίοις στρατηγήσαντος.

assigning the post to Plinta, though it cites the same passage of Sozomenos.[28] On the basis of these two reference works, Plinta is widely called an MMP in scholarship, often with citations to the same passage.[29] But here is all that the passage says, on which the entire case for Plinta's praesental command rests:

> But Plinta, a fellow believer [of the Arians], a man of consular rank, commander of cavalry and infantry, and at that time the most powerful man at court, reconciled [the Arians] in Constantinople after they had quarrelled with one another for thirty-five years.[30]

Although the phrase "at court" (ἐν τοῖς βασιλείοις) is similar to some later Greek formulations for the office of MMP,[31] it is clear that the phrase here is referring to Plinta's influence in the palace and not to his military command, which in any case has already been described simply as "the commander of the cavalry and infantry," that is, MVM. There is nothing here that would suggest that Plinta was MMP.

Following Plinta, Demandt and the *PLRE* agree in naming **Ardabur**, the father of Aspar, as MMP in the early 420s, but they disagree on the timing of the appointment.[32] Demandt wants Ardabur to be MMP during the Persian war of 421 because he thinks, based on the testimonies of Sokrates and Malalas, that the post of MMO was occupied by the general Procopius.[33] The *PLRE* instead argues that Ardabur was MMO during the war, yielding that office to Procopius in 422 when Ardabur was recalled to Constantinople to become MMP. But then the *PLRE* has to explain away Sokrates' reference to Procopius as a στρατηλάτης early in the war as an "anticipation," which is odd.[34] To be sure, the literary terms that mean "general" could be used in the sources for lesser ranks such as *dux* and *comes*. Moreover, Sokrates refers to

---

[28] Demandt, "Magister," 746.1–31; *PLRE* II, 893.
[29] See, among others, Heather, *Goths and Romans*, 183; McEvoy, "Becoming Roman?" 485; Elton, "Imperial Politics," 136; Lee, "Theodosius and His Generals," 104.
[30] Sozomenos, *Ecclesiastical History* 7.17.14: τοὺς δὲ ἐν Κωνσταντινουπόλει ἐπὶ τριάκοντα καὶ πέντε ἔτεσι διενεχθέντας πρὸς σφᾶς εἰς ὁμόνοιαν ὕστερον συνῆψεν ὁμόδοξος αὐτοῖς ὢν Πλίνθας, ἀνὴρ ὑπατικός, ἵππου τε καὶ πεζῆς στρατιᾶς ἡγεμών, δυνατώτατος τότε τῶν ἐν τοῖς βασιλείοις γεγονώς.
[31] τῶν ἀμφὶ βασιλέα in, among others: Priskos, *History* fr. 15.3; Malchos, *History* fr. 2; τῶν περὶ βασιλέα in ibid. fr. 18.4.
[32] *PLRE* II, 137–138 (Ardabur 3).
[33] Demandt, "Magister," 747.30–748.19; Malalas, *Chronicle* 14.23 calls Procopius στρατηλάτης Ἀνατολῆς; Sokrates, *Ecclesiastical History* 7.20.8 calls him a στρατηλάτης.
[34] *PLRE* II, 919–920 (Procopius 2). In addition to Ardabur and Procopius, there is also an Anatolius identified as MMO during this period: Kyrillos of Skythopolis, *Life of Saint Euthymios* 10 (p. 19.6–7); Prokopios, *Wars* 1.2.12. These passages are not addressed in any entry in the *PLRE*. It is possible that this is an otherwise unattested Anatolius or, perhaps, the Anatolius discussed later in the text, who is attested as MMO and later as MMP: *PLRE* II, 84–86 (Anatolius 10). If this (unlikely) identification is accepted, it would extend that Anatolius' attested career by almost a decade.

Ardabur's command during the Persian war as "a divisional force, which the general Ardabur commanded" (δύναμιν μερικήν, ἧς ἦρχεν ὁ στρατηγὸς Ἀρδαβούριος).[35] Μέρος would later become a technical term for a division of the late Roman field armies, and it is likely that Sokrates is using the term in a similar, though non-technical way.[36] We can therefore rule out Ardabur as MMP or MMO during the Persian war of 421 on the basis of his limited command, a conclusion that in turn undermines the *PLRE*'s implicit narrative that he was promoted from MMO to MMP for his service during that war. The most specific title that he is ever given occurs during the invasion of Italy in 424, when he is called "general of both forces" (στρατοπεδάρχης ἑκατέρας δυνάμεως), that is, MVM.[37] There is thus no reason to identify him as an MMP.

Ardabur is followed by **Areobindus**, a general at the court of Theodosius II remembered mostly as one of the five commanders who were sent to invade North Africa in 441.[38] Demandt argues that Areobindus was an MMP on the basis of his high social rank – he was consul in 434 and later a patrician – and also because he supposedly commanded the expedition of 441. Still according to Demandt, the consulship indicates that Areobindus already held the rank of MM by 434, while Theodosius II's *Novel* 7, which is addressed to Areobindus as MM, suggests the post of MMP, which is supposedly confirmed by his subsequent command of the African expedition of 441.[39] It should be noted that Demandt's prosopography of praesental generals runs into significant problems during the mid-fifth century due to its sheer abundance. As a result, he admits that Areobindus and Anatolius (who is specifically attested as MMP and discussed later) cannot be fitted into the scheme of the *Notitia* and considers them as irregular appointments.[40] For its part, the *PLRE* expresses doubt about Areobindus' praesental command in its entry on him and offers no argument in support of even this tentative assignment. What we have here are prosopographers trying, and failing, to fit the surviving evidence into the mold of the *Notitia*'s terminology. No source calls Areobindus anything more specific than στρατηγός nor is there any explicit evidence that he was commander-in-chief of the expedition of 441.[41]

---

[35] Sokrates, *Ecclesiastical History* 7.18.9.
[36] For the late Roman μέρη, see Treadgold, *Byzantium and Its Army*, 94–97.
[37] Olympiodoros, *History* fr. 43 = Photios, *Bibliotheca* 80 (63b.15–16).
[38] *PLRE* II, 145–146 (Ariobindus 2); for the aborted North African campaign, see Chapter 2.
[39] Demandt, "Magister," 752.37–753.53.
[40] Demandt, "Magister," 752.28–36, 753.44–53, and 754.31–53.
[41] For the expedition, see Prosper Tiro, *Chronicle* s.aa. 441 and 442 (pp. 478–479); Theophanes, *Chronographia* a.m. 5942, pp. 101–102 (misdated); Nikephoros Xanthopoulos, *Ecclesiastical History*

We are, finally, on firmer ground with the first attested MMP, **Apollonius**, whose office is explicitly mentioned in a law of Theodosius II (co-issued in the name of Valentinian III) preserved in the *Codex Justinianus*.⁴² The law is undated and so may have been issued at any time during the joint reign of Theodosius and Valentinian, that is, between 425 and 450, but almost certainly after 441, which is the firm date of the law that precedes it in the collection. The law deals with the retirement of *numerarii*, chief military accountants, which is unhelpful for dating purposes. We may, however, narrow the range further based on the other addressee of the law, the MMO Anatolius, who was active on the eastern frontier between 433 and 446 and is explicitly attested as MMO in 441.⁴³ The *PLRE* suggests that this law, along with *CJ* 12.59.7, may have been issued together with *CJ* 1.46.3, whose date, 28 January 443, is preserved. However, those other laws are addressed only to Anatolius, not to Apollonius, and Anatolius' title there is simply *magister militum*, a rank that he may have held before serving as MMO and continued to hold long after he had returned from the east. It is also possible, however, that the surviving version of those laws abbreviate his post of MMO as MM. At any rate, it seems that Apollonius was MMP somewhere in the years around 441–446.

Apollonius' office in *CJ* 12.54.4 is in fact the first extant attestation of the title *magister militum praesentalis* in the eastern empire (outside the *Notitia*). As for his duties, we can say virtually nothing save that he served as an ambassador to Attila in the aftermath of the Hun's failed invasion of Italy in 451. It is unclear if he was still MMP at that time. Priskos describes him as "holding command as a general" (τὴν στρατηγίδα λαχὼν ἀρχὴν), a common rendition of the post *magister militum*,⁴⁴ though it may encompass his being MMP too.

After Apollonius, the next attested MMP is **Anatolius**, whom we have already met as the MMO addressed jointly by *CJ* 12.54.4.⁴⁵ Like Apollonius, we find Anatolius as an ambassador to Attila, though Anatolius preceded Apollonius in this role, negotiating a treaty with Attila after the war in Thrace, around 447.⁴⁶ His rank at that time is unknown, but he reappears in 449 as one of the historian Priskos' companions on yet another embassy to Attila, where he is described as "the commander of the units at the court"

14.57 (1,170 ships). The number of generals varies. Prosper lists three, Theophanes five, and Nikephoros two, though Areobindus is the first mentioned in all three lists.
⁴² *PLRE* II, 121 (Apollonius 3); *CJ* 12.54.4: addressed to *Apollonio magistro militum praesentali et Anatolio magistro militum per Orientem*.
⁴³ Marcellinus Comes, *Chronicle* s.a. 441; his office is also known from Prokopios, *Wars* 1.2.12. For his activities in the east, see *PLRE* II, 84–86 (Anatolius 10).
⁴⁴ Priskos, *History* fr. 23.3.   ⁴⁵ *PLRE* II, 84–86 (Anatolius 10).
⁴⁶ Priskos, *History* fr. 9.3. For the date, see Maenchen-Helfen, *The World of the Huns*, 124. For the historical context, see Chapter 2.

(τῶν ἀμφὶ βασιλέα ἄρχοντα τελῶν), a phrase that closely matches other descriptions of confirmed praesental generals.[47]

At about the same time that Anatolius and Apollonius were engaged in their embassies to Attila, another possible praesental general was conspiring to murder the emperor Theodosius II. According to Photios' summary of Damaskios' *Life of Isidoros* (a.k.a. *The Philosophical History*, written in the early sixth century), one "**Lucius**, a man who held a military command in Byzantium under the emperor Theodosius" (Λούκιος, ἀνὴρ ἐν Βυζαντίῳ τὴν στρατηγίδα ἀρχὴν ὑπὸ βασιλεῖ Θεοδοσίῳ κοσμῶν), attempted to kill the emperor several times but was dissuaded by an apparition.[48] Lucius is otherwise unknown and, with only this praenomen, he is impossible to identify. His status as a praesental general is also uncertain as we would expect the phrase ἐν Βυζαντίῳ to be in the attributive position (τὴν ἐν Βυζαντίῳ στρατηγίδα), if the clause were specifying which military command he held.[49] However, it is possible that Photios' summary has distorted the syntax of the original passage. Lucius may have served as MMP but it is also possible that he was just an MM at court, whether *administrativus* or *vacans*.

A figure whose very historicity is tenuous is **Constantinus**, an otherwise unknown man attested as στρατηλάτης in Constantinople, under the emperor Marcian (450–457), by a much later saint's life, the *Life of Auxentios*.[50] He is not claimed by Demandt, and both his entry and the fasti in the *PLRE* are uncertain about his praesental status. Presumably he is included simply because he was a general present in Constantinople. But the AD 441 law of Theodosius II discussed in Chapter 2 breaks that connection.

The next praesental general claimed by both Demandt and the *PLRE* is **Aspar**, one of the most influential generals and politicians of the mid-fifth century, whose career and downfall have cast a long shadow over the historiography of the period.[51] He is uniformly described as a praesental general in modern scholarship; however, there is no positive evidence that he ever held this office, which is perhaps significant, seeing as we have now entered the period when the office actually existed. Demandt assigns Aspar's tenure as MMP to the reign of Theodosius II, while the *PLRE* prefers to place it in the reigns of Marcian (450–457) or Leo (457–474).

---

[47] Priskos, *History* fr. 15.3. Anatolius was one of the generals whom Attila asked for by name: ibid. fr. 13.1.
[48] Photios, *Bibliotheca* 242 (351b.30–38); *PLRE* II, 693 (Lucius 2).
[49] Compare Prokopios, *Wars* 1.8.2, describing the command of the MMP Hypatius: οἱ τῶν ἐν Βυζαντίῳ στρατιωτῶν ἄρχοντες.
[50] *PLRE* II, 312 (Constantinus 7); see the Bibliography for editions of the *Life of Auxentios*. The tenth-century Metaphrastic version, on which the *PLRE* relies, is in *PG* 114: 1375–1436. Constantinus appears in all versions.
[51] *PLRE* II, 164–169 (Ardabur Aspar).

This disagreement throws their respective reconstructions of the MMP fasti out of sync through the reign of Zeno.

Demandt makes the case for Aspar's status as MMP based on his high offices at court, his ability to secure a consulship for his son (Ardabur the Younger, in 447), and the existence of an MMT in the Hunnic war of 447/8 (when Aspar was a MM of some kind and was defeated, along with the other Roman generals, by Attila).[52] Demandt's precise reconstruction of Aspar's career, in particular the moment at which he first became MMP, is, however, frustratingly vague, perhaps as a result of his use of German rather than Roman military terminology.[53]

The *PLRE* makes the case for Aspar's praesental command on different grounds, namely a fragment of the historian Malchos that reports negotiations between the emperor Leo and Theoderic Strabo following the death of Aspar in 471.[54] Leo began negotiations by sending an ambassador to Strabo. According to Malchos, "the barbarians asked for three things: first, that Theoderic [Strabo], their leader, gain the inheritance that Aspar had given him; second, that it be permitted for him to administer Thrace; and third, that he become the general of the units which Aspar had commanded."[55] Leo rejected all of these requests except for the third, which he would grant only if Strabo "became his friend without duplicity." Strabo responded by ravaging Thrace in an attempt to extract further concessions. Eventually, he was forced back to the negotiating table by a famine, at which point an agreement was made on the following terms:

> That 2,000 lbs of gold be given to the Goths every year; that Theoderic [Strabo] be appointed general of the two armies around the emperor, the ones that are called senior; that [Strabo] be the ruler of the Goths; that the emperor not receive any of [Strabo's] followers who sought to desert into his territory; and that [Strabo] be the emperor's ally in everything that he should command, except against the Vandals.[56]

---

[52] Demandt, "Magister," 748.42–751.36.
[53] Demandt generally calls praesental generals *Hofgeneral* (i.e., "Court General") and is explicit that he believes Aspar was MMP by 433: "Magister," 753.52–53. However, in his actual discussion of Aspar, Demandt calls him *Oberkommandierender* (i.e., "Commander-in-Chief"), a position with no clear analog in the Roman system but which appears to include appointment as MMP: "Magister," 748.65–76.
[54] *PLRE* II, 165 (Ardabur Aspar).
[55] Malchos, *History* fr. 2: ἠτήσαντο δὲ τρία, πρῶτον [ἵνα] Θευδέριχον τὸν κατάρχοντα αὐτῶν τὴν κληρονομίαν ἀπολαβεῖν, ἣν ἀφῆκεν αὐτῷ Ἄσπαρ, δεύτερον νέμεσθαι τὴν Θράκην συγχωρηθῆναι αὐτῷ, τρίτον καὶ στρατηλάτην γενέσθαι τῶν ταγμάτων, ὧνπερ καὶ Ἄσπαρ ἡγήσατο.
[56] Malchos, *History* fr. 2: καὶ γίνεται ἡ σύμβασις τῶν ὅρκων ἐπὶ τούτοις, τοῖς μὲν Γότθοις δίδοσθαι κατ᾽ ἔτος χρυσίου λίτρας δισχιλίας, τὸν δὲ Θευδέριχον καθίστασθαι στρατηγὸν <τῶν> δύο στρατηγιῶν τῶν ἀμφὶ βασιλέα, αἵπερ εἰσὶ μέγισται, αὐτὸν δὲ τῶν Γότθων αὐτοκράτορα εἶναι,

The *PLRE's* argument for *Aspar's* praesental command relies on identifying the military office that *Strabo* requested in the *first* round of negotiations with the office (clearly the MMP I) that he received in the *second*.[57] However, we should be cautious before identifying the terms of the second deal with those of the first, as they were significantly different in both detail and circumstance. The final treaty makes no mention of Aspar's inheritance and does not give to Strabo rule over Thrace, an audacious request. Instead, Strabo receives a fixed yearly subsidy, a military title (MMP), and official support for his position among the Goths in return for military service to the emperor.[58] Strabo's first request makes it clear that he was aiming at command over actual soldiers (in addition to the Goths that he already led) and territories of the Roman state (specifically Thrace), and not just (as in the final concession) a sum of money that accompanied a court title that did not give him command over Roman armies or territories. The final treaty frustrated both of these desires by defining Strabo as a specifically Gothic political figure, making him dependent on the Roman state and severing his connection to the political legacy of Aspar. In sum, the two sets of terms were different and one should not be used to flesh out the other.

Of course, the possibility that Aspar held a praesental command, which Strabo claimed in the first round of negotiations and received in the second, cannot be ruled out. But if Malchos cannot be adduced as evidence of Aspar's praesental command, then the narrative of that command in the *PLRE* collapses. The only remaining detail that could link Aspar to the praesental armies is the emperor Leo, who served in the *Mattiarii*, a unit of the praesental armies that is attested in the *Notitia*.[59] Given the widespread belief that Aspar was a praesental general and his attested role in Leo's selection and elevation, scholars have attempted to link the selection of Leo (a praesental officer) to Aspar's command.[60] However, there is evidence that, in a separate capacity, Leo had previously served as Aspar's *curator* and, in any case, there are many ways in which a high-ranking officer such as Leo might have come into contact with one of the leading generals and politicians of his day, especially if we do not

καὶ μηδένας ἐξ αὐτῶν ἀποστῆναι εἰς τὴν σφετέραν γῆν θέλοντας τὸν βασιλέα δέχεσθαι· συμμαχεῖν δὲ τῷ βασιλεῖ εἰς πᾶν ὅ τι κελεύοι, πλὴν ἐπὶ μόνων τῶν Βανδίλων. See p. 141 for a discussion of the text at this point.

57 Demandt makes the same argument: "Magister," 775.35–65.
58 On this treaty, see Heather, *Goths and Romans*, 267–270.
59 For this unit and Leo's service in it, see Chapter 3.
60 For example, Croke, "Dynasty and Ethnicity," 150–151.

assume that it was necessary to hold the rank of MMP in order to command praesental soldiers.[61]

Demandt claims the office of MMP also for Marcian (before he became the eastern emperor in 450–457) and Anthemius (before he became western emperor in 467–472). Yet while **Marcian** appears in the list of MMPs at the end of Demandt's article, he is never discussed in the body of the article and there is no reason to associate him with the command.[62] Demandt similarly does not make an explicit case for Anthemius' appointment as MMP and there is no evidence linking him to the position.[63]

We have two more confirmed MMPs toward the end of the reign of Leo I, but their chronology is confused. This is a result of a short statement made in the *Chronicle* of Ioannes Malalas (sixth century):

> The emperor Leo chose husbands for his two daughters. For his elder daughter Leontia, he chose Marcianus the patrician, the son of Anthemius, the emperor of Rome. For Ariadne, he chose Zeno Kodissaios, the Isaurian. And he made both men praesental generals and patricians.[64]

This passage is our only explicit evidence that either of these men held praesental commands, and the report, coming at the end of Malalas' account of Leo's reign during a discussion of the succession, gives few chronological clues.

This is a problem especially for **Zeno**, whose career in the late 460s is notoriously difficult to pin down.[65] At issue are three explicitly attested military commands that Zeno held – MMP, MMT, and MMO – as well as the date of his marriage to Ariadne.[66] Scholars have proposed various reconstructions, but all of them must dismiss the testimony of one or more of the relevant sources. However, if Zeno was made MMP around the time of his marriage to Ariadne, which is generally dated to between 466 and 468, then it is possible that he still held the post during his

---

[61] Leo as Aspar's *curator*: Theophanes, *Chronographia* a.m. 5961, p. 116. The command of praesental units by non-praesental generals is explicitly attested in the late fifth century: see the Conclusions.

[62] *PLRE* II, 714–715 (Marcianus 8).

[63] Demandt, "Magister," 776.65–777.39; compare *PLRE* II, 96–98 (Anthemius 3).

[64] Malalas, *Chronicle* 14.46: Ὁ δὲ αὐτὸς Λέων βασιλεὺς ἔλαβε γαμβροὺς δύο ταῖς θυγατράσιν αὐτοῦ, Λεοντία τῇ μείζονι Μαρκιανὸν τὸν πατρίκιον, τὸν υἱὸν γενάμενον Ἀνθιμίου βασιλέως Ῥώμης, καὶ Ἀριάδνη Ζήνωνα τὸν Ἴσαυρον τὸν Κοδισσαῖον· καὶ ἐποίησεν ἀμφοτέρους στρατηλάτας πραισέντου καὶ πατρικίους.

[65] For two different reconstructions, see Croke, "Dynasty and Ethnicity," 163–190; and Kosiński, *The Emperor Zeno*, 57–70. *PLRE* II, 1200–1202 (Zenon 7).

[66] MMP: Malalas, *Chronicle* 14.46; MMT: *Life of Daniel the Stylite* 65; MMO: Theophanes, *Chronographia* a.m. 5962, p. 116; and Photios, *Bibliotheca* 79 (55b.10–13), drawn from the historian Kandidos.

consulship in 469, when the later historian Ioannes of Antioch reports that he "sent men to dislodge Indakos from the hill called 'Papirios'" in Isauria.[67] Such a mission is plausible for praesental units, as we see in the reign of Anastasius.[68] There are no other actions that we can link to Zeno's tenure as MMP, assuming Malalas is correct that he did actually hold the position.

We know nothing about the actions of **Marcianus** as MMP. His command is likewise attested only by Malalas.[69]

The case for **Basiliscus** as MMP is somewhat weaker and circumstantial, but not impossible.[70] Demandt argues for Basiliscus on the basis of his proximity to Constantinople; his defense of the City alongside Zeno following the assassination of Aspar; and his ability to successfully expel Zeno from the throne in 475.[71] The *PLRE* prefers to link his term as MMP to his failed command of the expedition to North Africa in 468, arguing that he probably ceased to be MMT and assumed the office of MMP instead.[72] No argument is provided for why we should prefer MMP to, say, MM *vacans*, the office that Germanus held in the African expedition of 441. Similarly, Belisarius was later sent against North Africa as MMO (along with Dorotheus as MM for Armenia, or MMA), which suggests that Basiliscus could also have sailed to North Africa while officially holding a Thracian command. The strongest argument for identifying Basiliscus as MMP is advanced by Demandt and only alluded to by the *PLRE*, namely his defense of Constantinople alongside Zeno after Aspar's assassination. This is precisely the function that we might expect of a praesental general, and Zeno is elsewhere attested as an MMP himself (see above), so the parallel mention of these two men as generals in the chronicle of pseudo-Zachariah may suggest a paired office such as the praesental command.[73] However, the uncertainty surrounding the chronology of Zeno's tenure of the office makes such an identification tenuous, while the same source that links Basiliscus to the defense of the city, Theophanes the Confessor, also makes it clear that his presence was a fortuitous consequence of his return from the failed North African expedition. No source actually calls Basiliscus a praesental general.

---

[67] Ioannes of Antioch, *History* fr. 229. For a survey of opinions on the date of Zeno's marriage, see Kosiński, *The Emperor Zeno*, 65 n. 55.

[68] See Chapter 3.   [69] *PLRE* II, 717–718 (Marcianus 17).   [70] *PLRE* II, 212–214 (Basiliscus 2).

[71] Demandt, "Magister," 777.64–778.63.   [72] *PLRE* II, 213 (Basiliscus 2).

[73] For the defense of Constantinople, see Theophanes, *Chronographia* a.m. 5964, p. 117. Service alongside Zeno: pseudo-Zachariah, *Chronicle* 5.1a: "[Basiliscus] who had been *strategos* with Zeno in the time of the emperor Leo" (trans. Phenix and Horn, p. 174, modified; they translate *strategos* as *magister militum* but make it clear that the word in question in the Syriac is *strategos*: 174 n. 11).

The later fifth century marks the beginning of much more reliable attestations of praesental generals, yet some dubious praesentals are still advanced. Demandt and the *PLRE* agree in listing **Idubingus** as a possible MMP, though both are hesitant. He is attested solely in the *Life of Daniel the Stylite*, where he is called στρατηλάτης and used to date an event in the life of a holy man named Anatolios. Demandt claims that Idubingus may have filled a gap in the roster of praesental generals between Anthemius and Basiliscus – though we consider neither of them to be confirmed – while the *PLRE*, which places him vaguely in "466 / 493," raises the same possibility on the basis of his local prominence.[74] These are weak arguments.

Demandt's account of the office of *magister militum* ends with the death of Leo, so the rest of our critical survey focuses on the *PLRE*. Among the more reliably attested MMPs are the Gothic leaders **Theoderic Strabo** and Theoderic the Amal. Theoderic Strabo was also known as the son of Triarios.[75] After he burned Philippi and besieged Arkadiopolis in 473, he forced the emperor Leo (as we saw earlier) to appoint him as "the general of the two armies at the court, the ones that are senior" (τὸν δὲ Θευδέριχον καθίστασθαι στρατηγὸν <τῶν> δύο στρατηγιῶν τῶν ἀμφὶ βασιλέα, αἵπερ εἰσὶ μέγισται).[76] The phrasing is awkward, seeming to imply that Strabo was made MMP of both praesental armies. But the best explanation, put forward by Peter Heather, takes "general of the two armies" as a translation of MVM, that is "of both the infantry and the cavalry," a relic of fourth-century titulature. That MMPs could refer to themselves as "masters of both infantry and cavalry" in this period is confirmed by the consular diptych of Justinian (AD 521), when he was MMP and before he became emperor, which does exactly that. This reading, in turn, allows μέγισται to refer, as it does in other contemporary sources, to the senior praesental army (see pp. 51, 54, 142, 144).[77] In other words, Strabo was made MMP I even though in practical terms he was not given actual command of any Roman armies at all. In his case, MMP I functioned effectively as a court title with salary perks.

Strabo was MMP for about a year before presumably losing the position when he revolted in 474. It is possible that Strabo was reappointed as MMP

[74] Demandt, "Magister," 777.40–63; *PLRE* II, 585–586 (Idubingus); *Life of Daniel the Stylite* 65.
[75] *PLRE* II, 1073–1076 (Theodericus Strabo 5).
[76] Malchos, *History* fr. 2. Blockley has removed the phrase εἰς τὴν ἑτέραν γῆν from the end of the clause, even though it is present in the manuscripts. Compare Cresci, *Malco di Filadelfia, ad. loc.* For the date, see Heather, *Goths and Romans*, 267.
[77] Heather, *Goths and Romans*, 268–269; diptych: Delbrueck, *Die Consulardiptychen*, 141–142: *mag[ister] eqq[uitum] et p[editum] praes[entalis]*.

during the usurpation of Basiliscus, which lasted from 475 to 476 and was supported in some way by Strabo, but our only evidence is Theophanes the Confessor, who simply calls Strabo στρατηγός, which is not definitive.[78] A circumstantial case for the office can be made on the basis of two fragments of Malchos, but the evidence is thin and vague. In any case, Strabo is not known to have played a military role in supporting Basiliscus' regime, though his cooperation may have freed up units under the MMT to march against Zeno in 476 (see p. 50).[79] In any case, he was reappointed to the position of MMP in 478 following Zeno's return to the throne. Malchos once again reports the terms of his agreement with Zeno, this time in a clearer way: "that he take one of the two generalships at the court" (λαβεῖν δὲ τὴν ἑτέραν τῶν δύο στρατηγιῶν τῶν περὶ βασιλέα).[80] He continued as MMP until 479, when he lost the post as a result of his support for Marcianus' failed putsch.[81] This was the same Marcianus whom Malalas says had been made MMP following his marriage to Leontia, Leo's daughter (see p. 140).

Theoderic Strabo's second term as MMP overlapped with that of **Armatus**, who was appointed to the position in 475/6.[82] According to Malalas, "at that time Verina [Leo's widow, Ariadne's mother] appointed [Basiliscus] emperor and consul along with Armatus, who had been advanced by Basiliscus to senior praesental general," that is, he was made MMP I.[83] When Zeno began his return from Isauria in 476, Basiliscus "sent Armatus, the praesental general, with all the military forces that he had in Thrace, Constantinople, and the palace."[84] Armatus swore not to betray Basiliscus, which he then promptly did, extracting from Zeno a perpetual military command and the appointment of his son as Caesar. What command Armatus was given by Zeno is confused in the sources. Thurn's edition of Malalas specifies that Armatus was made "general of the east," but the editor, based on the evidence of the *Paschal Chronicle*, has here supplied the word "east" (ἕως), which is omitted from several manuscripts. However, the *Paschal Chronicle* identifies the position as "praesental general

[78] Theophanes, *Chronographia* a.m. 5970, p. 126.12–13: οἰκειωθεὶς τῷ Βασιλίσκῳ καὶ στρατηγὸς ὑπ᾽ αὐτοῦ γεγονώς. For Strabo as MMP under Basiliscus, see Heather, *Goths and Romans*, 273–274.
[79] See Malchos, *History* fr. 14 and 18.1. The *PLRE* uses this evidence to argue for Strabo as MMP under Basiliscus: *PLRE* II, 1079.
[80] Malchos, *History* fr. 18.4; date: Heather, *Goths and Romans*, 258.
[81] Ioannes of Antioch, *History* fr. 234.4.
[82] He is also called Armatios, Harmatos, and Harmatios: *PLRE* II, 148–149 (Armatus).
[83] Malalas, *Chronicle* 15.3: ἡ δὲ αὐτὴ Βηρίνα ὅτε αὐτὸν βασιλέα ὠνόμασεν καὶ ὕπατον μετὰ Ἁρμάτου προαχθέντος παρὰ Βασιλίσκου στρατηλάτου τοῦ μεγάλου πραισέντου.
[84] Malalas, *Chronicle* 15.5: ἔπεμψεν Ἁρμᾶτον τὸν στρατηλάτην τοῦ πραισέντου μετὰ πάσης ἧς εἶχεν βοηθείας στρατοῦ ἐν Θράκῃ καὶ ἐν Κωνσταντινουπόλει καὶ εἰς τὸ παλάτιν. See Chapter 3 for a discussion of the identity of those units.

of the east" (στρατηλασίαν τοῦ πραισέντου ἕως), a wording that makes no sense; the information preserved in the *Chronicle* has likely been garbled in its intervening transmission.[85] Armatus reappears in our sources only once after this "lifetime appointment," namely on the occasion of his murder by Zeno in 476, at which point Malalas and the *Chronicon Paschale* both call him a "praesental general" (στρατηλάτης πραισέντου).[86] It appears that Zeno was, after a fashion, a man of his word.

As Theoderic Strabo was moving in and out of his praesental command and Armatus was securing his lifetime appointment, **Theoderic the Amal**, who would go on to establish the Ostrogothic kingdom in Italy in 493, also served his first term as MMP.[87] Malchos, when describing Theoderic Strabo's agreement with Zeno in 478, reports that, once the terms of the deal were agreed, "the emperor removed the kinsman of Valamir [i.e., Theoderic the Amal] from office and made Theoderic [Strabo] general in his place."[88] Because the office of MMP is specifically mentioned among the terms of Strabo's deal just a few lines prior, the generalship in question is almost certainly that of MMP. Unfortunately, we cannot say with certainty when Theoderic the Amal first became MMP, though a fragment of Malchos, in which the Senate of Constantinople states that the empire cannot afford to pay subsidies to both the Amal and Strabo, strongly suggests that he was in office by 477.[89]

Theoderic the Amal was again made MMP in 483 as part of an agreement that allowed his followers to settle in Moesia and Dacia.[90] Theoderic may have retained that position until 486, when he revolted and, the following year, marched on Constantinople. In 488, he agreed to emigrate to Italy, where he established his kingdom securely in 493. His status during his revolt and march west are unclear, though he was presumably stripped of office during his revolt.

Our next candidate is **Martinianus**, a general who replaced Illus, Zeno's *magister officiorum*, as the leader of a large army that the emperor had assembled to deal with Theoderic Strabo in 478.[91] After Illus was removed, the army grew mutinous and was disbanded on the suggestion of

[85] Malalas, *Chronicle* 15.5 (p. 302.42 with Thurn's note ad. loc.); *Paschal Chronicle* s.a. 478 (p. 601.7–8).
[86] Malalas, *Chronicle* 15.7; *Paschal Chronicle* s.a. 484 (p. 602.20–21).
[87] *PLRE* II, 1077–1084 (Theodericus 7).
[88] Malchos, *History* fr. 18.4: παύσας τὸν Βαλαμήρου τῆς ἀρχῆς ὁ βασιλεὺς στρατηγὸν ἀντ' ἐκείνου Θευδέριχον ποιεῖται.
[89] Malchos, *History* fr. 15.
[90] Marcellinus Comes, *Chronicle* s.a. 483, confirmed by Jordanes, *Romana* 348; Malalas, *Chronicle* 15.9. All three sources explicitly attest his praesental command and, notably, Jordanes does not closely follow the language of Marcellinus here, making him a possibly independent witness.
[91] *PLRE* II, 730 (Martinianus 3).

Martinianus himself.[92] As we will discuss, this army almost certainly contained praesental units, but this does not mean that Martinianus was himself a praesental general. Its previous commander, Illus, appears to have remained *magister officiorum* during his command of it, and Malchos calls Martinianus only a στρατηγός. Moreover, even if Martinianus was MMP during this period, his only recorded act was to propose the disbanding of his army. He is a possible, but not confirmed, MMP.

According to Ioannes of Antioch, **Illus Trocundes** (not to be confused with his more famous and eponymous brother, Illus, Zeno's *magister officiorum*),[93] was appointed as MMP to replace Theoderic Strabo following the latter's support for Marcianus in 479.[94] The duration of his command is uncertain. The *PLRE* argues that he remained as MMP until joining his brother Illus' rebellion against Zeno in 484, citing an inscription on a bronze tube that was found in Syria and dated to 482–484.[95] However, this inscription calls Illus only an MVM.

In addition to the two Theoderics, Armatus, and Illus Trocundes, we know of one more MMP in the 480s. In 485, **Longinus**, the brother of Zeno who had been held captive in Isauria by Illus (Zeno's *magister officiorum*) returned to the capital and was made "senior praesental general" (στρατηλάτης πραισέντου μεγάλου), that is, MMP I.[96] Although Zeno subsequently waged a campaign against Illus and his Isaurian followers, command of that army appears to have been given to the MMO, Ioannes the Scythian, and no source mentions a role for Longinus.[97] The *PLRE* argues for Longinus leading a campaign against the Tzanoi during the 480s, but the evidence for this is an undatable and off-hand reference in Prokopios' *Buildings*, and four other Longini with military credentials are known to have been active prior to the reign of Justinian.[98] It is unclear for how long Zeno's brother Longinus retained his post, but certainly not past his banishment by Anastasius in 491.[99]

---

[92] Malchos, *History* fr. 18.2–3.
[93] *PLRE* II, 1127–1128 (Appalius Illus Trocundes). For his brother, see *PLRE* II, 586–590 (Illus 1).
[94] Ioannes of Antioch, *History* fr. 234.4: Ὅθεν ὁ βασιλεὺς Θευδέριχον τὸν Τριαρίου παραλύσας τῆς ἀρχῆς, Τροκούνδην προχειρίζεται.
[95] *PLRE* II, 1127; the inscription is *L'Année épigraphique* 1972 (for years 1969–1970) 172, no. 609: *Fl(auius) Appalius Illus Trocundes, uir inl(ustris), | com(es) et mag(ister) utr(ius)q(ue) mil(itiae), patr(icius) et cons(ul) o|rd(inarius).*
[96] Malalas, *Chronicle* 15.12: ὁμοίως δὲ καὶ ὁ Λογγῖνος ὁ ἀδελφὸς τοῦ βασιλέως ἐγένετο στρατηλάτης πραισέντου μεγάλου εὐθέως καὶ ὕπατος. The dating is based on his consulship in 486. *PLRE* II, 689–690 (Longinus 6).
[97] *PLRE* II, 602–603 (Ioannes Scytha 34).
[98] Prokopios, *Buildings* 3.6.23. For other Longini, see *PLRE* II, 687 (Longinus 1), 688 (Longinus of Cardala 2), 688 (Longinus of Selinus 4), and 689 (Longinus 5).
[99] Ioannes of Antioch, *History* fr. 239.3.

The betrayals, usurpations, and assassinations that characterized the office of MMP during the reign of Zeno give way, with the accession of Anastasius, to a relatively stable succession of men in the office. The earliest attested office-holder under the new emperor is **Ioannes the Hunchback** (*gibbus* or κυρτός), who held it while leading Anastasius' Isaurian war in 492.[100] This command makes it likely that Ioannes the Hunchback is the Ioannes named as MMP in a law published in January 492.[101] As with many MMPs, it is unclear when his tenure in office ended, though Theophanes the Confessor implies that he served throughout the Isaurian war, which lasted until 498.[102]

We next find MMPs attested during the Persian war of 502–506, specifically **Patricius** and **Hypatius** in 503 (the latter was the emperor's nephew, who would be executed following the Nika Insurrection in 532).[103] Prokopios calls both men "commanders of the soldiers in Byzantion" (οἱ τῶν ἐν Βυζαντίῳ στρατιωτῶν ἄρχοντες), which was a way of referring to the position of MMP in Greek, and we are told that they led a combined army of 40,000 soldiers on the eastern frontier.[104] Due to his apparent incompetence, Hypatius was recalled in the winter of 503/4, but his soldiers appear to have remained behind and were placed under the command of his replacement, the MMP **Pharesmanes**, in 505.[105] Pharesmanes is not claimed as an MMP by the *PLRE* despite being explicitly named as Hypatius' successor by the *Chronicle* of pseudo-Joshua the Stylite, which was written by a well-informed author close to the events in both time and place. Pharesmanes is also given the title στρατηγός by Theophanes.[106] The *PLRE* has him replace Areobindus as MMO in 505, claiming that the *Chronicle* has confused Areobindus and Hypatius and supporting this interpretation by arguing that Prokopios likewise confused the two men when reporting the recall of Areobindus in the winter of 503/4.[107] But the

---

[100] Malalas, *Chronicle* 16.3, specifically names the office as "praesental general" (στρατηλάτης πραισέντου). Ioannes of Antioch, *History* fr. 239.5 confirms his command of the war but not his office. He is *PLRE* II, 617–618 (Ioannes qui et Gibbus).
[101] *CJ* 12.35.18.   [102] Theophanes, *Chronographia* a.m. 5986, p. 139; and 5988, p. 140.
[103] *PLRE* II, 577–581 (Hypatius 6) and 148–149 (Patricius 14).
[104] Prokopios, *Wars* 1.8.2, confirmed explicitly by Malalas, *Chronicle* 16.9. Numbers in pseudo-Joshua the Stylite, *Chronicle* 54. For an overview of this conflict through the sources, see Greatrex and Lieu, *The Roman Eastern Frontier*, 62–81. For our narrative, see Chapter 3.
[105] Recall: Theophanes, *Chronographia* a.m. 5998, p. 148, who misdates these events by a year. Pharesmanes: pseudo-Joshua the Stylite, *Chronicle* 88. *PLRE* II, 872–873 (Pharesmanes 3).
[106] Theophanes, *Chronographia* a.m. 5997, p. 146. Trombley and Watt, *The Chronicle of Pseudo-Joshua the Stylite*, 108 n. 503, are right to accept the plain meaning of the *Chronicle*, contra *PLRE* II, 872–873 (Pharesmanes 3), which says that Celer, the *magister officiorum*, had succeeded to the praesental command.
[107] Prokopios, *Wars* 1.8; *PLRE* II, 578, 873, and 143–144 (Areobindus Dagalaiphus Areobindus 1).

PLRE has invented a problem where none need exist. Anastasius could have recalled both Hypatius and Areobindus to report on the disastrous campaigning season of 503, then retained Hypatius while sending Areobindus back to the front in time for the spring campaign of 504.[108] The *magister officiorum* Celer, who had also been sent to the front, similarly reported in-person to the court during the winter of 504–505.

Nor is there any reason to assume that **Celer**, who was given command of the war in 504, was made MMP. The *PLRE* entry for Pharesmanes says that Celer replaced Hypatius as MMP. Yet neither Celer nor Pharesmanes appear as MMPs in the fasti of the *PLRE*, and Celer's own entry identifies him only (and correctly) as *magister officiorum* during this period.[109] Thus, following the plain testimony of the sources, Pharesmanes was promoted to MMP in 505 and seems to have stayed in this command at least until the construction of Dara.[110] Patricius, meanwhile, remained in his MMP command through the end of the war.[111] He is attested back in Constantinople in 512 when, along with the *magister officiorum* Celer, he unsuccessfully attempted to pacify a rioting crowd. Our sole source for this event, Marcellinus Comes, calls both Patricius and Celer only senators, so we cannot be sure whether Patricius was still MMP.

The *PLRE* argues that **Hypatius** may have been MMP again in 514 – he had been MMT in the meantime – when he was sent to confront the rebel Vitalianus in Thrace. Our sources are vague on his office in 514, but we are told that he was assisted by a new MMT named Alathar, which at least rules out that office.[112] The vagueness regarding Hypatius' position in our sources suggests that Anastasius had given him an empty title, perhaps *magister militum vacans*, so that Hypatius might gain credit for a victory but not contribute to a defeat by actually commanding any armies. Hypatius' record as a general was dismal.[113] **Patricius** also reappears during Vitalianus' revolt. According to Ioannes of Antioch, Patricius, described here only as a general (στρατηγός), was sent to negotiate with the rebel.[114] Malalas adds that Anastasius attempted to send Patricius, again simply called general (στρατηλάτης), against Vitalianus, but Patricius demurred, citing his former friendship with the rebel.[115] It is possible that Patricius was MMP during this

[108] Pseudo-Joshua the Stylite, *Chronicle* 87–88.
[109] Compare *PLRE* II, 872–873 (Pharesmanes 3) with 275–277 (Celer 2).
[110] Pseudo-Joshua the Stylite, *Chronicle* 90, 97.
[111] Marcellinus Comes, *Chronicle* s.a. 503; pseudo-Joshua the Stylite, *Chronicle* 87.
[112] Ioannes of Antioch, *History* fr. 242.6.
[113] For a summary of the sources for his command in 514, see *PLRE* II, 579. For the rebellion of Vitalianus, see Chapter 4.
[114] Ioannes of Antioch, *History* fr. 242.3.   [115] Malalas, *Chronicle* 16.17.

period, in fact during the entire period between 503 and 514, but we receive no direct confirmation of that. In a crisis, it would not be surprising to see Anastasius calling upon inactive military personnel and Malalas, who is usually keen to identify praesental generals, is uncharacteristically vague about Patricius' command during Vitalianus' revolt. Patricius appears once more in 518 during the struggle over Anastasius' successor, when he is once again identified simply as a general (στρατηλάτης) and supported as a candidate for the throne by the soldiers of the *scholae*.[116]

A dubious MMP is **Ioannes, son of Valeriana**, who was active during the reign of Anastasius.[117] He is attested in Malalas and Ioannes of Antioch, but only during Vitalianus' attack on Constantinople. He appears as a στρατηλάτης with consular status in an embassy to Vitalianus during the usurper's first march on Constantinople, and reappears during his last attack, refusing, along with Patricius, to take command of the emperor's forces against the rebel.[118] Yet Malalas, despite being a consistent source when it comes to labeling MMPs, does not give Ioannes the title, and none of Ioannes' actions would have been unusual for a high-ranking MM. On balance, then, we have opted to exclude him from the list.

The next confirmed MMP is the same **Vitalianus** against whom Hypatius and Patricius were fighting back in 514.[119] Reconciled to the regime of Justin in 518 as a fellow partisan of the Council of Chalcedon, Vitalianus was made MMP before being murdered by the regime during his own consulship in 520.[120] His only attested activity during this period is in Church affairs, helping to end the Acacian Schism (between Rome and Constantinople). Vitalianus may have overlapped in his position as MMP with the future emperor **Justinian**, though Justinian's tenure of this office is not certain for 520.[121] However, we can be certain that Justinian was MMP by 521 from the testimony of his consular diptych.[122] Once again, it is not clear when Justinian gave up the position of MMP. There are no other certain MMPs during the reign of his uncle Justin I (518–527).

---

[116] Konstantinos VII, *Book of Ceremonies* 1.102 (ed. Dagron and Flusin, vol. 2, 435).

[117] *PLRE* II, 608 (Ioannes 60). The *PLRE* erroneously identifies Ioannes as a relation of the emperor Anastasius, citing Ioannes of Antioch, *History* fr. 242.14 (= fr. 214e.13 of the older edition used by the *PLRE*), but the relative in question is the emperor's nephew, and erstwhile MMP, Hypatius, who was in Vitalianus' custody.

[118] Embassy: Ioannes of Antioch, *History* fr. 242.14. Refusal: Malalas, *Chronicle* 16.16.

[119] *PLRE* II, 1171–1176 (Vitalianus 2).

[120] MMP: Jordanes, *Romana* 361; Euagrios, *Ecclesiastical History* 4.3; Malalas, *Chronicle* 17.5, 17.8.

[121] Both are called *magister militum* in the *Collectio Avellana* no. 230: *filii quoque uestri magistri militum Uitalianus ac Iustinianus*. Prior to this point, Justinian referred to himself primarily as *comes*: see Hormisdas, *Letter* 68 (p. 864), dated to 519. *PLRE* II, 646 (Petrus Sabbatus Iustinianus 7).

[122] Delbrueck, *Die Consulardiptychen*, 141–142: *mag(ister) eqq(uitum) et p(editum) praes(entalis)*.

In the reign of Justinian, the *PLRE* identifies three men as MMP who we do not believe held the office. The first of these are **Leontius** and **Phocas**, two men addressed in Justinian's *Constitutio Haec* and *Constitutio Summa*, the imperial constitutions that initiated and promulgated the first *Justinianic Code* in 528 and 529 respectively.[123] Among the men charged with this task we find Leontius and Phocas, both of whom are addressed as MM in both laws. The *PLRE* makes them praesental generals on the basis of their presence in Constantinople, though oddly the fasti of *PLRE* III marks only Leontius' praesental status as questionable, despite the assignment for both men resting on identical evidence. In any case, we do not consider holding the title of MM while present in the city of Constantinople to be sufficient evidence for a praesental command, especially when their only attested actions were purely legal and administrative. As generals, they were quite likely *vacantes* or perhaps even *honorarii*. The third dubious praesental general under Justinian claimed by the *PLRE* is **Constantianus**, whose tenure is marked as questionable in the fasti and whose entry simply describes him as an MVM.[124]

In 528, the emperor Justinian created a new military command to oversee Roman forces in Armenia. The law creating the office of *magister militum per Armeniam et Pontum Polemoniacum et gentes* (MMA) is preserved in the *Codex* and is addressed to the first man to hold the new office, **Sittas**, who is identified by the newly created title.[125] We are told by both Justinian and Malalas that the new army was made up in part of praesental forces, although it is not clear whether Sittas held a praesental command prior to his appointment as MMA. Our narrative sources, writing about the aftermath of the battle of Kallinikon in 531, describe Sittas as a praesental general in charge of the forces in Armenia. It appears that he commanded the formerly-praesental-but-now-Armenian field army in his capacity as praesental general.[126] He continued to hold the position as late as 536, when he, along with two other men, is addressed as MMP in the Greek text of *Novel* 22, a marriage law that has several sections relevant to soldiers.[127] It is not clear if Sittas was still MMP two years later when he died fighting in Armenia.

---

[123] *PLRE* II, 673–674 (Leontius 27) and *PLRE* III, 1029 (Phocas 1).

[124] *PLRE* III, 334–337 (Constantianus 2) and 1501 (fasti).

[125] *CJ* 1.29.5; the date is also in Malalas, *Chronicle* 18.10; see *PLRE* III, 1160–1163 (Sittas 1).

[126] Prokopios, *Wars* 1.15.3: Σίττας δὲ ἀρχὴν μὲν τὴν στρατηγίδα ἐν Βυζαντίῳ εἶχε, παντὶ δὲ τῷ ἐν Ἀρμενίοις στρατῷ ἐφειστήκει; Malalas, *Chronicle* 18.60: καὶ ἐντυχὼν τοῖς γράμμασιν ὁ βασιλεὺς Ἰουστινιανός, κελεύσας διὰ γραμμάτων Τζίττα τῷ στρατηλάτῃ πραισέντου ἐν Ἀρμενίᾳ διάγοντι καταλαβεῖν τὴν ἀνατολὴν πρὸς συμμαχίαν.

[127] Justinian, *Novel* 22, epilogue: Ἐγράφη τὸ ἰσότυπον Τζίττᾳ τῷ ἐνδοξοτάτῳ στρατηγῷ τοῦ θείου πραισέντου, ἀπὸ ὑπάτων καὶ πατρικίῳ.

Of the two men listed alongside Sittas as praesental generals in *Novel* 22, one, **Maxentianus**, is otherwise unknown.[128] We argue in Chapter 4 that this was likely an honorary appointment, as the existence of the praesental armies in this period is increasingly in doubt. The other, **Germanus**, was, like Justinian himself, a nephew of the previous emperor, Justin I.[129] Germanus is not otherwise attested as MMP, but he was an accomplished general according to Prokopios and may have retained this position during the various campaigns that he carried out for Justinian before his death in 550. There is no evidence that he commanded actual praesental units on these missions.

After Germanus, there are only two men we can confirm as praesental generals during the reign of Justinian. The first is the Armenian **Artabanes**, who assumed the position after being recalled from Africa in 546/7.[130] He was stripped of his office after being suspected of conspiring against Justinian in 548/9 and later served as MMT.[131] Artabanes may have narrowly overlapped with the final MMP attested for the reign of Justinian, **Suartuas**.[132] A Herul resident in Constantinople, Suartuas was sent by Justinian to rule the Heruls when they asked for a king. He was subsequently deposed and fled to Constantinople where he was made MMP in 548/9,[133] presumably as a consolation prize. In 552, he was one of five generals in command of an army campaigning in the Balkans, but his office at that time is unspecified.[134] By this point in his reign, Justinian was clearly using the position of MMP as an empty court title with which to reward foreign nobles. As we argue in Chapter 4, the praesental armies no longer existed in their mid-fifth-century form. The office of their commander had become essentially a court rank.

We have evidence for the appointment of only one praesental general after 552, **Komentiolos**, a general of the emperor Maurikios (582–602), who was made MMP in 585 following his success against some Slavs in Thrace. The office is explicitly mentioned by the historian Theophylaktos, who treats it as if it were a court honor that enhanced Komentiolos'

---

[128] *PLRE* III, 864 (Maxentianus).   [129] *PLRE* II, 505–507 (Germanus 4).

[130] His post is explicitly specified in Prokopios, *Wars* 7.31.10; Addition to Marcellinus Comes, *Chronicle* s.a. 547; Jordanes *Romana* 385; see *PLRE* III, 125–130 (Artabanes 2).

[131] Prokopios, *Wars* 7.32.51 and 7.39.8 (MMT); Jordanes, *Romana* 385.

[132] *PLRE* III, 1205 (Suartuas).

[133] Prokopios' narrative of his career is broken up: *Wars* 6.15.32–36, 7.35.43 (date), and 8.25.11 (praesental command).

[134] Prokopios, *Wars* 8.25.11.

generalship.[135] Komentiolos continued to campaign against the Slavs after that, and there is some debate about whether he was the general of that name who was sent to Spain in 589 (he likely was not).[136] As always, it is unclear when his tenure of the MMP position ended. As we argue in Chapter 4, he was likely the recipient of an empty title, the praesental armies having been dismantled and dispersed more than thirty years prior, during the reign of Justinian.

Following the death of Justinian, the *PLRE* claims only two men as MMPs, but for these we feel there is insufficient evidence. The first is a **Germanos**, about whom the fasti express doubt and who is assigned to 582. However, the entry cited by the fasti, "Germanus 2," refers to an otherwise unknown bodyguard of Ioannes Troglita attested in 546/7 solely by a line from Corripus' epic poem *Ioannes*.[137] The right Germanos is probably the emperor Tiberios Konstantinos' son-in-law, whose entry describes him as MVM only on the basis of his description as στρατηγός.[138] This is insufficient to claim a praesental appointment. The final doubtful MMP is **Bonos**, who was charged with the defense of Constantinople during the emperor Herakleios' desperate campaigns against Persia in the 620s.[139] Bonos is identified variously as στρατηγός and μαγίστρος in the sources, and the *PLRE* makes a tentative argument for his status as MMP based solely on his presence in Constantinople. Once again, the evidence is insufficient.

Thus, of the forty-seven men who are claimed as praesental generals by either Demandt or the *PLRE*, only the following withstand scrutiny (with one addition, Pharesmanes). Most of the rest were just "generic" generals, a category that was always larger than has hitherto been realized. We include men for whom a good case can be made, even if they are not confirmed, with a question mark after their names. We also add their numbers in the relevant volumes of the *PLRE* for convenience of reference. The dates reflect the minimal period during which it is plausible to believe that they held the command, though it may have extended backward or forward in time, as our sources rarely disclose the entire duration of their tenure of office.

---

[135] Theophylaktos, *History* 1.7.4: διά τοι τοῦτο καὶ στρατηγὸς ὑπὸ τοῦ αὐτοκράτορος αὖθις χειροτονηθεὶς ἀποστέλλεται καὶ Ῥωμαϊκαῖς ἀξίαις λαμπρύνεται τήν τε τοῦ πραισέντου τὴν παρὰ Ῥωμαίοις λεγομένην ἔνοπλον ἡγεμονίας τιμὴν ἀποφέρεται. He is *PLRE* III, 321–322 (Comentiolus 1).

[136] "Comenciolus" in Spania province: *CIL* 2: 3420; see Wassiliou-Seibt, "From *magister militum* to *strategos*," 791 n. 16.

[137] *PLRE* III, 527 (Germanus 2).   [138] *PLRE* III, 529 (Germanus 5).

[139] *PLRE* III, 242–244 (Bonus 5).

Revised Fasti of the *magistri militum praesentales* (East)

440s	Apollonius 3
449	Anatolius 10
Mid-5th	Aspar?
ca. 470?	Zeno 7
ca. 470?	Marcianus 17
473	Theoderic 5 Strabo
475–476	Armatus
478	Theoderic 7 the Amal
478	Martinianus?
478–479	Theoderic 5 Strabo
479	Illus Trocundes
483–486	Theoderic 7 the Amal
485	Longinus 6
492–498	Ioannes 93 the Hunchback
503–506	Patricius 14
503–504	Hypatius 6
505	Pharesmanes
520	Vitalianus 2
521	Justinian
530–536	Sittas 1
536	Germanus 4
536	Maxentianus
546/7	Artabanes 2
548/9	Suartuas
585	Komentiolos (Comentiolus 1)

The Date of the Notitia dignitatum: Oriens

No account of the late Roman army can avoid the evidence and thorny problems of the *Notitia dignitatum* (henceforth *ND*), an illustrated document of uncertain date listing civilian offices, administrative structures, and military commands for both the west and east Roman empires. The *ND* lays out the "canonical" five-army system for the eastern empire, including the units under each command, that is generally agreed to have come into effect about 395 and that we, by contrast, argue came into effect later, toward the end of the reign of Theodosius II (408–450), in the 440s. This redating of the *ND* is an important corollary of our argument. Here we argue that there is no firm *terminus ante quem* for the *ND*, in particular for its military content, prior to the reign of the Leo I (457–474). This *terminus* is based on the attestation in a papyrus of a unit called the *Leontoclibanarii*, a unit of elite armored cavalry generally assigned to field armies and likely named for the emperor Leo. It is absent from the *ND* and first attested in 487 but was almost certainly raised or renamed during Leo's reign.[1] This unit can reasonably be expected to have been included in the *ND Or.* if it had existed at the time of that document's creation, thus its absence serves as the earliest *terminus ante quem* for the *ND*. As this conclusion differs significantly from the scholarship on the issue, a discussion of the earlier dates proposed by scholars in the past is necessary.

Most scholars understand the *ND* to be a composite document with the eastern and western materials drawn up at different times by the relevant officials, namely the *primicerii notariorum*, the officials in charge of maintaining the lists of high officeholders and perhaps issuing their codicils of appointment, for the eastern and western empires

---

[1] *Leontoclibanarii*: Palme, "Die Löwen des Kaisers Leon." Palme argues that we should identify the *Leontoclibanarii* with a unit of *equites clibanarii* attested in 454. However, there were a number of such units listed in the *ND Or.* and, even if this identification is accepted, it does not affect our dating of the *ND Or.* to the 440s.

respectively.[2] It should be noted, however, that the document itself gives no explicit indication of its author or function and that a wide variety of origins have been imagined for it, from a working document in the imperial administration to a lavishly illustrated imperial gift.[3] In addition to these uncertainties, the *ND Occ.* is thought to shows signs of later revision, making it impossible, on this reading, to assign a single date to the text as a whole.[4] The *ND Or.* is generally, but not universally, thought to have been composed at a single moment in the 390s or soon thereafter and taken to the west, where the document as we have it now was completed and preserved.[5] This narrative of the text's transmission reflects a broader trend in scholarship on the *ND*, which has traditionally focused on the western list, especially on the light that it can cast on Roman military retrenchment during the fifth century.

Given the uncertainty surrounding the origins and function of the *ND*, a recent line of scholarship has, following Peter Brennan, attempted to understand it as a primarily ideological document.[6] According to this interpretation, the *ND* is meant to project coherence and stability during a period of imperial dissolution (between east and west, and within the west separately). However, this line of argument both overstates the degree of imperial decline in the west prior to the Vandal conquest of Carthage in 439 and provides only a superficial ideological interpretation of the document.[7] Administrative documents, by their nature, present an image of order, so it is not clear what this reading adds to our understanding of this document in particular. Moreover, recent research has confirmed through papyrological evidence that the *ND Or.* contains accurate information about the units and command structure of Egypt.[8] Whatever its

---

[2] For the *primicerii*, see Jones, *Later Roman Empire*, 574–575; their role in composing the *ND*: ibid. 1417; Bury, "The *Notitia Dignitatum*," 131–133; Clemente, *La "Notitia Dignitatum*," 360–377. The function of the office is reconstructed largely on the basis of the *ND* itself, which placed under their supervision *omnis dignitatum et amministrationum notitia, tam militarium, quam civilium*: ND Or. 18.3–4; see also Claudian, *Epithalamium of Palladius and Celerina* 83–91; and Justinian, *Novel* 8 (notitia).

[3] For a survey and typology of the major schools of thought on the *ND*, see Purpura, "Sulle origini della Notitia Dignitatum." A new theory about the backstory of the text was subsequently proposed by Scharf, *Der Dux Mogontiacensis*, 309–316 (it was presented to the western usurper Ioannes upon his accession on November 20, 423).

[4] Kulikowski, "The *Notitia Dignitatum*," has recently revived the argument for a single original document of which only the western section was later updated.

[5] For the manuscript tradition, see Reeve, "The *Notitia Dignitatum*."

[6] Brennan, "The *Notitia Dignitatum*"; Kulikowski, "The *Notitia Dignitatum*," 358–361.

[7] For the western empire during this period, see Heather, *The Fall of the Roman Empire*.

[8] Kaiser, "Egyptian Units." These data are reconcilable with our revised date, see p. ix n. 2.

purpose and history, then, the *ND Or.* contains genuine information about the military forces of the east Roman empire.

For our purposes, the origins and function of the *ND* are secondary to the question of when it was produced or, more precisely, when the military arrangements described by the *ND Or.* came into effect. After all, scholars reconstruct the narrative of the text's origin, as well as its history and function, by bringing their imagination to bear on the document within the parameters of the dates to which they assign it. This is a critical point: Scholarly narratives of how and when the text was produced, updated in the west, and survived until Carolingian times, are exercises of the imagination. If the dates change, then so must these imaginative reconstructions, but the latter can by no means be used to check a new dating proposal if it is based on empirical evidence, as ours is. Instead, a new dating proposal should elicit a new round of reconstructions of the history of text. Put differently, in light of the evidence we have assembled demonstrating the late implementation of the military arrangements described by the *ND Or.*, the burden of proof now falls on those who wish to maintain an early date for the text, and this appendix seeks to increase that burden by addressing, in advance, likely counterarguments based on previous scholarship. Thus, objections cannot be raised to our dating based on past narrative reconstructions of the origin of the text.

We must acknowledge at the outset two recurring problems that bedevil attempts to pin down the date of the *ND*. The first of these is the problem of updating. Because scholars have struggled to align the details of the *ND* with any specific date, especially an early date, almost every reconstruction requires some portion of the *ND* to have been updated after the bulk of the document was first drafted. This updating is often linked to proposed (but unproven) theories of the *ND*'s history as a working document. However, this approach to the text creates an essentially unfalsifiable argument according to which the bulk of the *ND Or.* is assumed to date to 395 or shortly thereafter and anything that must come from after that date is explained as a later update.

The second problem builds on the first. It is a broad tendency in the scholarship to postulate or detect habits or tendencies in the text of the *ND*, harden them into formal rules, and then use the inevitable exceptions to these rules to excavate the compositional history of the text. In this way, the inconsistencies in the evidence for a particular theory of the document are transformed into supporting evidence or prompt the development of entirely new "rules" for how the text came into being.[9] All of these reconstructions rely

---

[9] See, in particular, Jones and Hoffmann on the lists of military units, discussed later.

on unproven and likely unproveable assumptions about the nature and history of the document.

Absent a major breakthrough in research on the *Notitia*, there is no way to know who wrote it, under what circumstances, or for what purpose. Our ignorance on these fundamental points imposes harsh limits on how we can use the document as a source for studying the later empire. But, as we will see, the failure to accept these limits has led generations of scholars to build sophisticated interpretive structures on evidentiary grounds that cannot support them.

In what follows, we aim to analyze the *ND* within the bounds imposed by our ignorance of the text's origin and purpose. Our goal is not to propose a definitive date for either half of the *ND* or the document as a whole. Instead, we seek to demonstrate through a survey of proposed *termini ante quem* that nothing prevents us from dating the eastern portion of the document, particularly its description of the five field armies, to the 440s, a date that we have settled on because it finally brings the *ND Or.* into alignment with all the available evidence for contemporary military arrangements in the eastern empire, as demonstrated by this book.

General Considerations

Before delving into the technical details of the *ND*, we first need to address some general issues that, in our mind, vitiate the traditionally early dating of the *ND Or.* to about 395. The first is that many scholars are entirely candid about the fact that the text cannot be precisely dated between 395 and 450 (or even later), but nevertheless persist in supposing an early date. This commitment to an early *ND Or.* then requires scholars to develop elaborate arguments to overcome the difficulties that their dating creates (as we will show). This indicates to us that the early date is not a conclusion at which otherwise impartial arguments have arrived, but rather a reflection of scholarly bias in favor of the consensus date. We will not speculate here as to the reasons for that bias beyond noting that it has proven useful for many historians to have a document that serves as a kind of "foundational charter" or even "quasi-constitutional layout" for the (ultimately permanent) division of the empire between east and west that occurred in 395.

Second, some scholars believe that, as the *ND* is a Latin document, it makes more sense for it to have had a western transmission, an assumption that is then used to argue that only the western portion of the text continued to be updated in the later fifth century. In assuming this, they forget that the bureaucracy and court of the eastern empire at Constantinople continued to operate in Latin down to at least 535, when Justinian began to issue laws primarily in Greek. The *Theodosian Code*, for example, was compiled in Constantinople in 438, drawing on legal texts from both east and west, and then sent from Constantinople to Rome. Mere Latinity should not be a factor in the reconstruction of the text's history before the seventh century. In a similar vein, scholars have pointed to the manuscript tradition, which can be traced back to a ninth-century Carolingian codex, as evidence that the *ND* was fundamentally a western document. But the eastern empire was not sealed off from the west between 395 and the 800s: It intervened to establish western emperors in the fifth century, reconquered and occupied Africa and Italy beginning in the sixth century, and then later engaged in diplomacy with the court of Charlemagne and his successors. This is to say nothing of the *Theodosian Code*, a Latin document of eastern origin completed within a decade or so of our proposed date for the *ND Or.* and under the same emperor that is also preserved in a western manuscript tradition.[10] Like Latinity, the circumstances of the text's transmission, which are unknown and unknowable before the ninth century, cannot clinch (or even vaguely support) any argument concerning the document's origin or, on that basis, its date.

Third, contrary to the scholarly bias in favor of an early *ND*, the major differences in the document between the organization of the western and eastern military commands can be taken to suggest that the original template of the text reflects decades of divergent evolution between the two halves of the empire and thus was drawn up long after 395. It is difficult to understand why Theodosius I would set up a western command dominated by two *magistri militum*, one of infantry and one of cavalry (using fourth-century titles and practices) but divide the eastern command among five *magistri utriusque militiae* who are given specific regional commands. It is easier to imagine that those differences evolved over the years after 395, as Stilicho established the precedent for unitary command in the west, where *magister utriusque militiae* effectively meant supreme commander, while the quite different politics of the eastern court resulted over time in a more regionally divided (and so more easily controlled) military hierarchy. On its face, the *ND* appears to describe those two systems only after the complex and tense political history of the empire in the years and decades after 395 had given rise to them.

---

[10] Matthews, *Laying Down the Law*, 85–97.

We will now survey the major arguments that have been advanced in favor of an early date for the *ND Or.* and argue that they are wrong, unconvincing, or inconclusive. When those arguments fail, we must fall back on the actual empirical evidence for armies and titles, which favor a date in the 440s.

Internal Inconsistencies in the Notitia

As mentioned, scholars have often attempted to reconstruct the compositional history of the *ND* on the basis of "problems" detected in the text. Most go further and attempt to use these problems as a basis for recovering the date of the *ND* or at least the bulk of its information. The logic generally runs as follows: Scholars detect a problem, they link that problem to a datable event, usually about 395, and then they argue that the problem is a result of the hasty or incomplete editing of *ND*, which allows them to date the majority of the document prior to the datable event in question.

For example, the *ND Or.* identifies two provinces governed by *correctores*, Augustamnica and Paphlagonia, and these provinces appear under the jurisdiction of their appropriate *vicarii*, but they do not appear in the list of provinces under the supervision of the praetorian prefect of Oriens (PPO).[11] Because these offices are first attested independently of the *ND* in 393 (Augustamnica) and 395 (Paphlagonia), the omission is understood to be the result of hasty editing and indicates a Theodosian date for the bulk of the *ND Or.*[12]

To begin with, we should note that the identification of problems in the *ND* is fraught. To designate something a problem we must assume that it either reflects a genuine factual error or undermines the function of the document. However, the *ND* is our sole source for a large amount of information about the structure of late Roman government, therefore its contents can only rarely be confirmed. If we had the ability to verify its contents, we would not depend on it nearly so much. In the same vein, scholars necessarily base their arguments on completely hypothetical reconstructions of the nature and function of the *ND*, which cannot be confirmed by any empirical means. Thus it is impossible to tell whether the inconsistencies they detect would have posed any problems for the author(s) or user(s) of the *ND*. In reality, these "problems" reflect failures of the text to align with modern scholarly standards of consistency, but these cannot be used to argue

---

[11] Augustamnica: *ND Or.* 1.27, 2.24–29, 23.14; Paphlagonia: *ND Or.* 1. 28, 2.30–40, 25.17.

[12] Augustamnica: *CTh* 1.7.2; Paphlagonia: ibid. 2.8.22; dating: Jones, *Later Roman Empire*, 1417; Clemente, *La "Notitia dignitatum,"* 31, 57–58; Ward, "The Notitia Dignitatum." For a slightly later dating on the same grounds, see Clemente, "La *Notitia Dignitatum*," 125–126.

for hasty or incomplete corrections and therefore cannot be used to establish the date of the document. Taken together, these two factors make any arguments based on these "problems" inherently suspect.

To illustrate these points, consider the case of the *correctores* described above. We cannot actually prove that their provinces were under the supervision of the PPO (and, therefore, that they "should" have been listed under his bailiwick in the *Notitia*) because we have virtually no evidence regarding the matter. Moreover, Roman government was full of ad hoc or exceptional bureaucratic structures. To be clear, we are not arguing that Augustamnica and Paphlagonia were not under the PPO, only that we cannot prove that they were at the moment when the document was drafted, whenever that was. Therefore, we cannot prove that their absence from the corresponding list in the *ND* is an error or a problem. Even if provinces governed by *correctores* were under the PPO, we nevertheless remain uncertain about the purpose or function of the *ND*, so it is conceivable that the omission of these two provinces did not affect the document's utility, which would undermine the case for a hasty revision and therefore the value of this "problem" for establishing the date of the document.

More can be said against the value of the *correctores* as evidence for the date of the *ND Or.*, and we return to the matter later, but our point here is more general. Apparent errors or internal inconsistencies in the *ND Or.* cannot be used to date the document unless we have independent evidence that is able to 1) confirm that they were in fact errors, and 2) provide grounds for dating them. In these matters, the *ND* cannot be checked against itself in order to provide that information. Other commonly cited problems include the governors of provinces in Dacia and Macedonia being listed under Illyricum, the varying composition of the staffs assigned to different *magistri militum*, and the governors of Isauria and Arabia being given both civilian and military offices. But these "problems" or "inconsistencies" (if that is what they are) can just as well have been features of the late Roman imperial administration as of the *ND* itself.

The Transfer of Dalmatia

J. B. Bury, who began the modern discussion of the *ND*'s date, proposed a *terminus ante quem* of 437 on the grounds that the province of Dalmatia is listed in the *ND Occ.* and not the *ND Or.*[13] Bury believed that Dalmatia had been transferred from the western to the eastern empire by Valentinian

[13] Bury, "The *Notitia Dignitatum*," 142.

III on the occasion of his marriage to Licinia Eudoxia, the daughter of Theodosius II. The evidence for this transfer comes from two sixth-century sources, Cassiodorus' *Variae* and Jordanes' *Romana*, both of which refer to the transfer of "Illyricum" from the western to the eastern empire on the occasion of this wedding.[14] However, Illyricum is frequently a broad and vague term in late Roman usage, and we cannot be certain that either source understood the term to include the territory of Dalmatia specifically. Moreover, we now have an inscription from Lopud in modern Croatia definitively demonstrating that Dalmatia was under the authority of the western Roman empire in 452.[15] So, even if Dalmatia was ceded to the east in 437, it was back in western control by 452, and thus this event does not provide a firm *terminus ante quem* for the *ND Or.*

The comes *of Pontus*

A. H. M. Jones, whose magisterial survey in *The Later Roman Empire* includes an appendix that sought to counter Bury and down-date the *ND Or.*, posits a firm *terminus ante quem* of 413 on the basis of a law of that year that refers to a *comes* of Pontus, an office not attested in the *ND Or.*[16] His assumption seems to be that the office came into being after the *ND* was created. Jones simply does not consider the possibility that the office might instead predate the *ND*. In addition to being an argument from absence, and thus inherently weak when dealing with a document of uncertain function such as the *ND*, this *comes* is exceptional in several respects. First, dioceses, as Jones himself knew, were typically governed by a *vicarius*, which is precisely the office listed for the diocese of Pontus in the *ND Or.*, and we have explicit attestation of *vicarii* for that diocese in 435 and 471/2.[17] Thus the *ND* faithfully reflects later fifth-century practice. Moreover, Pontus continued to be governed by *vicarii* until the reign of Justinian, who briefly abolished and then restored the office.[18] If we understand the *comes* of Pontus in the law of 413 to be a civilian official, then, given the consistent attestation of *vicarii* in the diocese after 435, the likeliest interpretation is that the *comes* of the law of 413 represents an *earlier* moment in the administrative history of the province. That is, Jones' *terminus ante*

---

[14] Cassiodorus, *Variae* 11.1.9; Jordanes, *Romana* 329.
[15] Basić and Zemon, "What Can Epigraphy Tell Us."
[16] Jones, *Later Roman Empire*, 1420; the law is *CTh* 6.13.1.
[17] Jones, *Later Roman Empire*, 373–374; *ND Or.* 1.32 and 25.1; 435: *CTh* 6.28.8.2; 471/2: *CJ* 12.59.10.4.
[18] Jones, *Later Roman Empire*, 374; Justinian, *Novel* 8.3.

quem is more likely a *terminus post quem*, and this would favor our argument.

However, the *comes* of Pontus mentioned in 413 was almost certainly a military official, probably a *dux* for whom the title of *comes* was an honorific. The law in question is concerned with the status of retiring *praepositi* and *tribuni* of the *scholarii*, that is, with military affairs. Moreover, *CTh* 6.14.3, which was issued on the same date and was likely part of the same original law as *CTh* 6.13.1 (i.e., the law of 413 under discussion), makes *comites primi ordinis* ("*comites* of the first rank") who have performed certain military duties equal in status to "the *duces* who have administered in the other provinces except Egypt and Pontus (*Pontica*)."[19] The implication is that the military affairs of Egypt and Pontus were also managed by *duces* in 413, who held the honorary rank of *comites primi ordinis* and were to retain greater prestige than the ad hoc *comites* with whom the law is concerned. There is robust documentary evidence for such *comites et duces* in Egypt in the late fourth century as well as an inscription, firmly dated to the joint reign of Honorius and Arcadius (395–408), that references a *comes primi ordinis et dux* of Isauria.[20] In other words, the *comes* of the law regarding Pontus is best understood as reflecting the rank of the individuals who held the office (*duces* treated for legal purposes as *comites*), rather than as a blanket promotion of the status of their office. It is therefore not the sort of thing that is listed in the *ND*.

This reconstruction fits our broader evidence for the military administration of the diocese of Pontus, which consistently points toward its command by *duces* rather than *comites*. The *ND Or.* lists only one military commander in the diocese, the *dux* of Armenia, who has command of four units in Pontus.[21] Similarly, a law of Leo I dated to 471/2 lists the *duces* and *comites* in the empire at that time and we find there a *dux* in Armenia I and II and a *dux* for the provinces of Pontus Polemoniacus and Helenopontus; these are all the provinces in the diocese of Pontus with military officials.[22] The *dux* of Pontus Polemoniacus continued to operate until he was subordinated to the new *magister militum per Armeniam* by Justinian in 538.[23]

---

[19] *CTh* 6.14.3: *ducibus, qui praeter Aegyptum et Ponticam in aliis provinciis administraverint, adaequamus.*
[20] Egypt: Zuckerman, "Comtes et ducs," 137; Isauria: *MAMA* 3: 73.   [21] *ND Or.* 38.15–19.
[22] On this evidence, Jones himself argued for a *dux* of Pontus in the fifth and sixth centuries: *Later Roman Empire*, 44, 271.
[23] *CJ* 1.29.5; for the creation of the MMA, see Chapter 4.

To summarize, if we understand the *comes* of Pontus in 413 to be either a civilian or military official, then his appointment is a unique deviation from established patterns in the period and so cannot provide a firm *terminus ante quem* for the *ND Or.* Moreover, if we understand him as a *dux* with the rank of *comes primi ordinis* – a combination that is widely attested leading up to the publication of *CTh* 6.13.1 and 6.14.3 – then we have a *dux* of Pontus attested in 413 whose office does not appear in the *ND Or.* There are a multitude of potential explanations for this discrepancy, but the likeliest explanation is that the *dux* of Pontus mentioned in 413 is identical to the *dux* of Armenia mentioned in the *ND Or.*[24] Both *CTh* 6.13.1 and 6.14.3 refer to *Pontica*, not *Pontus Polemoniancus* or *Helenopontus*. The distinction is important as *Pontica* is used in the *ND Or.* to refer only to the diocese of Pontus, and this usage is echoed by the text of *CTh* 6.13.1. The *ND Or.* specifically states that the *dux* of Armenia is the only *dux* in the diocese of Pontus.[25] Thus the law of 413 and the *ND Or.* agree that there is a single *dux* in the diocese of Pontus but differ slightly in his nomenclature. In any case, there is nothing here that provides a firm *terminus ante quem* for the *ND Or.*

Macedonia Salutaris

In addition to the *comes* of Pontus, Jones also finds evidence for a *terminus ante quem* in the province of Macedonia Salutaris, whose existence is attested only by the *ND Or.* This province is given a *praeses* for its governor in the index of the *ND*, but, in the chapter on the praetorian prefecture of Illyricum, this province has its territory divided between the province of Epirus Nova in the diocese of Macedonia and the province of Praevalitana in the diocese of Dacia.[26] The traditional interpretation of this evidence is that the *ND Or.* was composed around the time that the province of Macedonia Salutaris was abolished and reabsorbed into the surrounding provinces, an event dated prior to 412 on the basis of an episcopal letter (discussed on p. 164).[27] However, this interpretation faces two major problems. First, the only source for the existence of Macedonia Salutaris is the *ND* itself, so any attempt to date the document using the province is manifestly circular. Second, Macedonia Salutaris should almost certainly be identified with the later province of Macedonia Secunda, making 412 a *terminus post quem* for the *ND Or.*, rather than a *terminus ante quem*.

[24] *ND Or.* 28.1.   [25] *ND Or.* 1.49–50.   [26] *ND Or.* 1.125, 3.13, and 3.19.
[27] Jones, *Later Roman Empire*, 1420.

The first document that might shed light on the history of Macedonia Salutaris is a *Laterculus*, or list of provinces, composed by Polemius Silvius, an official at the western court whose floruit was the late 440s.[28] Despite this relatively late date, Mommsen argued that his coverage of the east Roman empire was based on an earlier source, likely from the reign of Theodosius I, and was subsequently incompletely updated.[29] Mommsen postulated this early date based on the absence from the *Laterculus* of a number of provinces attested in the *ND* (such as Macedonia Salutaris) that reflect the subdivision of earlier provinces (in this case, Macedonia).[30] These inconsistencies created a problem for Mommsen because he, like other scholars, sought to link the proliferation of provinces to the dominance of the eastern court by the eunuch Eutropius in 396–399 on the basis of an accusation in Claudian's invective poem *Against Eutropius* that Eutropius needlessly multiplied the provinces.[31] Thus, for Mommsen, the *ND* reflected Eutropius' reforms, which meant that Polemius' information must have predated the *ND*. Based on these and other inconsistencies, Mommsen conceded that Polemius' *Laterculus* was unreliable for the eastern empire and could not be assigned to a single date. In any case, it is apparent that the *Laterculus* is incapable of providing a firm *terminus ante quem* for the *ND* given the difficulties surrounding its own date and the circularity of any argument based on a comparison between it and the *ND*.

The second relevant document is the *Synekdemos* of Hierokles, another list of provinces, this one dating early in the reign of Justinian (527–565) but thought to be based on a mid-fifth-century prototype.[32] Here again, on account of its own chronological inconsistencies, the evidence of the *Synekdemos* cannot be used to definitively date the *ND*. Nevertheless, it is worth noting how much more closely the *Synekdemos* corresponds to the *ND* than does Polemius' *Laterculus*. Both the *Synekdemos* and the *ND Or.* report subdivisions of the following provinces which are not found in Polemius: Macedonia, Galatia, Cilicia, and Cappadocia. Likewise, where

---

[28] He is dated on the basis of the last entry in his *Names of All the Emperors of the Romans*, which ends with the consulship of Postumianus and Zenon in 448: Polemius Silvius, *Laterculus* 1.84 (p. 523). See also, *PLRE* II, 1012–1013 (Polemius Silvius).

[29] See Mommsen's notes accompanying his edition of the *Laterculus*, pp. 532–533.

[30] Other missing provinces include Cilicia Secunda and Cappadocia Secunda, the existence of both of which is implied by the mention of a Cilicia Prima and Cappadocia Prima at the Council of Ephesus I in 431: *ACO* 1.1.2, p. 3.14–15.

[31] Bury, "The *Notitia Dignitatum*," 135; Claudian, *Against Eurtropius* 2.20.585–588: *ne quid tamen orbe reciso | venditor amittat, provincia quaeque superstes | dividitur geminumque duplex passura tribunal | cogitur alterius pretium sarcire peremptae.*

[32] Jones, *Cities*, 514–521.

the *ND* and *Synekdemos* agree on the existence of two Syrias and three Palestines, Polemius has three Syrias: Coele, Palaestina, and Phoenice. Given the supposed dates of the archetypes of Polemius and Hierokles, these correspondences suggest a later date for the *ND Or.*, though we would not press the point too far.

These three texts, Polemius' *Laterculus*, the *ND Or.*, and Hierokles' *Synekdemos*, along with the earlier *Laterculus Veronensis* (dated to the reign of Constantine) provide a basis on which to rewrite the administrative history of Macedonia. Both the *Laterculus Veronensis* and Polemius' *Laterculus* report the existence of a single province of Macedonia, while both the *Synekdemos* and the *ND Or.* mention two Macedonias, though the *Synekdemos* calls them Prima and Secunda, whereas the *ND* calls them Prima and Salutaris.[33] In order to preserve an early date for the *ND*, or rather taking that early date for granted, many scholars have attempted to argue that Macedonia Secunda and Macedonia Salutaris were different provinces. This line of argument postulates an early division of Macedonia and the creation of Salutaris at some point between 380 and 386 followed by the reunification of Macedonia (as required by a papal letter discussed on p. 164), and then a second split into Macedonia Prima and Secunda before 449.[34] The arguments in favor of this history include the alleged early date of the *ND Or.* (ca. 395) and the difference between the names Salutaris and Secunda. In reality, this is an improbable fiction motivated by the desire to maintain an early date for the *ND*.

There is clear evidence that Salutaris was a common epithet used to distinguish between provinces with the same name, as our provincial lists amply demonstrate: Phrygia Prima and Phrygia Secunda in the *Laterculus Veronensis* are listed as Phrygia Prima and Phrygia Salutaris by Polemius, and as Phrygia Pacatiana and Phrygia Salutaris by the *ND* and *Synekdemos*.[35] Thus we can see a general evolution in the nomenclature of Phrygia in these documents, one that corresponds with external evidence: Phrygia Salutaris is found in the *Acta* of the Council of Ephesus I in 431, whereas Phrygia Pacatiana appears in the *Ecclesiastical History* of Sokrates, which was completed before 450.[36] In the *ND Or.* we likewise find Syria and Syria Salutaris, Galatia and Galatia Salutaris, and Palaestina,

---

[33] *Laterculus Veronensis* 44; Polemius Silvius, *Laterculus* 3.5.18 (p. 539).

[34] Papazoglou, *Les villes de Macédoine*, 94–98; Konstantakopoulou, Ἱστορική γεωγραφία, 74–81. The latter is based on Konstantakopoulou, "Ἡ ἐπαρχία Μακεδονία Salutaris," whose reconstruction of the territory of Salutaris (as a different and earlier province from Macedonia II) is wholly conjectural, and it accepts, dismisses, or emends the evidence of the sources in a seemingly arbitrary way.

[35] *Laterculus Veronensis* 26–27; Polemius Silvius, *Laterculus* 3.7.9–10 (p. 540); *ND Or.* 1.98–99; Hierokles, *Synekdemos* 664.6 and 676.7.

[36] *ACO* 1.1.2, p. 62.17; Sokrates, *Ecclesiastical History* 7.3.1.

Palaestina Secunda, and Palaestina Salutaris. In each of these cases, the same provinces are listed as Prima and Secunda in the *Synekdemos*, with the sole exception of the third Palestine, which is given no number or epithet.[37] Nevertheless, Palaestina Salutaris is attested in the *Acta* of Ephesus I (431) and as Tertia Palaestina Salutaris in papyri from the sixth century.[38] To conclude, Salutaris was a common and generic way to refer to newly subdivided provinces in late antiquity, which could alternately be called Secunda or Tertia.[39]

Scholars who wish to use Macedonia Salutaris to establish an early date for the *ND Or.* do so on the basis of a letter from pope Innocent I of Rome to Rufus, the bishop of Thessalonike, securely dated to 412. In this letter, Innocent lists all of the provinces in the diocese of Macedonia and Dacia that are found in the *ND Or.* except for Macedonia and Macedonia Salutaris.[40] Moreover, he reveals, through his placement of the word *et* in his list, an awareness of which provinces belong to which diocese, which again agrees completely with the *ND Or.* The absence of Macedonia from this list is understandable because Rufus, to whom the pope is writing, is the bishop of the metropolitan see of Macedonia (namely the city of Thessalonike), so the presence of his province is assumed. However, this cannot explain the absence of Macedonia Salutaris and the most reasonable interpretation of the letter is that this province did not exist in 412. However, the *ND Or.* is our *only evidence* for the existence of a "Macedonia Salutaris," so the entire case for using this letter to establish a *terminus ante quem* for the *ND Or.* relies on an a priori assumption that the *ND Or.* was composed prior to 412. This reasoning is manifestly circular.

In fact, Innocent's letter of 412 is likely a *terminus post quem* for the *ND Or.* As we have seen, Salutaris was a common epithet for subdivided provinces and used interchangeably with an ordinal designation. In 449, in the *Acta* of the second Council of Ephesus (cited in the *Acta* of the Council of Chalcedon of 451), we find a series of bishops from the province of

---

[37] *ND Or.* 2.11 and 2.20 (Syria), 2.42 and 2.51 (Galatia), 2.9 and 2.16–17 (Palestine); Hierokles, *Synekdemos* 711.1 and 712.1 (Syria), 696.4 and 697.3 (Galatia), 717.8, 719.12, and 721.1 (Palestine).

[38] *ACO* I.1.2, p. 24.33; papyri: see *inter alia*, P.Petra I.1 (AD 537), ed. in J. Frösén et al., *The Petra Papyri*, vol. I.

[39] For a survey of the evidence for the provincial epithet Salutaris in late antiquity, see Pietri, "Les provinces 'Salutaires'."

[40] Innocent, *Letter* 13.2 (= *PL* 20: 515–516): *Divinitus ergo haec procurrens gratia ita longis intervallis disterminatis a me ecclesiis discat consulendum, ut prudentiae gravitatique tuae committendam curam causasque, si quae exoriantur per Achaiae, Thessaliae, Epiri veteris, Epiri novae, et Cretae, Daciae Mediterraneae, Daciae Ripensis, Moesia, Dardaniae et Praevali ecclesias, Christo Domino annuente, censeant.*

Macedonia Prima (Μακεδονία Πρώτη).[41] Although no bishops are named from Macedonia Secunda or Macedonia Salutaris, the designation clearly implies the existence of a second province of Macedonia, which is further attested by the chronicler Marcellinus for 482 and 512, as well as by one of Justinian's *Novels* in 535.[42] Therefore, the province of Macedonia was permanently divided sometime between 412 and 449 into Macedonia Prima and Macedonia Secunda (which was alternately called Salutaris, as in the *ND*). Those who posit an early date for the *ND Or.* and take 412 as a *terminus ante quem* must argue that the province of Macedonia was split in the late fourth century (to enable an early date for the *ND Or.*), reunified just in time to avoid the pope's letter in 412, and split again before 449 in order to match the division reflected in the Council Acts. While not impossible, this reconstruction is needlessly complicated, circularly premised on an early date for the *ND Or.*, and finds external confirmation only from a vague comment in a work of poetic invective against Eutropius that does not even refer to Macedonia (namely, the vague accusation that Eutropius "multiplied provinces"). It is far likelier that Macedonia was divided only once, in the period between 412 and 449, into Prima and Secunda, also called Prima and Salutaris, and that this single division is reflected in the *ND Or.* Far from being evidence of the dissolution of Macedonia Salutaris, then, the *ND Or.* appears to reflect the moment of its creation, with a new, low-ranking governor dispatched to the province, whose territories are marked as coming from the provinces of Epirus Nova and Praevalitana.

The Order and Status of the correctores

It is widely assumed in scholarship on the *ND* that the order in which offices, provinces, and units are mentioned reflects their hierarchies of status.[43] There is something to this, especially in the military lists, where we generally find older units listed before units named after members of the Valentinian or Theodosian dynasties, and in the index of the text, where all offices of *spectabilis* rank appear before those of *clarissimus* rank. However, scholars have taken a general tendency and hardened it into an ironclad rule that can be used to excavate the compositional history, and from this the date, of the *ND*.[44] The most important example of this process involves

---

[41] *ACO* 2.1.1, pp. 79.34–80.1.

[42] Marcellinus Comes, *Chronicle*, s.aa. 482 and 517; Justinian, *Novel* 11, preface.

[43] For civilian offices: Bury, "The *Notitia Dignitatum*," 134–135; for military units: Jones, *Later Roman Empire*, 1418–1419. Virtually all modern scholarship follows their lead.

[44] The most extensive such reconstruction is Ward, "The Notitia Dignitatum," 399–414.

the *correctores* that the *ND Or.* assigns to govern the provinces of Paphlagonia in Pontus and Augustamnica in Egypt. The argument runs as follows: The post of *corrector* outranks that of *praeses*, but the index lists the *correctores* after the *praesides*, therefore the *correctores* must have been added to a preexisting document which was not subsequently updated to appropriately reflect the relative ranks of these two offices. On this reconstruction, the bulk of the index must have been drafted before 393, when a law confirms that, by that year at the latest, the province of Augustamnica was governed by a *corrector*.[45]

Although this is not a firm *terminus ante quem* for the *ND*, the *correctores* are part of the argument for dating the bulk of the *ND Or.* to the end of the reign of Theodosius I. However, it should be noted that this argument relies on unproven (and, given the state of the text, likely unproveable) assumptions about the nature and compositional history of the *ND*, especially the idea that offices of the same rank would have to be listed in order of precedence in the index. Even accepting these assumptions, however, there is no firm evidence that *correctores* outranked *praesides* in the early fifth century. *Correctores* are thought to outrank *praesides* in the fourth century on the grounds of the court ranks of attested officeholders: As a rule, the *correctores* whom we know were *clarissimi*, and thus senators, while the *praesides* were *perfectissimi*, and thus equestrians.[46] Yet, by the early fifth century, the office of *praeses* was widely associated with the rank of *clarissimus*, while an inscription from the reign of Theodosius I confirms that at least one *corrector* was merely *perfectissimus*, albeit in the western empire.[47] In other words, the relative ranks of *praesides* and *correctores* were not fixed, and the ranks implied by the order in the index of the *ND* actually matches an early fifth-century date better than a late fourth-century date, albeit on slight evidence. There is also a temporal discontinuity between the original introduction of the post of *corrector* under the Tetrarchy (late third–early fourth century), when it was generally assigned to territories in the western empire, and its reintroduction for the eastern empire in the reign of Theodosius I. All of this undermines the case for a clearly established hierarchy among these offices, especially across both halves of the empire. Their rough equivalence in status may explain why the two halves of the *ND* record different orders for *praeses* and *correctores* or it may reflect a divergence of their relative status in the two halves of the

[45] Ward, "The Notitia Dignitatum," 412; Bury, "The *Notitia Dignitatum*," 134–135; Augustamnica: *CTh* 1.7.2; the *corrector* of Paphlagonia is attested two years later: *CTh* 2.8.22.

[46] Jones, *Later Roman Empire*, 45.

[47] Jones, *Later Roman Empire*, 526–527; *perfectissimus*: *CIL* 9: 333.

empire after 395. The two offices were treated as interchangeable in Justinian's *Novels*.[48] Be that as it may, we cannot be certain enough of their relative status to confidently label the position of the *correctores* in the *ND Or.* as a discrepancy, much less use it to recover the date of the index or the document as a whole.

Finally, the law of 393 that first attests a *corrector* for Augustamnica does not institute that office but treats it as an established part of the administration. This means that the office was instituted at least a few years prior to the law, possibly many years prior to it, which in turn means that this method of dating the *ND* would push the date far earlier than most scholars would like, even proponents of an early date. 393 is already too early for some of them, especially in light of C. Zuckerman's compelling argument that the *terminus post quem* of the *ND Or.* must be 399 (see p. 174), so their arguments have to assume that *correctores* were only just recently assigned to Augustamnica in 393, but for this they have no proof.

The Hoffmann Thesis

Among the most compelling chronological indicators in the *ND* are the names of military units. Since the early empire, it had been standard practice to name or rename military units after reigning emperors or dynasties. This practice is well-represented in the *ND Or.*, which lists twenty units named after a Theodosius (either I or II) and four each for Arcadius and Honorius. The fact that no units in the *ND Or.* have names that can be linked to an emperor after Theodosius II is strong evidence for a *terminus ante quem* around 450. However, some scholars have attempted to use this information to build the case for an early date for the *ND Or.* In particular, Dietrich Hoffmann argued that the appearance of certain unit names proves that the *ND Or.* was composed prior to 395.

Hoffmann argues that the units listed under the MMP I and II in the *ND Or.* represent a distortion of the original composition of these armies, which he sets out to reconstruct. Hoffmann bases his reconstruction on two features that he detects operating in the *ND*: the pairing of units based on their armaments, history, or (most often) names and the generally parallel composition and structure of the two praesental armies. Hoffmann hardens these features into fixed rules that reflect formal policies, which allows him to reconstruct an earlier, more precisely parallel

---

[48] Justinian, *Novel* 8.33–34.

form of the praesental lists in the *ND Or.*[49] In other words, he reconstructs an earlier, more orderly structure of lists and units (and, by extension, a cleaner "proto-*ND*") by fixing the messiness that he detects in the *ND* that we have. For example, Hoffmann believes that the units of *Felices Arcadiani* and *Felices Honoriani* were originally formed in linked pairs, with each army having one unit named after each child, but always in chiastic pairs of one senior and one junior unit, so the *Felices Arcadiani seniores* and the *Felices Honoriani iuniores* operated together as did the *Felices Arcadiani iuniores* and *Felices Honoriani seniores*. He then combines this assumption with a belief that, in their original form, the two praesental armies were perfectly symmetrical in having six *vexillationes palatinae*, six *vexillationes comitatenses*, six *legiones palatinae*, and eighteen *auxilia palatina* in order to create his reconstructed list in which each of these unit pairs (*seniores-iuniores*) is found in one of the praesental armies. (In the actual *Notitia*, only the two *iuniores* units are in the praesental armies; the *seniores* of each name are under the MMO.)[50] Every element of this reconstruction is speculative, and Hoffmann's "rules" are, as far as we can see, entirely arbitrary.

In Hoffmann's (entirely hypothetical) original *Notitia* – a document, we should note, that we neither have nor have any reason to believe ever existed – units named after Arcadius and Honorius were evenly distributed between the two praesental armies, and it is on these grounds that he assigns this proto-*ND* to the reign of Theodosius; he assumes that the emperor would have named an equal number of units after each of his two sons (disregarding the fact that Arcadius, who was made Augustus in 383, was co-emperor for a decade longer than his younger brother Honorius, who was made Augustus in 393). Meanwhile, the *ND Occ.* contains many units named after Honorius, but no units named after Arcadius or Theodosius, suggesting that the western half of the *Notitia* was composed during the sole reign of Honorius and thus, for Hoffmann, after the *ND Or.* Having used this argument to establish that the *ND Or.* is older than the *ND Occ.*, Hoffmann goes on to argue that a number of units whose names appear in both lists, such as the *Comites seniores*, reflect a transfer of units, which must have moved from east to west given the relative chronology of the two lists.[51] It should be noted that Hoffmann must emend the

---

[49] For Hoffmann's proto-*ND* lists for the praesental armies, see *Das spätrömische Bewegungsheer*, vol. 1, 492–493.
[50] *Felices Arcadiani iuniores*: *ND Or.* 6.62; *Felices Honoriani iuniores*: 5.62; *Felices Honoriani seniores* and *Felices Honoriani seniores*: 7.36–37.
[51] *Comites seniores*: *ND Or.* 6.28 and *ND Occ.* 6.43.

text of the *ND* in order to create six of his eighteen duplications, usually by adding epithets to units that are not present in the text. For example, the *Victores* of the *ND Or.* are made into *Victores iuniores* in order to match the *ND Occ.*, and, in one case, Hoffmann invents a unit, the *Comites iuniores*, that is not attested anywhere in the *ND Or.*[52] Thus, he not only invents an earlier form of the document, he embellishes reality in order to make it conform to textual principles that he has invented.

In other words, Hoffmann believes that units whose names appear in both halves of the *ND*, including those that only appear in both halves on his arbitrary reconstruction, are in fact the same units and that they are being recorded twice because they moved from east to west after the composition of the *ND Or.* but before the composition of the *ND Occ.* According to him, this transfer must have happened after Theodosius I left for the west in 394, which is Hoffmann's *terminus ante quem* for the *ND Or.* (albeit excluding Illyricum), and before the death of Honorius in 423, his *terminus ante quem* for the *ND Occ.*[53] Given the tense relationship between the two empires in the early fifth century, Hoffmann argues that the most likely point for the permanent transfer of these units was early in 395, when Zosimos reports that Stilicho retained the best soldiers from the combined army that Theodosius I led to the west against the usurper Eugenius, before sending back the worst units to Constantinople.[54]

Hoffmann's massive two-volume work, published over fifty years ago, is one of the main reasons why research not only on the *Notitia* but on the late Roman army generally has languished in a largely fossilized state for the past half-century. His tomes give off an appearance of magisterial and intimidating authority and Teutonic thoroughness. Merely to understand his convoluted arguments is achievement enough, but to actually critique their basis is asking too much of the twenty-first-century scholar who is not inclined to wade through hundreds of pages of stilted German prose. The universal consensus of almost all subsequent scholars to an early date for the *ND* makes that exercise seem pointless. Why go to all the trouble? Yet in reality Hoffmann's argument relies on a series of arbitrary conjectures about the operation of the late Roman military that are by turns unproven,

---

[52] *Victores: ND Or.* 5.63; *Victores iuniores: ND Occ.* 5.185; *Comites iuniores: ND Occ.* 6.75; see Hoffmann, *Das spätrömische Bewegungsheer*, vol. 1, 25–28.

[53] Hoffmann's *terminus ante quem* for the *ND Occ.* is based in part on an erroneous dating of the Golden Gate to the reign of Theodosius II: *Das spätrömische Bewegungsheer*, vol. 1, 55–60. For the Golden Gate, see now Bardill, "The Golden Gate."

[54] This summarizes the arguments of the first two chapters of Hoffmann's work. For his own summary of these arguments, see *Das spätrömische Bewegungsheer*, vol. 1, 525–536.

unproveable, or simply wrong. The whole edifice – both Hoffmann's argument and the half-century of scholarship that is erected upon it – is a house of cards.

For example, there is no evidence to support the theory that "paired" units such as the *Felices Honoriani iuniores* (MMP I) and *Felices Arcadiani iuniores* (MMP II) were raised at the same time or given parallel postings. We do not claim that this was not the case, only that there is no evidence for it, just as there is no reason to believe that the praesental armies were once mirror images of one another. Moreover, even if we accept that such paired units were raised at the same moment and for a common purpose, there are no grounds to argue, as Hoffmann does, that we can recapture an earlier moment in the organization of the praesental armies by "restoring" as many pairings and parallels as possible. It is on these grounds, for instance, that he argues that the *Felices Honoriani seniores* and *Felices Arcadiani seniores*, both assigned to the MMO in the *ND*, were originally assigned to the MMP II and MMP I respectively, so that each praesental army would have one unit named after each of Theodosius' sons.[55] It is important to note how much weight Hoffmann's argument places on the completely conjectural and unattested proto-*Notitia* that he has reconstructed on the basis of these two features: strict parallelism and pairing. If either of these features is a mirage, did not function in the way or to the extent that Hoffmann imagines, or is an artifact of Hoffmann's mind, then his proposed original distribution of units is arbitrary and, by extension, so is his dating of the *ND Or.* because that dating relies on the concentration and relative distribution of units named after the sons of Theodosius in the praesental armies.

There is, moreover, no compelling reason to accept the features on which Hoffmann's thesis rests *unless* one wants to use them to argue for an early date for the *ND*. That is, there is no problem in need of solving, no earlier configuration of units in need of recovery, unless one assumes that the *ND* has an early date and that the *ND* that we have rests on an even earlier, slightly different (but more orderly) proto-*ND*. Thus, the argument is perfectly circular: Hoffmann assumes that the *ND Or.* reflects an early date, then postulates "rules" for the document that allow him to reconstruct a hypothetical, earlier form of the document, and, finally, he uses this hypothetical document to make the case for the early date of the *ND* that we have. This circularity is necessary, however, in order to extract a *terminus ante quem* from the names of units, information that is logically

---

[55] Hoffmann, *Das spätrömische Bewegungsheer*, vol. I, 15–16.

more relevant to the *terminus post quem* of the document. Moreover, even on its own terms his argument provides a date only for the hypothetical proto-*ND*, not the *ND Or.* that we actually have. In order to assign the extant *ND Or.* to the period before 395, Hoffmann relies on his argument for unit transfers between east and west.

Hoffmann's transfer argument is based on the fact that units with the same name appear in both lists (i.e., of east and west), but Hoffmann restricts his argument to a small selection of even these, dismissing, for instance, duplications among the frontier legions and across unit ranks.[56] It is worth noting that, absent these caveats, the full number of duplications across the entire document would make it impossible to credit the idea that every duplication represents a unique unit that was transferred between the two empires; there are simply too many.[57] Hoffmann has to restrict his use of the duplication-and-transfer argument only to those units that best suit his case for the purposes of the date that he wants to establish, and that is why he focuses almost exclusively on a few elite units of the praesental armies. Moreover, even for the duplications he considers valid, Hoffmann's reconstruction continues to rely on his assertions of parallelism and pairing, as well as the (false) theory that units with the epithet *seniores* are strictly from the west, while those called *iuniores* are strictly from the east.[58] It is illustrative of Hoffmann's approach that he considers units of *iuniores* to be categorically inferior to *seniores* and he views this inferiority as a major factor in the Roman defeat at Adrianople.[59] Hoffmann's transfer theory is also undermined by the continued presence of at least one of his transferred units in the east in the ninth century, the *Victores.*[60]

Hoffmann makes no positive case for why we should understand these duplications as transfers (rather than, for instance, as the division of previously integral units into two descendant units with the same name) other than by making a vague appeal to the unique status of units in the *comitatus*. Finally, his entire history of these units relies on a single line of Zosimos, in which the historian accuses Stilicho of retaining the cream of

---

[56] Hoffmann, *Das spätrömische Bewegungsheer*, vol. 1, 25.
[57] For a list of duplicate units, see Hoffmann, *Das spätrömische Bewegungsheer*, vol. 2, 8–9.
[58] For the erroneous nature of this assumption, see Kulikowski, "The *Notitia Dignitatum*," 370–371; for the epithet *seniores* before 364, see Drew-Bear, "A Fourth-Century Latin Soldier's Epitaph."
[59] Hoffmann, *Das spätrömische Bewegungsheer*, vol. 1, 425–429.
[60] Hoffmann, *Das spätrömische Bewegungsheer*, vol. 1, 27; *ND Or.* 5.63; Konstantinos VII, *Book of Ceremonies* 2.45. Hoffmann is aware of this passage and discusses the other unit mentioned, the *Theodosiaci*, but appears to have missed the *Victores*.

the eastern army for himself in 395, a polemical and unreliable claim that cannot bear the weight of Hoffmann's argument.[61]

None of Hoffmann's arguments provide a firm *terminus ante quem* for the *Notitia dignitatum* because they are based on unproven or unproveable suppositions about the military organization of the later Roman empire and on unit names that more logically reflect a *terminus post quem* than *ante quem*. Moreover, a later date for the *ND* can account for all of the features Hoffmann highlights and even provide more compelling explanations than his. To start with, there is nothing unusual about units that might have been raised together under Theodosius I being stationed far apart almost fifty years later, toward the end of the reign of Theodosius II. Likewise, if we assume that the duplications of units in the two halves of the *ND* represents an original splitting of those units, then we can account for the large number of units that appear in both lists with different statuses. Far from being unrelated coincidences, as Hoffmann would have it, these duplications represent the divergent trajectories of these units during the first half of the fifth century. Admittedly, these reconstructions are entirely theoretical and there is no positive evidence for them, but the same is true for Hoffmann's dating scheme. However, our proposal is recommended by its correspondence to the independent evidence for the military structure of the *ND Or.*, on which our argument ultimately rests: empirical verification rather than abstract schematizing.

Hoffman's arguments for the date of the *ND* must be discarded along with many other arguments he advances on similar grounds. We hope that the study of the late Roman army will soon be freed from the stultifying influence of his work.

Unit Order and Status

As mentioned, there is a general tendency in the *ND* to list offices and units in order of seniority. In the *ND Or.*, for instance, offices of *spectabilis* rank precede those of *clarissimus*, while military units that are named by the Tetrarchic emperors or that are otherwise attested prior to the reign of Theodosius I generally come before those named after members of the Theodosian dynasty. Once again, however, scholars have hardened a general tendency into an absolute rule and applied it to all of the institutions in the *ND*, including civilian offices, military units, and even

---

[61] Hoffmann, *Das spätrömische Bewegungsheer*, vol. 1, 33–41; Zosimos, *New History* 5.4.2; see Chapter 2 for our discussion of this passage.

provinces. In the case of military units, our particular interest here, Jones went so far as to elaborate (totally unattested) rules for promotion and status.[62] Meanwhile, deviations from the expected order are explained by Jones through a system of demotions (labeled by other scholars as "errors") and analyzed to reconstruct the history of the text, as in the case of the *correctores* discussed earlier.[63] The imposition of this system of precedence serves a critical function for scholars who want to maintain an early date, for it allows them to use the names of units, which are logically *termini post quem* for the document, to extract *termini ante quem*. Yet, because there is no positive evidence for the system they propose, this theoretical hierarchy cannot be used to provide a firm *terminus ante quem* for the *Notitia*.

Units Labeled nuper constituta

The *ND Or.* contains six units, all of them *limitanei*, listed with the notation *nuper constituta* or *constituta*.[64] Of these, two are named after emperors, the *Alae Theodosiana* and *Arcadiana*, both of which were under the command of the *comes* of Egypt. Scholars have interpreted the phrase *nuper constituta* to mean "recently formed" and, based on the names of the units, argued that the "recently" in question must refer to the period between Arcadius' accession as Augustus in 383 and Theodosius I's departure for the west in 394.[65] Yet even if we accept that the phrase refers to the creation of these units, there is nothing to prevent both of these units from having been established under Theodosius II and named after the reigning emperor and his father.

However, it is much more likely that the participle *constituta* should be understood to refer to the stationing, rather than the initial recruitment, of these units. This usage is common in the *Theodosian Code* for both soldiers and other officials, indicating that it was a standard idiom in government circles.[66] Moreover, this explains why four of the units designated as

---

[62] Jones, *Later Roman Empire*, 1418.

[63] Demotions: Jones, *Later Roman Empire*, 1418; other errors: Ward, "The Notitia Dignitatum," 404, 408.

[64] *Nuper constituta*: *ND Or.* 28.20–21 (*ala Theosodiana, ala Arcadiana*); *constituta*: *ND Or.* 34.37 (*ala idiota*), 35.34 (*ala prima salutaria*), 38.25 (*ala castello Tablariensi*). At *ND Or.* 38.26 there is a textual difficulty with the unit that Seeck reconstructs as the *ala prima praetoria nuper constituta*, but multiple manuscripts have as *pretorica* or *praetorica*.

[65] Lot, "La *Notitia Dignitatum*," 310; Clemente, *La "Notitia dignitatum*," 58. However, Clemente himself notes that the term *constituta* is likely a reference to the stationing, rather than the formation, of these units: ibid. 40–41. Jones follows this reading of *nuper constituta* but relies on the order, and thus supposed seniority, of the units for dating, despite citing several exceptions: Jones, *Later Roman Empire*, 1419.

[66] Soldiers: *CTh* 7.4.2, 7.4.3, 7.4.15, 8.5.30, 8.5.33.1; other officials: ibid. 1.28.4, 6.22.5, 6.36.1.

constituta or *nuper constituta*, including the *Alae Theodosiana* and *Arcadiana*, are not listed alongside a place-name as is virtually every other unit of the *limitanei* in the *ND Or.* The *ND* is therefore likely recording that these units have been reassigned to a region (not newly created) but have either not arrived or have not yet taken up their permanent station. In either case the adverb *nuper* cannot be used to establish the date of the *ND.*

Evidence for a post-395 ND Or.

Our survey demonstrates that there are no firm *termini ante quem* for the eastern *Notitia* that require us to date its contents earlier than the reign of Leo I (457–474). However, the arguments for a later date are not merely negative, and we survey here the evidence that argues positively for a date after 395.

C. Zuckerman has demonstrated that the promotion of the *praefectus Augustalis* of Egypt to the court rank of *spectabilis* can be dated rather precisely between 398 and 399 on the basis of Theophanes and papyrological evidence.[67] Because this is the rank of the office in the *ND Or.*, this promotion appears to be a firm *terminus post quem* for the *ND Or.*[68] Note, by the way, that this discovery invalidates the whole of Hoffmann's mode of reasoning about the text, unless one resorts to supplementary arguments about later redactions, which is an ad hoc approach deployed in *Notitia* studies solely in order to dispense with later evidence in an ostensibly early text.

Tassilo Schmitt has argued for a similar date based on his reconstruction of attacks on the region of Cyrene reported in the letters of Synesios (late fourth–early fifth century). According to Schmitt's reconstruction, Cerealius, the military commander whom Synesios accuses of incompetence and corruption, was made the first independent *dux Libyarum* in 405, an arrangement that is reflected in the *ND Or.*[69] It must be admitted, however, that Schmitt's chronology of the office cannot be definitely established on the basis of current evidence.

The most concrete evidence for the date of the *ND Or.* is papyrological, though it can generally be brought to bear only in Egypt. A. M. Kaiser, comparing units attested in papyri to those found in the *ND Or.*, has

---

[67] Zuckerman, "Comtes et ducs," 143–147. Zuckerman goes on to link this promotion to a broader promotion of civilian officials during this period and proposes a date of 401 for the *ND Or.* on the basis of other arguments, but the *terminus post quem* is what interests us here. Zuckerman's date has found widespread acceptance in recent scholarship, for example, Kaiser, "Egyptian Units," 245 n. 13.

[68] *ND Or.* 23.8. [69] Schmitt, *Die Bekehrung des Synesios*, 607–621; the office is *ND Or.* 30.1–6.

demonstrated that there are no units attested in the papyri from the period around 400 that are not also listed in the *ND Or.* as posted to Egypt or under the command of a *magister militum* (whose units, as we have seen, could be widely dispersed). Kaiser looks specifically at the period around 400 because she follows the dating of Zuckerman and Schmitt, but her conclusions hold true even if we redate the *ND Or.* to the 440s. In fact, only one military unit is first attested in the papyri in the period between 399 and the 440s: the *Transtigritani* under the MMO.[70] So the papyrological evidence is entirely reconcilable with a late dating of the *ND Or.*

There is also positive evidence for a significantly later date. The *ND Or.* mentions a *tabularium dominarum augustarum*, an office apparently charged with managing the finances of the empresses under the supervision of the *castrensis sacri palatii.*[71] Bury took the plural *augustarum* literally as evidence for the presence of two *augustae* and argued for a *terminus post quem* of 423, as this was the first year in which Eudocia and Pulcheria both held the title Augusta.[72] Scholars have pushed back on this argument in a variety of ways. Jones asserted that if the *ND* dated from after 414, then we would expect to find a full *cubiculum* in it for the Augusta and suggests that the plural *augustarum* was the result of a mistake or correction by a western updater of the text.[73] But this is an argument from absence concerning a text of uncertain purpose that is defective at many points, including for the office of *praepositus sacri cubiculi*, and thus it is inherently weak. Meanwhile, his theory of a western mistake/correction is pure supposition, as is the suggestion by Ward that the plural *augustarum* was a result of custom or tradition.[74] None of these attempted refutations is

---

[70] Kaiser, "Egyptian Units," 245–249. Kaiser also lists the *Felices Theodosiaci Isauri*, but see our discussion at pp. 62–64.

[71] *ND Or.* 17.8.   [72] Bury, "The *Notitia Dignitatum*," 136.

[73] Jones, *Later Roman Empire*, 1419–1420. Jones bases his argument for a full *cubiculum* on the mention of a *castrensis* for Eudoxia, Honorius' empress: Markos the Deacon, *Life of Porphyrios of Gaza* 37 (although we now know that this is a later and problematic text: Barnes, *Early Christian Hagiography*, 260–284); on the mention of two *praepositi* who received gifts from Cyril of Alexandria in the 430s: *ACO* 1.4, p. 224; and on a story in Theophanes the Confessor about the struggle between Eudocia and Pulcheria for control over a *praepositus*: Theophanes, *Chronographia* a.m. 5940, pp. 99–100. However, there were multiple different officials with the title καστρήσιος, so the identity of the specific official under Eudoxia is unclear (cf. *Life of Daniel the Stylite* 32). The same is true for the *praepositi*, whose precise titles are not mentioned. And, moreover, the struggle between Eudocia and Pulcheria dates to 447/8 – Jones redates it without explanation – and it was in any case likely connected to a fictional set of stories, something like the Romance of Theodosius and Eudocia, on which Malalas and, through him, Theophanes relied. For this "Romance," see Malalas, *Chronicle* 14.3–8; *Paschal Chronicle* s.aa. 420, 421, 444; Ioannes of Nikiou, *Chronicle* 87; and Braccini, "An Apple."

[74] Ward, "The Notitia Dignitatum," 400–401; endorsed by Kulikowski, "The *Notitia Dignitatum*," 368 n. 28.

more compelling than the plain meaning of the text as written, though again we would not insist on it too much. Ultimately, our argument for a late *ND* is empirical: It is only in the 440s that the military system it describes is reflected in other sources (narrative, legal, papyrological, etc.).

Concluding Remarks: Notitia *of the West and* Notitia *of the East*

Much scholarship on the *Notitia* tries to generate the text's "backstory": who wrote the text and why, in what historical context, and how it was subsequently transmitted.[75] Yet all such stories – and many have been devised – are purely conjectural and cannot be used as a basis for further research. Ultimately, these exercises in narrative fiction have to be restrained by the likeliest dating of the text, even if this eliminates back-stories that we would like to be true, such as that the *Notitia* served as a blueprint for the division of the empire in 395. By following a rigorous empirical approach that, for the first time, compares the testimony of this text to all the external evidence for the command structures of the eastern empire, we conclude that only a date in (or slightly after) the 440s can work for the eastern *Notitia*. If that means that we have to jettison existing backstories, so be it. But we are not inclined to add to the store of fiction about the text with a new narrative of how it was generated. Among other concerns, our analysis has had little to say about the western *Notitia*, so that a unified theory is beyond our reach. But our research on the evolution of the late Roman army does offer new insights into the divergent trajectories of east and west, as reflected in the *Notitia* and other sources, and this might point others toward a "unified theory" of the *Notitia* as a whole.

Specifically, at the top of its command structure the western *Notitia* preserved the "conservative" title forms of the fourth century, that is, *magister peditum* and *magister equitum*, and to them is added a *magister equitum per Gallias* (for Gaul). This was the sort of arrangement that a Julian, Valens, or Theodosius I might have. By contrast, the eastern *Notitia* reflects an army that had developed beyond this fourth-century model in both its titles and organization, with three regional *magistri militum* and two *magistri militum praesentales*. The last *possible* attestation of *magistri peditum* and *magistri equitum* in the east comes in 409 (Varanes and Arsacius liaising between the palace and the populace, who were angry over a grain shortage). But even so, the trend in the east was already for all

---

[75] Most recently: Scharf, *Der Dux Mogontiacensis*, 309–316 (presented to the western usurper Ioannes on November 20, 423).

generals to be MMs or MVMs (with the latter office rarely "unpacked" as *magister equitum et peditum*, for example regarding Plinta [ca. 418–438] and in Justinian's consular diptych). However, *magistri peditum* and *magistri equitum* are still attested in the west as late as 423 and possibly beyond.[76] This divergence between east and west is compelling evidence that the *Notitia* was drawn up after the two halves of the empire had evolved along separate trajectories for some time: One (the west) had, at least on paper, stuck to older forms, while the other (the east) had evolved in a different direction. It is hard to imagine that Theodosius I devised this asymmetrical diptych. There is a simpler solution, namely that the *Notitia* reflects decades of divergent evolution between east and west.

We do not mean to suggest that, just because it preserves conservative forms, the western *Notitia* was necessarily drawn up before the eastern one. The western empire may have simply kept those forms active for longer, while the eastern empire developed in a different direction. We also note that the evident divergence in the military structures described by the two halves of the *Notitia* stands in contrast to the unified bureaucratic logic of the document. Both halves of the *Notitia* discuss similar offices in a similar order and preserve similar information. This points to an abiding conception of the unity of the empire when the *ND* was finalized; after all, its final version encompasses both halves of the empire in as parallel a fashion as possible. This is consistent with the relations between Rome and Constantinople in the mid-fifth century. It was, after all, Theodosius II who installed Valentinian III on the western throne in 425. The *Theodosian Code* was created in Constantinople and sent to Rome, where it was accepted by the Senate. The east repeatedly sent armies to the west, making many efforts to save it from its spiraling dissolution and conquest by the barbarians. The most spectacular of these attempts, albeit a catastrophic failure, was made by Leo I in 468. Leo also sent the eastern senator Anthemius (467–472) to be emperor of the west in 467. Many more such ties can be mentioned, but these suffice to show that the two halves remained close enough to explain why a conjoined and unified *Notitia* made sense.

However, the tension remains between the relatively unified structure of the document, which points to a shared bureaucratic context, and the divergent information about the structures of command in east and west. Perhaps the most striking example of this tension is found in the lists of military units. In the east, as we have seen, the *Notitia* lists individual units under their respective *magistri* (in the case of field army units) or local

---

[76] See p. 178.

officials (in the case of *limitanei*). The eastern *Notitia* does not preserve a "master" list of military units. In the western half, on the other hand, units and subcommanders such as *comites* and *duces* are found in a master list under either the *magister peditum* or *equitum*, and then in lists organized by province. This reduplication is noteworthy because it both distinguishes and unifies the two halves of the *Notitia*. That is, both halves are attempting to preserve the same information about military units, namely their chain of command and station, but do so in different ways reflecting their divergent organizations.

Complicating any analysis of the broad similarities of the two halves of the *Notitia* is the simple fact that the document reflects two empires that shared a common organizational heritage. They also periodically interfaced with one another, as when both empires brought their legal codes into theoretical uniformity in 438. As a result, it is difficult to distinguish between similarities imposed by the author(s) of the *Notitia* in pursuit of the document's agenda (whatever that may be), similarities that persisted as a result of the conservatism of Roman imperial government, and similarities that resulted from the mutual adoption of the *Theodosian Code*. This final complication has not previously been considered by scholars because it falls far outside the consensus date for the composition of the *Notitia*. But, in light of the arguments advanced in this book, scholars must now consider if and how the information contained in the western *Notitia* can be reconciled with an eastern document that reflects military arrangements around 450.

Unfortunately, a full comparison of western practice to the "theory" of the western *Notitia* has yet to be carried out and is beset with problems. One problem with the western empire is that its practice may have deviated from its theory (treating here the western *ND* as the "theory"). In the fifth century, the western empire periodically came under the power of a single general, often called a "generalissimo" in the scholarship, who concentrated military authority in his hands and essentially ruled from behind the throne. The first of these men was Stilicho (395–408), but in the sources Stilicho is consistently called an MM or MVM, never *magister peditum* or *magister equitum*, though he had at least one subordinate *magister equitum*.[77] After Stilicho's violent overthrow, the western military leadership seems to have reverted to a division between *peditum* and *equitum* commands until at least 423.[78] Yet

[77] *PLRE* I, 855 (Stilicho); see the *magister equitum* Iacobus in 401–402: *PLRE* II, 581–582 (Iacobus 1).
[78] Vincentius was *magister equitum* in 408: Zosimos, *New History* 5.32.4; *PLRE* II, 1168 (Vincentius 1). Turpilio was *magister equitum* later in 408 with Varanes as *magister peditum*: Zosimos, *New History* 5.36.3; *PLRE* II, 1133 (Turpilio) and 1149 (Varanes 1). Ulphilas was *magister equitum* in 411 (on campaign) while Constantius (the later Augustus) was *magister peditum*: Sozomenos, *Ecclesiastical*

periodically, a generalissimo would appear with an "overarching" command-title MVM or MM, such as Constantius in the 410s, who went on to become Augustus briefly in 421.[79] After the mid-420s, the titles MVM or MM seem to have become common among western generals, though careful and nuanced sifting would be required to recover official usage from the some-times loose terminology used by literary sources.[80]

This does not mean, however, that the western *ND* can or should be dated precisely to the interludes during which the army of the western empire was led in practice by *magistri peditum* and *equitum* (to match the "theory" of its *Notitia*). The generalissimos who periodically concentrated the power of both offices into their hands as MVMs may have been doing so independently of the separation of those two positions in theory; in fact, maintaining the theory that there were really two commands, albeit concentrated now in the hands of one MVM (which literally meant "*magister peditum* and *magister equitum* combined"), may have enhanced their authority and marked it as extraordinary (in both senses). The dating of the western *Notitia* has always posed thornier problems of dating and interpretation than its eastern counterpart, such as, for example, the fact that parts of the text seem to date to the early 420s while the document treats Britain as still belonging to the empire.[81] We happily leave these problems, along with the backstory of the *Notitia* as a whole, to others. For our purposes, as in the history of this period, the east can stand on its own.

History 9.14.2; *PLRE* II, 1181 (Vlphilas) and 322 (Constantius 17). Crispinus was *magister equitum* in 423: *CTh* 2.23.1; *PLRE* II, 329 (Crispinus).

[79] These titles are attested for him in the sources cited by the *PLRE* II, 322 (Constantius 17).

[80] Especially for Castinus in the early 420s (*PLRE* II, 269: Castinus 2); Constantius Felix in the late 420s (*PLRE* II, 461–462: Constantius Felix 14); and Aetius down to 455 (*PLRE* II, 22–28: Aetius 7).

[81] The latest gateway into the problems of the western *Notitia* is Scharf, *Der Dux Mogontiacensis*.

Bibliography

Primary Sources

We reference below the critical editions of the Greek and Latin sources that we
have used, along with the English or other modern translations of sources in other
eastern languages. For the convenience of the readers, we also reference English
translations of the Greek and Latin sources, but we have generally quoted our own
translations, unless otherwise indicated in the notes.

Agathias, *Histories*; ed. R. Keydell, *Agathiae Myrinaei Historiarum Libri Quinque*
(Berlin 1967 = *Corpus Fontium Historiae Byzantinae* vol. 2); English trans.
J. D. Frendo, *Agathias: The Histories* (Berlin 1976 = *Corpus Fontium Historiae
Byzantinae* vol. 2A).

Ambrose, *Commentary on the Gospel of Luke*; ed. and French trans. G. Tissot,
Ambroise de Milan: Traité sur l'Evangile de S. Luc. 2 vols. (Turnhout 1971–2006
= *Sources chrétiennes* 45 and 52); English trans. T. Tomkinson, *Exposition of the
Holy Gospel According to Saint Luke* (Etna, CA 1998).

Ambrose, *Letter 1**; ed. M. Zelzer, *Sancti Ambrosi Opera, Pars X: Epistulae et Acta;
Tomus III Epistularum Liber Decimus, Epistulae extra Collectionem, Gesta Concili
Aquileiensis* (Vienna 1982 = *Corpus Scriptorum Ecclesiasticorum Latinorum* 82.3) =
PL 16: 1113–1121 (*Letter* 1.41); English trans. J. H. W. G. Liebeschuetz, *Ambrose of
Milan: Political Letters and Speeches* (Liverpool 2005 = *Translated Texts for
Historians* vol. 43).

Ammianus Marcellinus, *Res gestae*; ed. W. Seyfarth, *Ammiani Marcellini Rerum
gestarum libri qui supersunt*, 2 vols. (Leipzig 1978); text and English trans.
J. C. Rolfe, *Ammianus Marcellinus*, 3 vols. (Cambridge, MA 1935–1940 = Loeb
Classical Library).

Anonymous, *Funeral Oration for John Chrysostom*; ed. M. Wallraff with Italian trans.
by C. Ricci, *Oratio Funebris in Laudem Sancti Iohannis Chrysostomi: Epitaffio
attribuito a Martirio di Antiochia (BHG 871, CPG 6517)* (Spoleto 2007 = *Quaderni
della Rivista di bizantinistica* vol. 12); English trans. T. D. Barnes and G. Bevan,
The Funerary Speech for John Chrysostom (Liverpool 2013 = *Translated Texts for
Historians* vol. 60).

Basil of Caesarea, *Letters*; ed. and French trans. Y. Courtonne, *Saint Basile: Lettres*, 3 vols. (Paris 1957–1966); text and English trans. R. J. Deferrari, *Saint Basil: The Letters*, 4 vols. (London and New York 1926–1934 = Loeb Classical Library).

Cassiodorus, *Variae*; ed. T. Mommsen, *Cassiodori Senatoris Variae* (Berlin 1894 = *Monumenta Germaniae Historica: Auctores Antiquissimi* vol. 12); English trans. M. S. Bjornlie, *Cassiodorus, The Variae: The Complete Translation* (Oakland, CA 2019).

Chronicon Paschale; ed. L. Dindorf, *Chronicon paschale*, vol. 1 (Bonn 1832 = *Corpus Scriptorum Historiae Byzantinae*); English trans. M. and M. Whitby, *Chronicon Paschale 284–628 AD* (Liverpool 1989 = *Translated Texts for Historians* vol. 7).

Chronicle to 1234 7–8; English trans. A. Palmer, *The Seventh Century in the West-Syrian Chronicles* (Liverpool 1993 = *Translated Texts for Historians* vol. 15) 111–221.

Claudian; ed. J. B. Hall, *Claudii Claudiani Carmina* (Leipzig 1985 = *Bibliotheca scriptorum graecorum et romanorum Teubneriana*); text and English trans. M. Platnauer, *Claudian*, 2 vols. (Cambridge, MA 1922 = Loeb Classical Library).

Collectio Avellana; ed. O. Guenther, *Epistulae imperatorum, pontificum, aliorum . . . Avellana quae dicitur Collectio*, 2. vols. (Prague 1895–1898 = *Corpus scriptorum ecclesiasticorum Latinorum* vol. 35).

Consular History of Constantinople; ed. and English trans. R. W. Burgess, *The Chronicle of Hydatius and the Consularia Constantinopolitana: Two Contemporary Accounts of the Final Years of the Roman Empire* (Oxford 1993).

Euagrios, *Ecclesiastical History*; ed. J. Bidez and L. Parmentier, *The Ecclesiastical History of Evagrius* (London 1898); English trans. M. Whitby, *The Ecclesiastical History of Evagrius Scholasticus* (Liverpool 2000 = *Translated Texts for Historians* vol. 33).

Eunapios, *History*; ed. and English trans. R. C. Blockley, *The Fragmentary Classicising Historians of the Later Roman Empire: Eunapius, Olympiodorus, Priscus and Malchus*, 2 vols. (Liverpool 1981–1983) vol. 2, 2–150.

Georgios of Pisidia, *Heracliad* and *Avar War*; ed. and Italian trans. A. Pertusi, *Giorgio di Pisidia: Poemi*, vol. 1: *Panegirici epici* (Ettal 1959).

Greek Anthology; ed. and English trans. W. R. Paton, *The Greek Anthology*, 5 vols. (London 1916–1918 = Loeb Classical Library).

Gregory of Nazianzos, *Letters*; ed. and French trans. P. Gallay, *Saint Grégoire de Nazianze: Lettres*, 2 vols. (Paris 1964–1967); English trans. B. K. Storin, *Gregory of Nazianzus' Letter Collection: The Complete Translation* (Berkeley 2019).

Hierokles, *Synekdemos*; ed. A. Burckhardt, *Hierocles Synecdemus* (Leipzig 1893); ed. also by E. Honigmann, *Le Synekdèmos d'Hiéroklès et l'opuscule géographique de Georges de Chypre* (Brussels 1939).

Hormisdas, *Letter 68*; ed. A. Thiel, *Epistolae romanorum pontificum genuinum* (Braunsberg/Braniewo 1868) 64.

Hydatius, *Chronicle*; ed. and English trans. R. W. Burgess, *The Chronicle of Hydatius and the Consularia Constantinopolitana: Two Contemporary Accounts of the Final Years of the Roman Empire* (Oxford 1993).

Ioannes of Antioch, *History*; ed. and English trans. S. Mariev, *Ioannis Antiocheni fragmenta quae sypersunt omnia* (Berlin and New York 2008 = *Corpus Fontium Historiae Byzantinae* vol. 47).

Jerome, *Letter* 60; ed. and French trans. J. Labourt, *Saint Jérôme: Lettres*, vol. 2 (Paris 1951) 90–110; text and English trans. F. A. Wright, *Select Letters of St. Jerome* (London and New York 1933 = Loeb Classical Library) 264–309.

John Chrysostom, *Homilies on the Statues to the People of Antioch* 17; ed. *PG* 49: 171–180; English trans. W. R. W. Stevens in P. Schaff and H. Wace, eds., *A Select Library of the Nicene and Post-Nicene Fathers of the Christian Church: First Series*, vol. 9: *Saint Chrysostom: On the Priesthood; Ascetic Treatises; Select Homilies and Letters; Homilies on the Statues* (Buffalo, NY 1889) 665–676.

John of Nikiu, *Chronicle*; English trans. R. H. Charles, *The Chronicle of John, Coptic Bishop of Nikiu* (Amsterdam 1916).

John Rufus, *Plerophoriae*; ed. and French trans. F. Nau, *John Rufus, Évêque de Maïouma: Plérophories*, in *Patrologia Orientalis* 8.1 (1911).

Jordanes, *Romana* and *Getica*; ed. T. Mommsen, *Iordanis Romana et Getica* (Berlin 1882 = *Monumenta Germaniae Historica, Auctores Antiquissimi* vol. 5); English trans. P. Van Nuffelen and L. Van Hoof, *Jordanes: Romana and Getica* (Liverpool 2020 = *Translated Texts for Historians* vol. 75).

Justinian, *Novels*; ed. R. Schoell and G. Kroll, *Corpus Iuris Civilis*, vol. 3: *Novellae* (Berlin 1899); English trans. D. J. D. Miller and P. Sarris, *The Novels of Justinian: A Complete Annotated English Translation*, 2 vols. (Cambridge 2018).

Justinianic Code; ed. P. Krueger, *Corpus Iuris Civilis*, vol. 2: *Codex Iustinianus* (Berlin 1892); English trans. ed. B. W. Frier, *The Codex of Justinian: A New Annotated Translation, with Parallel Latin and Greek Text*, 3 vols. (Cambridge 2016).

Kallinikos, *Life of Hypatios*; ed. and French trans. G. J. M. Bartelink, *Callinicos: Vie d'Hypatios* (Paris 1971 = *Sources chrétiennes* vol. 177).

Kandidos, *History*; ed. and English trans. R. C. Blockley, *The Fragmentary Classicising Historians of the Later Roman Empire: Eunapius, Olympiodorus, Priscus and Malchus*, 2 vols. (Liverpool 1981–1983) vol. 2, 463–473.

Konstantinos VII Porphyrogennetos, *Book of Ceremonies*; older ed. J. J. Reiske, *Constantini Porphyrogeniti imperatoris de cerimoniis aulae byzantinae*, 2 vols. (Bonn 1829–1830 = *Corpus Scriptorum Historiae Byzantinae*); older text and trans. A. Moffatt and M. Tall, *Constantine Porphyrogennetos: The Book of Ceremonies*, 2 vols. (Canberra 2012 = *Byzantina Australiensia* vol. 18); newer ed. G. Dagron and B. Flusin, *Constantin VII Porphyrogénète: Le livre des cérémonies*, 5 vols. (Paris 2020 = *Corpus fontium historiae Byzantinae* vol. 52.1–5).

Kyrillos of Skythopolis, *Life of Sabas* and *Life of Saint Euthymios*; ed. E. Schwartz, *Kyrillos von Skythopolis* (Leipzig 1939); English trans. R. M. Price, *Cyril of Scythopolis: The Lives of the Monks of Palestine* (Kalamazoo, MI 1991 = *Cistercian Studies Series* vol. 114).

Laterculus Veronensis; ed. O. Seeck, *Notitia dignitatum* (Berlin 1876) 244–253.

Libanios, *Letters*; ed. R. Foerster, *Libanii opera*, vol. 10–11 (Leipzig 1921–1922).

Libanios, *Orations*; ed. R. Foerster, *Libanii opera*, vol. 1–4 (Leipzig 1903–1908).

Life of Auxentios; ed. P. Varalda, *Vita sancti Auxentii (BHG 199)* (Alessandria, Italy 2017); L. Clugnet, "Vie de Saint Auxence," *Revue de l'Orient chrétien* 8 (1903) 3–14.

Life of Daniel the Stylite; ed. H. Delehaye, *Les saints stylites* (Brussels 1923 = *Subsidia hagiographica* vol. 14) 1–94; English trans. E. Dawes and N. H. Baynes, *Three Byzantine Saints: Contemporary Biographies of St Daniel the Stylite, St Theodore of Sykeon and St John the Almsgiver* (Crestwood, NY 1977) 1–84.

Lydos, Ioannes, *On the Magistracies of the Roman State*; ed. and English trans. A. Bandy, *Ioannes Lydus: On Powers or the Magistracies of the Roman State* (Philadelphia 1983).

Malalas, Ioannes, *Chronicle*; ed. I. Thurn, *Ioannis Malalae Chronographia* (Berlin and New York 2000 = *Corpus Fontium Historiae Byzantinae* vol. 35); English trans. E. Jeffreys et al., *The Chronicle of John Malalas* (Melbourne 1986 = *Byzantina Australiensia* vol. 4).

Malchos, *History*; ed. and English trans. R. C. Blockley, *The Fragmentary Classicising Historians of the Later Roman Empire: Eunapius, Olympiodorus, Priscus and Malchus*, 2 vols. (Liverpool 1981–1983) vol. 2, 401–462.

Marcellinus Comes, *Chronicle*; ed. and English trans. B. Croke, *The Chronicle of Marcellinus* (Sydney 1995 = *Byzantina Australiensia* vol. 7).

Markos the Deacon, *Life of Porphyrios of Gaza*; ed. and French trans. H. Gregoire and M. A. Kugener, *Marc le Diacre: Vie de Porphyre* (Paris 1930); English trans. G. F. Hill, *The Life of Porphyry, Bishop of Gaza by Mark the Deacon* (Oxford 1913).

Menandros, *History*; ed. and English trans. R. C. Blockley, *The History of Menander the Guardsman* (Liverpool 1985).

Michael the Syrian, *Chronicle*; French trans. J.-B. Chabot, *Chronique de Michel le Syrien, Patriarche Jacobite d'Antioche (1166–1199)*, 4 vols. (Paris 1899–1910); English trans. M. Moosa, *Michael the Syrian: The Syriac Chronicle of Michael Rabo (the Great), A Universal History from the Creation* (Archdiocese of the Syriac Orthodox Church for the Eastern United States, New Jersey 2014).

Movses Dasxuranci, *History of the Caucasian Albanians*; English trans. C. J. F. Dowsett (London 1961).

Nikephoros, Patriarch of Constantinople, *Short History*; ed. and English trans. C. Mango, with S. Efthymiades (Washington, DC 1990 = *Corpus Fontium Historiae Byzantinae* vol. 13).

Nikephoros Xanthopoulos, *Ecclesiastical History*; ed. *PG* 145–147.

Notitia dignitatum, ed. O. Seeck, *Notitiae dignitatum* (Berlin 1876); ed. C. Neira Faleiro, *La Notitia dignitatum* (Madrid 2005).

Olympiodoros, *History*; ed. and English trans. R. C. Blockley, *The Fragmentary Classicising Historians of the Later Roman Empire: Eunapius, Olympiodorus, Priscus and Malchus*, 2 vols. (Liverpool 1981–1983) vol. 2, 151–219.

Orosius, *Seven Books of History against the Pagans*; ed. and French trans. M.-P. Arnaud-Lindet, *Orose: Histoires (contre les païens)*, 3 vols. (Paris 1990–1991); English trans. A. T. Fear, *Orosius: Seven Books of History against the Pagans* (Liverpool 2010 = *Translated Texts for Historians* vol. 54).

Pacatus, *Oration in Praise of Theodosius I* (= *Panegyrici Latini* 2); text and English trans. C. E. V. Nixon and B. S. Rodgers, *In Praise of Later Roman Emperors: The Panegyrici Latini, Introduction, Translation, and Historical Commentary* (Berkeley 1994).

Palladius, *Dialogue on the Life of John Chrysostom*; ed. P. R. Coleman-Norton, *Palladii dialogus de vita S. Joanni Chrysostomi* (Cambridge 1928).

Philostorgios, *Ecclesiastical History*; ed. J. Bidez, *Philostorgius: Kirchengeschichte, mit dem Leben des Lucian von Antiochien und den Fragmenten eines arianischen Historiographen*, 3rd ed., rev. by F. Winkelmann (Berlin 1981 = *Die Griechischen christlichen Schriftsteller der ersten drei Jahrhunderte* vol. 21); English trans. P. R. Amidon, *Philostorgius: Church History* (Atlanta 2007 = *Writings from the Greco-Roman World* vol. 23).

Photios, *Bibliotheca*; ed. R. Henry, *Photius: Bibliothèque*, 8 vols. (Paris 1959–1977); partial English trans. N. G. Wilson, *Photius: The Bibliotheca* (London 1994).

Polemius Silvius, *Laterculus*; ed. T. Mommsen, *Chronica Minora saec. IV. V. VI. VII.*, vol. 1 (Berlin 1892 = *Monumenta Germaniae Historica: Auctores Antiquissimi* vol. 9) 511–552.

Priskos, *History*; ed. and English trans. R. C. Blockley, *The Fragmentary Classicising Historians of the Later Roman Empire: Eunapius, Olympiodorus, Priscus and Malchus*, 2 vols. (Liverpool 1981–1983) vol. 2, 222–400.

Prokopios, *Wars* and *Secret History*; ed. J. Haury, rev. G. Wirth, *Procopii Caesariensis opera omnia*, 4 vols. (Leipzig 1962–1964); English trans. H. B. Dewing, *Procopius*, 6 vols. (Cambridge, MA and London 1914–1935); rev. English trans. H. B. Dewing and A. Kaldellis, *Prokopios: The Wars* (Indianapolis 2014); English trans. A. Kaldellis, *Prokopios: The Secret History with Related Texts* (Indianapolis 2010).

Prosper Tiro, *Chronicle*; ed. T. Mommsen, *Chronica Minora saec. IV. V. VI. VII.*, vol. 1 (Berlin 1892 = *Monumenta Germaniae Historica: Auctores Antiquissimi* vol. 9) 385–485.

pseudo-Joshua the Stylite, *Chronicle*; English trans. F. R. Trombley and J. W. Watt, *The Chronicle of Pseudo-Joshua the Stylite* (Liverpool 2000 = *Translated Texts for Historians* vol. 32).

pseudo-Sebeos, *History*; English trans. R. W. Thomson, with notes by J. Howard-Johnston, *The Armenian History Attributed to Sebeos*, 2 vols. (Liverpool 1999 = *Translated Texts for Historians* vol. 31).

pseudo-Zacharias, *Ecclesiastical History*; English trans. R. R. Phenix and C. B. Horn, ed. G. Greatrex, *The Chronicle of Pseudo-Zachariah Rhetor: Church and War in Late Antiquity* (Liverpool 2011 = *Translated Texts for Historians* vol. 55).

Rufinus, *Ecclesiastical History*; PL 21: 461–540; English trans. P. R. Amidon, *The Church History of Rufinus of Aquileia, Books 10 and 11* (Oxford 1997).

Sidonius Apollinaris, *Carmina*; ed. A. Loyen, *Sidoine Apollinaire*, vol. 1: *Poèmes* (Paris 1960); text and English trans. W. B. Anderson, *Sidonius: Poems and Letters*, 2 vols. (Cambridge, MA 1936–1965 = Loeb Classical Library).

Sokrates, *Ecclesiastical History*; ed. and French trans. P. Maraval and P. Périchon, *Socrate de Constantinople: Histoire ecclésiastique (Livres I–VII)*, 4 vols. (Paris 2004–2007 = *Sources chrétiennes* vols. 477, 493, 505, 506); English trans. A. C. Zenos in P. Schaff and H. Wace, eds., *A Select Library of the Nicene and Post-Nicene Fathers of the Christian Church: Second Series*, vol. 2: *Socrates and Sozomenus Ecclesiastical Histories* (Edinburgh 1891).

Sozomenos, *Ecclesiastical History*; ed. J. Bidez and G. C. Hansen, *Sozomenus: Kirchengeschichte* (Berlin 1960 = *Die griechischen christlichen Schriftsteller* vol. 50); English trans. C. D. Hartranft in P. Schaff and H. Wace, eds., *A Select Library of the Nicene and Post-Nicene Fathers of the Christian Church: Second Series*, vol. 2: *Socrates and Sozomenus Ecclesiastical Histories* (Edinburgh 1891).

Themistios, *Oration* 16; ed. G. Downey and H. Schenkl, *Themistii orationes quae supersunt*, vol. 1 (Leipzig 1965) 287–304; English trans. P. Heather and D. Moncur, *Politics, Philosophy, and Empire in the Fourth Century: Select Orations of Themistius* (Liverpool 2001 = *Translated Texts for Historians* vol. 36) 255–284.

Theodoretos, *Ecclesiastical History*; ed. L. Parmentier and F. Scheidweiler, *Theodoret: Kirchengeschichte*, 2nd ed. (Berlin 1954 = *Die griechischen christlichen Schriftsteller* vol. 44); English trans. B. Jackson in P. Schaff and H. Wace, eds., *A Select Library of the Nicene and Post-Nicene Fathers of the Christian Church: Second Series*, vol. 3: *Theodoret, Jerome, Gennadius, And Rufinus: Historical Writings* (Edinburgh 1892).

Theodoros Anagnostes, *Ecclesiastical History*; ed. G. C. Hansen, *Theodoros Anagnostes: Kirchengeschichte*, 2nd ed. (Berlin 1995 = *Die griechischen christlichen Schriftsteller der ersten Jahrhunderte: Neue Folge* vol. 3).

Theodoros Synkellos, *On the Attack by the Atheist Barbarians and Persians on This God-Protected City*; ed. L. Sternbach with French trans. by F. Makk in Makk, *Traduction et commentaire de l'homélie écrite probablement par Théodore le Syncelle sur le siège de Constantinople en 626* (Szeged 1975).

Theodosian Code; ed. T. Mommsen, *Theodosiani libri XVI* (Berlin 1905); trans. C. Pharr, *The Theodosian Code and Novels and the Sirmondian Constitutions* (Princeton 1952).

Theodosius II, *Novels*; ed. and trans. with the *Theodosian Code* (q.v.).

Theophanes, *Chronographia*; ed. C. de Boor, *Theophanis Chronographia*, 2 vols. (Leipzig 1883–1885); English trans. C. Mango and R. Scott, *The Chronicle of Theophanes Confessor: Byzantine and Near Eastern History, AD 284–813* (Oxford 1997).

Theophylaktos Simokattes, *History*; ed. C. de Boor, rev. P. Wirth, *Theophylacti Simocattae Historiae* (Stuttgart 1972); English trans. M. and M. Whitby, *The History of Theophylact Simocatta* (Oxford 1986).

Thomas Artsruni, *History of the House of the Artsrunik'*; English trans. R. W. Thomson (Detroit 1985).

Victor of Vita, *History of the Vandal Persecution*; ed. and French trans. S. Lancel, *Histoire de la persécution vandale en Afrique* (Paris 2002); English trans.

J. Moorhead, *Victor of Vita: History of the Vandal Persecution* (Liverpool 1992 = *Translated Texts for Historians* vol. 10).

Zonaras, Ioannes, *Chronicle*; ed. *PG* 134–135; also ed. M. Pinder and T. Büttner-Wobst, *Ioannis Zonarae Epitomae historiarum*, 3 vols. (Berlin 1841–1897); partial English trans. T. Banchich and E. N. Lane, *The History of Zonaras from Alexander Severus to the Death of Theodosius the Great* (London 2009).

Zosimos, *New History*; ed. and French trans. F. Paschoud, *Zosime: Histoire nouvelle*, 3 vols. (Paris 1971–1989); English trans. J. J. Buchanan and H. T. Davis, *Zosimus: Historia nova. The Decline of Rome* (San Antonio, TX 1967); English trans. R. T. Ridley, *Zosimus: New History* (Sydney 2004 = *Byzantina Austaliensia* vol. 2).

Modern Scholarship

Adontz, N., *Armenia in the Period of Justinian: The Political Conditions Based on the Naxarar System*, trans. N. G. Garsoïan (Lisbon 1970).

Banaji, J., *Agrarian Change in Late Antiquity: Gold, Labour, and Aristocratic Dominance* (Oxford 2001).

Bang, P., "The Roman Empire II: The Monarchy," in P. Bang and W. Scheidel, eds., *The Oxford Handbook of the State in the Ancient Near East* (Oxford 2013) 412–472.

Bardill, J., "The Golden Gate in Constantinople: A Triumphal Arch of Theodosius I," *American Journal of Archaeology* 103 (1999) 671–696.

Barnes, T. D., *Early Christian Hagiography and Roman History* (Tübingen 2010).

Basić, I., and M. Zemon, "What Can Epigraphy Tell Us about *Partitio Imperii* in Fifth-Century Dalmatia?" *Journal of Late Antiquity* 12.1 (2019) 88–135.

Benaissa, A., "The Size of the Numerus Transtigritanorum in the Fifth Century," *Zeitschrift für Papyrologie und Epigraphik* 175 (2010) 224–226.

Blaudeau, P., *Alexandrie et Constantinople 451–491: De l'histoire à la géo-ecclésiologie* (Rome 2006).

Blockley, R. C., *East Roman Foreign Policy: Formation and Conduct from Diocletian to Anastasius* (Leeds 1992).

Blockley, R. C., *The Fragmentary Classicising Historians of the Later Roman Empire: Eunapius, Olympiodorus, Priscus and Malchus*, 2 vols. (Liverpool 1981–1983).

den Boeft, J., J. W. Drijvers, D. den Hengst, and H. C. Teitler, *Philological and Historical Commentary on Ammianus Marcellinus XXVI* (Leiden 2008).

den Boeft, J., J. W. Drijvers, D. den Hengst, and H. C. Teitler, *Philological and Historical Commentary on Ammianus Marcellinus XXXI* (Leiden 2018).

Braccini, T., "An Apple between Folktales, Rumors, and Novellas: Malalas 14.8 and Its Oriental Parallels," *Greek, Roman, and Byzantine Studies* 58 (2018) 299–323.

Brennan, P., "The *Notitia Dignitatum*," in C. Nicolet, ed., *Les littérateurs techniques dans l'antiquité romain: Statut, public et destination, tradition* (Geneva 1996) 147–178.

Brennan, P. "Zosimos II.34.1 and the 'Constantinian Reform'," in A. S. Lewin and P. Pellegrini, eds., *The Late Roman Army in the Near East from Diocletian to the*

Arab Conquest: Proceedings of a Colloquium Held at Potenza, Acerenza, and Matera, Italy (May 2005) (Oxford 2007) 211–218.

Brown, T. S., *Gentlemen and Officers: Imperial Administration and Aristocratic Power in Byzantine Italy* A.D. *554–800* (London 1984).

Bury, J. B., "The *Notitia Dignitatum,*" *Journal of Roman Studies* 10 (1920) 131–154.

Cameron, A., *Claudian: Poetry and Propaganda at the Court of Honorius* (Oxford 1970).

Cameron, A., *Porphyrius the Charioteer* (Oxford 1973).

Cameron, A., and J. Long, with S. Lee, *Barbarians and Politics at the Court of Arcadius* (Berkeley, CA 1993).

Casey, P. J., "Justinian, the *limitanei*, and Arab-Byzantine Relations in the 6th C.," *Journal of Roman Archaeology* 6 (1996) 214–222.

Chatziantoniou, E., *Η θρησκευτική πολιτική του Αναστασίου Α΄ (491–518): Η στάση του αυτοκράτορα απένταντι στο μονοφυσιτικό ζήτημα και το ακακιανό σχίσμα* (Thessaloniki 2009).

Clemente, G., *La "Notitia Dignitatum"* (Cagliari 1968).

Clemente, G., "La *Notitia Dignitatum*: L'immagine e la realtà dell'impero tra IV e V secolo," in G. Bonamente and R. L. Testa, eds., *Istituzioni, carisimi, ed esercizio del potere (IV–V secolo d.C.)* (Bari 2010) 117–136.

Cresci, L. R., *Malco di Filadelfia: Frammenti* (Naples 1982).

Croke, B., "The Date of the 'Anastasian Long Wall' in Thrace," *Greek, Roman, and Byzantine Studies* 23 (1982) 59–78.

Croke, B., "Dynasty and Ethnicity: Emperor Leo and the Eclipse of Aspar," *Chiron* 35 (2005) 147–203.

Croke, B., "Evidence for the Hun Invasion of Thrace in A.D. 422," *Greek, Roman, and Byzantine Studies* 18 (1977) 347–367.

Croke, B., "The Imperial Reigns of Leo II," *Byzantinische Zeitschrift* 96 (2003) 559–575.

Cronin, H. S., "First Report of a Journey in Pisidia, Lycaonia, and Pamphylia. II," *Journal of Hellenic Studies* 22 (1902) 339–376.

Crow, J., and A. Ricci, "Investigating the Hinterland of Constantinople: An Interim Report on the Anastasian Long Wall," *Journal of Roman Archaeology* 10 (1997) 235–262.

Dana, D., "Notices épigraphiques et onomastiques IV.," *Zeitschrift für Papyrologie und Epigraphik* 210 (2019) 159–179.

Decker, M. J., *The Byzantine Art of War* (Yardley, PA 2013).

Delbrueck, R., *Die Consulardiptychen und verwandte Denkmäler* (Berlin 1929).

Demandt, A., "Magister Militum," *Real-Encyclopädie* (Pauly-Wissowa) Suppl. 12: 553–790.

Drew-Bear, T., "A Fourth-Century Latin Soldier's Epitaph at Nakolea," *Harvard Studies in Classical Philology* 81 (1977) 257–274.

Elton, H., "Imperial Politics at the Court of Theodosius II," in A. Cain and N. Lenski, eds., *The Power of Religion in Late Antiquity* (Ashgate 2009) 133–142.

Elton, H., *Warfare in Roman Europe,* AD *350–425* (Oxford 1996).

Errington, R. M., "The Accession of Theodosius the Great," *Klio* 78.2 (1996) 438–453.

Errington, R. M., "Theodosius and the Goths," *Chiron* 26 (1996) 1–27.

Feissel, D., "La requète d'Appion, évêque de Syène, à Théodose II: P. Leid. Z révisé," in D. Feissel, *Documents, droit, diplomatique de l'Empire romain tardif* (Paris 2010) 339–362.

Fisher, G., *Between Empires: Arabs, Romans, and Sassanians in Late Antiquity* (Oxford 2011).

Fourlas, B., "Early Byzantine Church Silver Offered for the Eternal Rest of Framarich and Karilos: Evidence of 'the Army of Heroic Men' Raised by Tiberius II Constantine?" in S. Esders, Y. Fox, Y. Hen, and L. Sarti, eds., *East and West in the Early Middle Ages: The Merovingian Kingdoms in Mediterranean Perspective* (Cambridge 2019) 87–107.

Fournet, J. -L., *Hellénisme dans l'Égypte du VIe siècle: la bibliothèque et l'oeuvre de Dioscore d'Aphrodité* (Cairo 1999).

Frösén, J., A. Arjava, and M. Lehtinen, *The Petra Papyri*, vol. 1 (Amman 2002).

Gallay, P., *Saint-Grégoire de Nazianze: Lettres*, 2 vols. (Paris 1964–1967).

Gândilă, A., "Heavy Money, Weightier Problems: The Justinianic Reform of 538 and Its Economic Consequences," *Revue numismatique* 6.168 (2012) 363–402.

Geogakakis, G., "Το κίνημα του Βιταλιανού (513–515): Μια πρόταση ερμηνείας των στόχων του επαναστάτη," *Byzantiaka* 31 (2014) 87–105.

Gilliver, K., "The Augustan Reform and the Structure of the Imperial Army," in P. Erdkamp, ed., *A Companion to the Roman Army* (Malden, MA 2007) 183–200.

Goldsworthy, A., *Pax Romana: War, Peace, and Conquest in the Roman World* (New Haven, CT 2016).

Greatrex, G., "The Nika Riot: A Reappraisal," *Journal of Hellenic Studies* 117 (1997) 60–86.

Greatrex, G. and M. Greatrex, "The Hunnic Invasion of the East of 395 and the Fortress of Ziatha," *Byzantion* 69 (1999) 65–75.

Greatrex, G., and S. Lieu, *The Roman Eastern Frontier and the Persian Wars: Part II, AD 363–630* (London 2002).

Haarer, F. K., *Anastasius I: Politics and Empire in the Late Roman World* (Liverpool 2006).

Haldon, J., *Byzantine Praetorians: An Administrative, Institutional and Social Survey of the Opsikion and Tagmata, c. 580–900* (Bonn 1984).

Haldon, J., *The Empire That Would Not Die: The Paradox of Eastern Roman Survival, 640–740* (Cambridge, MA 2016).

Haldon, J., "More Questions about the Origins of the Imperial Opsikion," in A. Beihammer, B. Krönung, and C. Ludwig, eds., *Prosopon Rhomaikon* (Berlin 2017) 31–41.

Haldon, J. F., *Warfare, State and Society in the Byzantine World, 565–1204* (London 1999).

Halsall, G., *Barbarian Migrations and the Roman West, 376–568* (Cambridge 2008).

Heather, P., "The Anti-Scythian Tirade of Synesius' De Regno," *Phoenix* 42 (1988) 152–172.

Heather, P., *Empires and Barbarians: The Fall of Rome and the Birth of Europe* (Oxford 2010).

Heather, P., *The Fall of the Roman Empire: A New History of Rome and the Barbarians* (Oxford 2005).

Heather, P., *Goths and Romans, 332–489* (Oxford 1991).

Heather, P., *Rome Resurgent: War and Empire in the Age of Justinian* (Oxford 2018).

Hoffmann, D., *Das spätrömische Bewegungsheer und die Notitia Dignitatum*, 2 vols. (Düsseldorf 1969–1970).

Howard-Johnston, J., "Heraclius' Persian Campaigns and the Revival of the East Roman Empire, 622–630," *War in History* 6 (1999) 1–44.

Hoyland, R. G., "Insider and Outsider Sources: Historiographical Reflections on Late Antique Arabia," in J. H. F. Dijkstra and G. Fisher, eds., *Inside and Out: Interactions between Rome and the Peoples on the Arabian and Egyptian Frontiers in Late Antiquity* (Leuven 2014) 267–280.

Jacobs, I., "The Creation of the Late Antique City: Constantinople and Asia Minor during the 'Theodosian Renaissance'," *Byzantion* 82 (2012) 113–164.

Jones, A. H. M., *Cities of the Eastern Roman Provinces*, 2nd ed. (Oxford 1971).

Jones, A. H. M., *The Later Roman Empire 284–602: A Social, Economic, and Administrative Survey*, 2 vols. (Baltimore 1990).

Kaiser, A. M., "*Daci* und *Sextodalmati*: Zwei Truppen des magister militum praesentalis II Orientis in den Papyri," posted online with the Imperium and Officium Working Papers (IOWP), at https://iowp.univie.ac.at/sites/default/fil es/IOWP%20-%20Daci%20und%20Sextodalmati.pdf (accessed July 23, 2021).

Kaiser, A. M., "Egyptian Units and the Reliability of the Notitia Dignitatum, Pars Oriens," *Historia* 64 (2015) 243–261.

Kaldellis, A. "Classicism, Barbarism, and Warfare: Prokopios and the Conservative Reaction to Later Roman Military Policy," *American Journal of Ancient History* n.s. 3–4 (2004–2005 [2007]) 189–218.

Kaldellis, A., "The Politics of Classical Genealogies in the Late Antique Roman East," in I. Tanaseanu-Döbler and L. von Alvensleben, eds., *Athens II: Athens in Late Antiquity* (Tübingen 2020) 259–277.

Kaldellis, A., *Streams of Gold, Rivers of Blood: The Rise and Fall of Byzantium, 955* A.D. *to the First Crusade* (Oxford 2017).

Kaldellis, A., *New Roman Empire: A History of Byzantium from Constantine to the Fall* (Oxford, in preparation).

Kelly, G., "Adrien de Valois and the Chapter Headings in Ammianus Marcellinus," *Classical Philology* 104.2 (2009) 233–242.

Keppie, L., *The Making of the Roman Army: From Republic to Empire* (London 1984).

Koehn, C., *Justinian und die Armee des frühen Byzanz* (Berlin 2018).

Koehn, C., "Justinian στρατηγός," in G. Greatrex and S. Janniard, eds., *Le Monde De Procope* (Paris 2018) 215–228.

Konstantakopoulou, A., "Ἡ ἐπαρχία Μακεδονία Salutaris: Συμβολή στὴ μελέτη τῆς διοικητικῆς ὀργάνωσης τοῦ Ἰλλυρικοῦ," *Δωδώνη* 10 (1981) 85–100.

Konstantakopoulou, A., *Ἱστορικὴ γεωγραφία τῆς Μακεδονίας (4ος–6ος αἰώνας)* (PhD dissertation: University of Ioannina 1983).

Kosiński, R., *The Emperor Zeno: Religion and Politics* (Krakow 2010).

Kraemer, C., *Excavations at Nessana*, vol. 3: *Non-Literary Papyri* (Princeton 1958).

Kulikowski, M., "The *Notitia Dignitatum* as a Historical Source," *Historia* 49 (2000) 358–377.

Laniado, A., "Jean d'Antioche et les débuts de la révolte de Vitalien," In P. Blaudeau and P. Van Nuffelen, eds., *L'historiographie tardo-antique et la transmission des savoirs* (Berlin 2015) 349–369.

Le Bas, P., and W. H. Waddington, *Voyage archéologique en Grèce et en Asie Mineure . . . pendant 1834 et 1844, vol. 3, pt. 5: Inscriptions grecques et latines recueillies en Grèce et en Asie Mineure* (Paris 1870–1876).

Lebek, W. D., "Die Landmauer von Konstantinopel und ein neues Bauepigramm," *Epigraphica Anatolica* 25 (1995) 110–119, 138.

Lee, A. D., "Theodosius and His Generals," in C. Kelly, ed., *Theodosius II: Rethinking the Roman Empire in Late Antiquity* (Cambridge 2013) 90–108.

Lee, A. D., *War in Late Antiquity: A Social History* (Malden, MA 2007).

Lenski, N., *Failure of Empire: Valens and the Roman State in the Fourth Century A. D.* (Berkeley 2002).

Lenski, N., "*Initio mali Romano imperio*: Contemporary Reactions to the Battle of Adrianople," *Transactions of the American Philological Association* 127 (1997) 129–168.

Leppin, H., *Theodosius der Grosse* (Darmstadt 2003).

Liebeschuetz, J. H. W. G., *Barbarians and Bishops: Army, Church, and State in the Age of Arcadius and Chrysostom* (Oxford 1990).

Liebeschuetz, J. H. W. G., *Decline and Fall of the Roman City* (Oxford 2001).

Lot, F., "La *Notitia Dignitatum Utriusque Imperii*: ses tares, sa date de composition, sa valeur," *Revue des études anciennes* 38 (1936) 285–338.

Maenchen-Helfen, J. O., *The World of the Huns: Studies in their History and Culture* (Berkeley 1973).

Marciak, M., *Sophene, Gordyene, and Adiabene: Three Regna Minora of Northern Mesopotamia between East and West* (Leiden 2017).

Mason, H. J., *Greek Terms for Roman Institutions: A Lexicon and Analysis* (Toronto 1974).

Maspero, J., *Papyrus grecs d'époque byzantine: Catalogue général des antiquités égyptiennes du Musée du Caire*, vol. 2 (Cairo 1913).

Matthews, J., *Laying Down the Law: A Study of the Theodosian Code* (New Haven 2000).

Matthews, J., *Western Aristocracies and Imperial Court, AD 364–425* (Oxford 1975).

McEvoy, M., "Becoming Roman? The Not-So-Curious Case of Aspar and the Ardaburii," *Journal of Late Antiquity* 9 (2016) 483–511.

McLynn, L., "'*Genere Hispanus*': Theodosius, Spain, and Nicene Orthodoxy," in K. Bowes and M. Kulikowski, eds., *Hispania in Late Antiquity: Current Perspectives* (Leiden 2005) 77–120.

Millar, F., *A Greek Roman Empire: Power and Belief under Theodosius II, 408–450* (Berkeley 2006).

Mitthof, F., *Annona militaris. Die Heeresversorgung im antiken Ägypten: Ein Beitrag zur Verwaltungs- und Heeresgeschichte des Römischen Reiches im 3. bis 6. Jh. n. Chr.* (Florence 2001).

Omissi, A., *Emperors and Usurpers in the Later Roman Empire: Civil War, Panegyric, and the Construction of Legitimacy* (Oxford 2018).

Palme, B., "Die Löwen des Kaisers Leon: Die spätantike Truppe der *Leontoclibanarii*," in H. Harrauer and R. Pintaudi, eds., *Gedenkschrift Ulrike Horak (P. Horak)*, vol. 1 (Florence 2004) 311–332.

Palme, B., *Dokumente zu Verwaltung und Militär aus dem spätantiken Ägypten* (Vienna 2002).

Palme, B., "*Theodosiaci Isauri* in Alexandria," in J. M. S. Cowey and B. Kramer, eds., *Paramone: Editionen und Aufsätzen von Mitgliedern des Heidelberger Instituts für Papyrologie zwischen 1982 und 2004* (Munich 2004) 157–173.

Palme, B., "Verstärkung für die fortissimi Transtigritani," in D. Minutoli, ed., *Inediti offerti a Rosario Pintaudi per il suo 65°Compleanno* (Florence 2012) 172–179.

Papazoglou, P., *Les villes de Macédoine à l'époque romaine* (Paris 1988).

Paschoud, F., *Zosime: Histoire nouvelle*, vol. 2, pt. 1 (Paris 1979).

Pellegrini, P., "Una guarnigione bizantina a Roma nell'età di Gregorio Magno: i Theodosiaci," in A. S. Lewin and P. Pellegrini, eds., *The Late Roman Army in the Near East from Diocletian to the Arab Conquest* (Oxford 2007) 357–366.

Pietri, C., "Les provinces 'Salutaires': géographie administrative et politique de la conversion sous l'Empire chrétien (IVe s.)," in M. Van Uytfanghe and R. Demeulenaere, eds., *"Aevum inter utrumque": Mélanges offerts à Gabriel Sanders* (The Hague 1991) 319–338.

Pillon, M., "Armée et défense de l'Illyricum byzantin de Justinien à Héraclius (527–641): de la réorganisation Justinienne á l'émergence des 'armées de cité'," *Erytheia* 26 (2005) 7–85.

Pohl, W., *The Avars: A Steppe Empire in Central Europe, 567–822* (Ithaca, NY 2018).

Popescu, E., *Inscripțiile grecești și latine din secolele IV-XIII descoperite în România* (Bucarest 1976).

Pringle, D., *The Defence of Byzantine Africa from Justinian to the Arab Conquest* (Oxford 1981).

Purpura, G., "Sulle origini della Notitia Dignitatum," *Annali dell'Università di Palermo* 42 (1992) 469–484.

Rance, P., "The Battle of Taginae (Busta Gallorum) 552: Procopius and Sixth-Century Warfare," *Historia* 54 (2005) 424–472.

Reeve, M. D., "The *Notitia Dignitatum*," in L. D. Reynolds, ed., *Texts and Transmissions* (Oxford 1983) 253–257.

Rendina, S., *La prefettura di Antemio e l'Oriente romano* (Pisa 2021).

RouECHÉ, C., *Performers and Partisans at Aphrodisias in the Roman and Late Roman Periods* (London 1993).

Sarantis, A., *Justinian's Balkan Wars: Campaigning, Diplomacy and Development in Illyricum, Thrace and the Northern World,* A.D. *527–565* (Liverpool 2016).

Sarantis, A., "The Socio-Economic Impact of Raiding on the Eastern and Balkan Borderlands of the Eastern Roman Empire, 502–602," *Millennium* 17 (2020) 203–264.

Sarris, P., *Empires of Faith: The Fall of Rome to the Rise of Islam, 500–700* (Oxford 2011).

Scharf, Ralf, *Der Dux Mogontiacensis und die Notitia Dignitatum: eine Studie zur spätantiken Grenzverteidigung* (Berlin 2005).

Schmitt, T., *Die Bekehrung des Synesios von Kyrene: Politik und Philosophie, Hof und Provinz als Handlungsräume eines Aristokraten bis zu seiner Wahl zum Metropoliten von Ptolemais* (Leipzig 2001).

Schoolman, E. M., "Greeks and 'Greek' Writers in the Early Medieval Italian Papyri," *Medieval Worlds* 9 (2019) 139–159.

Seeck, O., *Regesten der Kaiser und Päpste für die Jahre 311 bis 476 n. Chr.: Vorarbeit zu einer Prosopographie der christlichen Kaiserzeit* (Stuttgart 1919).

Shlosser, F. E., "The Exarchates of Africa and Italy," *Jahrbuch der österreichischen Byzantinistik* 53 (2003) 27–45.

Sivan, H., *Palestine in Late Antiquity* (Oxford 2008).

Sivan, H., "Was Theodosius I a Usurper?" *Klio* 78.1 (1996) 198–211.

Southern, P., and K. R. Dixon, *The Late Roman Army* (New Haven 1996).

Stathakopoulos, D., *Famine and Pestilence in the Late Roman and Early Byzantine Empire: A Systematic Survey of Subsistence Crises and Epidemics* (Birmingham 2004).

Strobel, K., "Strategy and Army Structure between Septimius Severus and Constantine the Great," in P. Erdkamp, ed., *A Companion to the Roman Army* (Malden, MA 2007) 267–285.

Teall, J. L., "The Barbarians in Justinian's Armies," *Speculum* 40 (1965) 294–322.

Treadgold, W., *Byzantium and Its Army 284–1081* (Stanford 1995).

Treadgold, W., *The Early Byzantine Historians* (New York 2007).

Treadgold, W., "Paying the Army in the Theodosian Period," in I. Jacobs, ed., *Production and Prosperity in the Theodosian Period* (Leuven 2014) 303–318.

Trombley, F. R., and J. W. Watt, *The Chronicle of Pseudo-Joshua the Stylite* (Liverpool 2000).

Vinogradov, A. Yu., "Von der antiken zur christlichen Koine: typische und untypische Inschriften des nördlichen Schwarzmeerraums," in A. Bresson, A. Ivanchik, and J.-L. Ferrary, eds., *Une koiné pontique: Cités grecques, sociétés indigènes et empires mondiaux sur le littoral nord de la mer Noire (VIIe s. a.C. – IIIe s. p.C.)* (Bordeaux 2007) 255–267.

Ward, J. H., "The Notitia Dignitatum," *Latomus* 33.2 (1974) 397–443.

Wassiliou-Seibt, A.-K., "From *magister militum* to *strategos*: The Evolution of the Highest Military Commands in Early Byzantium (5th–7th c.)," *Travaux et mémoires* 21 (2017) 789–802.

Whitby, M., "The Long Walls of Constantinople," *Byzantion* 55 (1985) 560–582.

Whitby, M., *The Emperor Maurice and His Historian: Theophylact Simocatta on Persian and Balkan Warfare* (Oxford 1988).

Whitby, M., "Recruitment in Roman Armies from Justinian to Heraclius (ca. 565–615)," in A. Cameron, ed., *The Byzantine and Early Islamic Near East*, vol. 3 (Princeton 1995) 61–123.

Whitby, M., and M. Whitby, *Chronicon Paschale, 284–628* AD (Liverpool 1989).

Woods, D., "Dating Basil of Caesarea's Correspondence with Arintheus and His Widow," *Studia Patristica* 37 (2001) 301–307.

Youtie, H. C., "P. Mich. Inv. 6223: Transtigritani," *Zeitschrift für Papyrologie und Epigraphik* 21 (1976) 25–26.

Zuckerman, C., "Cappadocian Fathers and the Goths," *Travaux et mémoires* 11 (1991) 473–486.

Zuckerman, C., "Comtes et ducs en Égypte autour de l'an 400 et la date de la *Notitia Dignitatum Orientis*," *Antiquité tardive* 6 (1998) 137–147.

Zuckerman, C., *Du village à l'empire: autour du registre fiscal d'Aphroditô (525/526)* (Paris 2004).

Zuckerman, C., "Le haute hiérarchie militaire en Afrique byzantine," *Antiquité tardive* 10 (2002) 169–175.

Zuckerman, C., "Heraclius in 625," *Revue des études byzantines* 60 (2002) 189–197.

Zuckerman, C., "Two Reforms of the 370s: Recruiting Soldiers and Senators in the Divided Empire," *Revue des études byzantines* 56 (1998) 79–139.

Index

For EU product safety concerns, contact us at Calle de José Abascal, 56–1°,
28003 Madrid, Spain or eugpsr@cambridge.org.

www.ingramcontent.com/pod-product-compliance
Ingram Content Group UK Ltd.
Pitfield, Milton Keynes, MK11 3LW, UK
UKHW020352140625
459647UK00020B/2427